Canada and the U.S.: Continental Partners or Wary Neighbours?

CANADA

Issues & Options

_____

A series designed to stimulate intelligent inquiry into crucial Canadian concerns

Canada and the U.S.: Continental Partners or Wary Neighbours?

RICHARD P. BOWLES
Associate Professor, College of Education, University of Toronto

JAMES L. HANLEY
Educator-Producer, History and Social Science, Ontario Educational Communications Authority

BRUCE W. HODGINS
Professor, Department of History, Trent University

WILLIAM N. MACKENZIE
Teacher, Department of History, Sydney Academy, Sydney, Nova Scotia

GEORGE A. RAWLYK
Professor, Department of History, Queen's University

PRENTICE-HALL OF CANADA, LTD
Scarborough Ontario

PRENTICE-HALL, INC., ENGLEWOOD CLIFFS, NEW JERSEY
PRENTICE-HALL INTERNATIONAL, INC., LONDON
PRENTICE-HALL OF AUSTRALIA, PTY., LTD., SYDNEY
PRENTICE-HALL OF INDIA, PVT., LTD., NEW DELHI
PRENTICE-HALL OF JAPAN, INC., TOKYO

Library of Congress Catalog No. 73-7184

ISBN   013-112780

1 2 3 4 5   77 76 75 74 73

PRINTED IN CANADA

Contents

Preface

The *Canada: Issues and Options* series focusses on a number of vital continuing Canadian concerns. Each volume probes the nature of a complex issue in both its contemporary and historical contexts. The issues were chosen because of their relevance to the life of the Canadian teenager as well as the general Canadian public.

Every volume in the series provides a wide variety of primary and secondary source materials. These sources are interdisciplinary as well as analytical and descriptive. They embody many divergent points of view in order to provoke critical in-depth consideration of the issue. They are arranged in a manner designed to personally involve and confront the reader with the clash of opinions and options inherent in the various issues. The historical sources have been carefully selected to provide a better understanding of the roots of the issue under consideration. It is hoped that this method will establish in the reader's mind a meaningful relationship between the past and the present.

The organization is flexible. If a chronological study of the development of the issue is desired, this can be accomplished by treating the historical sources first and later examining the contemporary manifestations of the issue. By reversing this procedure, the reader can first deal with the contemporary section. This approach will provide the reader with a brief overview of the issue, a case study designed to put it into personal and immediate terms, and a more detailed examination of the issue in its contemporary setting, prior to examining its historical roots.

Questions designed to stimulate further research are also included. These questions do not limit examination or prescribe answers, but raise more questions and suggest aspects of the issue which might be further investigated.

Throughout these volumes, a conscientious effort has been made to avoid endorsing any one viewpoint. No conclusions are drawn. Rather, the reader is presented with information which has been arranged to encourage the drawing of his own tentative conclusions about the issue. The formation of these conclusions involve the use of the skills of inquiry and the examination and clarification of personal values.

Acknowledgments

The authors are particularly indebted to Dr. John Weaver for his considerable help in the assembling of basic material for this volume. Further research was also carried out by Patricia Johnson.

Particular thanks are due Wendy Cuthbertson for her help, advice and hard work in the final preparation of this material. Without her assistance this volume might never have been published.

The authors also thank the many writers and publishers who have granted them permission to use various materials. Source references are provided with the documents.

Introduction

One of the most controversial issues facing Canadians today is Canada's relationship with the United States. The issue is not a new one, far from it, but certain events and developments in the last decade have revitalized it: Canadians seem to be more concerned about this question than ever before, and their concern is often reflected in sharp debate.

This volume provides the reader with a variety of source materials to enable him to probe many of the contemporary and historical dimensions of the issue. The authors hope that the reader will be stimulated and provoked by the diversity of opinion expressed in the volume and will attempt answers to such crucial questions as:

—What is my attitude towards the U.S. and why?

—How much of Canada is owned by U.S. investors and what are the implications for Canada's economy, culture, and politics?

—Does Canada have a culture distinct from that of the United States?

—How has the past contributed to the present situation and what does the future hold?

The Issue:
Some Opinions

The following selection of documents provides a collage of differing Canadian attitudes towards the United States. Do you have particularly strong views about the United States and about Americans? What do you think about Canada's "special relationship" with the United States? Why do you feel the way you do?

SECOND-CLASS AMERICANS

This selection is from an article by Mr. Dennis Braithwaite, presently a columnist for the Toronto Star. The article appeared in the now defunct Toronto Telegram.

Why should remaining Canadians be the *sine qua non* of our existence? To what extent is our independence, or even our separateness, a reality?

As I see it, we are Americans now in everything but name, but second-class Americans. It's not just that most of our resources are American-owned; that wouldn't really matter if we still possessed a distinct national identity. But, of course, we don't. Our whole culture, everything we think and do and feel, every aspiration and hope we have is part of the mainstream of America.

WE ARE AMONG FRIENDS

This selection, by Hugh Garner, a Canadian novelist, is taken from an article Mr. Garner wrote for The New Romans: Candid Canadian Opinions of the U.S. *(Edmonton: M. J. Hurtig, 1968).*

Since I was six years old I have lived in a country that is a northern annex to the world's most powerful state, and my attitude towards it is coloured not only by propinquity but also by comparison. Despite their sometime faults and the arrogance that comes from financial and muscular strength, I like and admire the American people. My box score to date as both a hobo and a car-driving tourist is thirty-eight of the continental United States, and in a couple of weeks my wife and I hope to raise this by visiting some northwestern states we have yet to see. We will drive out there secure in the knowledge that we are among friends who speak our language, are friendly and generous towards us, and will make us feel at home. What more could we ask?

THERE IS AN AMERICAN DREAM

On May 18, 1970, the following Letter to the Editor appeared in the Globe and Mail.

To put it very bluntly, I've had it! I love Canada deeply and I truly am proud to be called a Canadian. But my family and I are going to the United States, a country, thank God, which will still stand up and be counted.

Yes, it is racked with injustice and violence, but I can promise you that there is an American dream, where strength of character and the healthy understanding that if a man is industrous, his merit is rewarded and not with a bilingual cheque from Ottawa.

Yes, my sons may be drafted, may have to fight and may die, in "pursuit of foreign aggressions" (truly a despicable statement) so that some Canadians can sit on cold and bleak afternoons, gloating and knowing full well, as Prime Minister Pierre Trudeau so pointedly reminded us, that the United States will defend our "sovereignty."

FEET OF CLAY

Duncan Macpherson, the Toronto Star's award-winning political cartoonist, depicts one attitude that some Canadians have about the U.S. How would you describe this attitude?

CANADA: SOLD TO THE HIGHEST BIDDER?

This Letter to the Editor, written by Bernard Bennell of Scarborough, Ontario, was published in the Toronto Star, *October 13, 1971.*

As an immigrant to this nation I love, I am sickened to see the way Canada has sold her heritage and sovereignty for dollars, her resources and labour force for pennies, and her self-respect for nothing.

Canada, in your quest to become just as affluent as your southern cousins, you have lost everything. Why did you (the people) allow this to happen? Did you really believe you could be as wealthy as the United States without losing anything? Wake up, Canadians, you will never be as affluent as the U.S., because you neglect the greatest resource the United States has, the ability to buy nations, suck their very blood like some giant vampire, and, after all life has been drawn, sell the shattered remains like a black slave in days gone by.

Canada is under the spell of this vampire which takes on the appearance of an eagle. Are you going to stand by and be finally sold to the highest bidder (if there is one), or are you prepared to re-evaluate your political thinking? I wonder.

THERE WAS A CANADIANISM, ONCE

In his novel, In High Places, *Arthur Hailey described an argument between a prime minister of Canada and an American admiral. The admiral is protesting a Canadian demand made during a meeting with the president of the United States. This demand concerned a proposed act of union between the two countries.*

"No!" The word snapped back from the admiral as though a needle had been jabbed. "I said you were a greedy nation and so you are." His thin voice rose. "Thirty years ago you wanted an American standard of living, but you wanted it overnight. You chose to ignore that American standards took a century of sweat and belt-tightening to build. So you opened up your raw wealth that you might have husbanded instead; and you let Americans move in, develop your birthright, take the risks, and run the show. That way you bought your standard of living — then you sneered at the things we had in common."

"Levin . . ." the President remonstrated.

"Hypocrisy, I said!" As if he had not heard, the admiral stormed on, "You sold your birthright, then went searching for it with talk about distinctive Canadianism. Well, there was a Canadianism once, but you got soft and lost it, and not all your Royal Commissions piled on end will ever find it now."

MAN MARVELS AT U.S. GENEROSITY

Toronto Star reporter John Saunders wrote the following news item which was published in the Star on February 12, 1973.

Elated by what he feels is a major victory in a struggle to prevent a United States oil tanker fleet from fouling Canada's west coast, David Anderson praises the "generosity" of Americans and their legal system.

Anderson, a 35-year-old bachelor who leads British Columbia's Liberal party, is carrying on a personal crusade against plans to move Alaskan oil to U.S. markets by an ocean route off British Columbia. He is one of six plaintiffs in a lawsuit against Rogers Morton, the U.S. secretary of the interior. Anderson is the only individual among the six—most of the rest are environmental organizations—and he shares responsibility for the heavy costs of the U.S. Court of Appeals case. On Friday the court ruled in Washington that Morton may not issue permits for construction of a controversial oil pipeline across Alaska.

Anderson says he is amazed by the way the United States has responded to his efforts. He conjures up the vision of a U.S. politician coming to Canada and helping to take a Canadian cabinet minister to court to stop a giant project strongly favoured by Ottawa and a number of provincial governments.

"In Canada," he says, "the American would be greeted with hostility. But in the States they don't seem to care who argues a case. If he's right, he's right; if he's wrong, he's wrong."

A STATE OF THE UNION?

This article is from the Toronto Star, *October 2, 1971.*

When a pretty information officer at Information Canada's headquarters here opened a letter from an Ohio schoolgirl the other day, she was at first amused and then, after consideration, mildly upset. The letter stated simply that each member of the girl's class had been asked to write an essay about one of the states of the Union.

"The one chosen for me was Canada," the girl wrote. "Please send me some information."

DON'T WORRY, MR. PRESIDENT

Ottawa physician and free-lance writer, Wayne A. Howell, wrote the following spoof in the Toronto Star, *November 2, 1971.*

Richard Nixon, Treasury Secretary John Connally, and Attorney-General John Mitchell are gathered in the White House.

"This report is dynamite!" exclaims John Connally, waving a copy of *Canadian Forum* that contains the secret Herb Gray Report recommending that Canada curb foreign investment.

"Maybe Ken Galbraith can shed some light on this," says Richard Nixon. Air Force 1 is dispatched to Harvard and whisks the lanky Canadian-born economist to Washington. The report is thrust into his hands; Galbraith breaks out laughing.

"We've got another Cuba on our northern border. What's so funny about that?" roars the president. Galbraith sobers up with difficulty.

"Trudeau was right when he said Americans don't know much about Canada. The Herb Gray Report is just part of a quaint Canadian custom that got started way back in 1957 with Walter Gordon's Royal Commission on Canada's Economic Prospects. Lately they've been churning out a 'nationalist' report every year or so. They had the Watkins Report in 1968, the Wahn Report in 1970 and now the Gray Report for 1971," explains Galbraith.

"You mean the reports are a tradition like our Easter-egg hunt on the White House lawn," says a relieved Richard Nixon.

"Exactly. All the economic reports say the same thing: that we Americans own Canada, lock, stock and barrel. But their governments are never so foolish as to act on the recommendations in the reports," explains Galbraith.

"But isn't there a danger that some Canadians might start taking the recommendations of these reports and speeches seriously?" asks a worried John Mitchell, thinking of all the problems too many civil rights speeches have caused.

"They're very careful about that in Canada. Walter Gordon got out of control back in 1963 and he actually introduced a nationalist budget, it only lasted a week," explains Galbraith.

"All the same I'm worried about this Herb Gray Report," says John Connally.

"Look, if the Canadians kick out American investment they'll have to get by without Glad-bags, electric can openers, stretch-and-seal, astro-turf, coloured toilet paper, pop tarts, and Wayne and Shuster Gulf Oil commercials," says Galbraith.

"In that case, gentlemen, we don't have a thing to worry about," says Richard Nixon.

What do you think?

1. What issues in Canada-U.S. relations did you find in the above documents? What issues do you think have been omitted? In your opinion what is the most important problem today in Canada-U.S. relations? Why?

2. (a) Of the documents you have just read, which come closest to expressing your views? Why?

   (b) Which seemed to you to be the most logical and reasonable? Why?

   (c) Was your choice the same in (a) and (b)?

   (d) Describe what you consider to be the typical Canadian view of the United States.

The U.S. and You

How does Canada's "special relationship" with the United States affect your life? To what extent is your life-style set by patterns which have been "made in the U.S.A."? How much of this influence do you resent? How much do you welcome?

The following questionnaire is designed to help show you the extent of your involvement in the U.S. way of life.

What do you think the results will show?

	Item	Country
Favorite movie:		
Favorite magazine:		
Favorite music group:		
Favorite singer/musician:		
Favorite TV programme:		
Favorite TV news programme:		
Favorite hockey team:		
Favorite football team:		
Make of family car:		
Brands of your clothing:		
(a) jeans:		
(b) footwear:		
(c) shirt:		
Breakfast food:		

Most admired political figure (living or dead):

Most admired woman (living or dead):

Most admired man (living or dead):

City you would most like to visit:

Place of last vacation:

What do you think?

1. *Analyze your responses to the questionnaire items.*
   (a) *How "American" is your life-style? How do you feel about this and why?*
   (b) *What parts of your life-style do you consider to be uniquely Canadian? Why?*
   (c) *Using your own case, as shown by the questionnaire, estimate to what extent you think Canadian life has been Americanized. How can you account for this?*
2. *Do you think the findings of the questionnaire would have been the same had it been taken ten years ago? Do you think the findings might be different in the future? Why?*

The Contemporary Problem

Will Canada survive? For many Canadians this question has become as crucial as it is dramatic. They feel that Canada's close involvement in the U.S. economy and culture poses a very real threat, not merely to a distinct Canadian identity, but to Canada's very existence as a separate nation. For many others, the fact that this question is asked by Canadians does not signify so much that the threat is real, but that Canadian fears of U.S. domination is a factor of paramount importance in Canadian life. These people are concerned about what these fears will do to Canada's future well-being.

It is not the intention of the authors in this section dealing with contemporary Canada-U.S. relations to take sides in this debate or even to deal with the question of Canadian "survival" directly. Rather they hope to raise a few of the issues that must be examined before such a large problem "Will Canada survive" can be examined with any effectiveness. Contemporary Canada-U.S. relations will be dealt with in three major areas: economics, culture and politics. Each area provides an opportunity to probe some of the specific questions involved in the larger one of Canadian "survival": Why exactly are many Canadians convinced that the U.S. presence in this country's economy poses a threat to Canadian independence? Are their convistions based on sound reasons or on an emotional Canadian chauvinism? What is the nature of the concern over the U.S. influence on Canadian cultural independence?

Is the U.S. cultural influence bad or good, inevitable or avoidable? What is the impact of the U.S. economic and cultural presence in Canada on this country's political scene? Do U.S.-owned firms or the U.S. government help mould Canadian policy, domestic and foreign?

The examination and discussion of such questions will enable you to assess more accurately the significance of the question, "Will Canada survive?" Will you feel that this question merits serious concern and attention or rather that it is only an example of national paranoia?

The Economic Debate

Many Canadians are deeply concerned about the extent to which Americans effectively control the economic life of this country. It is felt by some that if this trend continues, not only will Canada's economic well-being be threatened but also its cultural identity and its political sovereignty.

Are Canadian fears about the U.S. economic presence in Canada based on a real danger, or are they merely a modern manifestation of an old Canadian tradition of anti-Americanism? What effects does U.S. investment have on Canada's economy? What benefits do Canadians derive from American investment? What price, if any, do they have to pay for it? What government action has been taken to deal with the problem? What answers are being suggested today by concerned Canadians?

This section will deal specifically with the debate over the impact of U.S. investment on the Canadian *economy*. The cultural and political aspects of the controversy over U.S. investment will be dealt with later.

The authors have made no attempt to answer any of the questions raised in the following readings. Their intent has been to expose you to some of the complexities of the issue surrounding U.S. ownership of much of Canada's natural resources and industry. Perhaps you will reach some conclusions. More likely, some important questions will be raised in your mind about this critical issue.

You will first examine the extent of U.S. involvement in the Canadian economy, its nature and the reasons for it. There will then be a probe into the cost-benefit dilemma of U.S. investment: What are the advantages and disadvantages? Are the economic benefits real or imagined? Is it possible to enjoy the benefits without incurring costs?

However, before starting your examination of these topics, you should try to define your present views on this subject. Below are a few documents which present some of the major themes in the debate, concluding with a survey into Canadian views on U.S. investment.

Where do you stand in this debate? Why?

1. WE'RE NOT IN CHARGE HERE ANYMORE

In an editorial of April 11, 1972, the Toronto Star *commented on the findings of the* Gray Report on the Domestic Control of the Economic Environment *(Information Canada, 1971).*

Canada chose the easy road to a modern industrial economy and high living standards. We let the Americans provide the capital and the business leadership.

Now, while reaping the expected benefits, we have discovered that the easy road is also a greased slope leading to domination by the United States. Already we have lost much of our capacity to pursue full employment and the kinds of economic growth we want. At the bottom of the slope lies tame captivity in which Canada's separate economic and cultural identity would disappear.

Canada's openness to direct foreign investment means, according to the Gray Report, "that Canadian industrial development and priorities have in large part been determined by foreign corporate interests and the industrial policies of other governments." (In our case, the U.S. government.)

In other words, we Canadians aren't really in charge here any more — and our grip on our own future is getting looser.

2. INTEGRATION INEVITABLE

Former American Undersecretary of State, George Ball, described what he saw as Canada's future relationship with the United States in his book, The Discipline of Power *(Boston: Little, Brown and Company, 1968).*

Canada, I have long believed, is fighting a rearguard action against the inevitable. Living next to our nation, with a population ten times as large as theirs and a Gross National Product fourteen times at great, the Canadians recognize their need for United States capital; but at the same time they are determined to maintain their economic and political independence. Their position is understandable and the desire to maintain their national integrity is a worthy objective.

Thus, while I can understand the motivating assumptions of the Canadian position, I cannot predict a long life expectancy for her present policies. The great land mass to the south exerts an enormous gravitational attraction while at the same time tending to repel, and even without the divisive element of a second culture in Quebec, the resultant strains and pressures are hard to endure. Sooner or later, commercial imperatives will bring about free movement of all goods back and forth across our long border; and when that occurs, or even before it does, it will become unmistakably clear that the countries with economies so inextricably intertwined must also have free movement of the other vital factors of production — capital, services and labour. The result will inevitably be substantial economic integration, which will require for its full realization a progressively expanding area of common political decision.

3. THE AMERICAN EMPIRE IS CANADA'S CENTRAL REALITY

This selection is the preamble to the Waffle Manifesto of 1969. The "Waffle" a left-wing section of the NDP (New Democratic Party), was strongly in favour of economic nationalism.

The major threat to Canadian survival today is American control of the Canadian economy. The major issue of our times is not national unity but national survival, and the fundamental threat is external, not internal.

American corporate capitalism is the dominant factor shaping Canadian society. In Canada, American economic control operates through the formidable medium of the multi-national corporation. The Canadian corporate elite has opted for a junior partnership with these American enterprises. Canada has been reduced to a resource base and consumer market within the American empire.

4. FLAG WAVING IS FOR KIDS

Executive, a Canadian monthly business magazine, published an editorial on Canadian economic nationalism in July, 1970 issue.

Here, in Canada, we seem to be building walls — preparing to huddle emotionally above the northern border and to yell, "You can't have it," at the United States. We have failed to acknowledge, it seems, that our destiny is, has been, and will be, inevitably bound up with theirs.

As we said last month, we have had it too good so far. Prosperity has been too easy for us. And it stands fair to ruin us. Much of our achievement (if we have the guts to recognize it), is due directly to our proximity to the American nation.

Whether we like it or not, rationalization of productive effort and of resources will, and must, take place continentally. Unending choruses of nationalistic rantings will not alter the fact. In a.world of gigantic economic groupings we cannot go it alone.

Flag waving may provide a momentary thrill — but it's basically the action of children.

5. HOW CANADIANS FEEL ABOUT U.S. INVESTMENT

The poll below, conducted by the Toronto Star, *was published December 30, 1972.*

IS U.S. OWNERSHIP OF CANADIAN COMPANIES GOOD OR BAD FOR OUR ECONOMY?

	Total Canada	Maritimes	Que.	Ont.	Prairies	B.C.
1972						
Bad	47.0%	36.0%	47.0%	46.0%	50.4%	55.3%
Good	37.8	41.8	41.9	36.9	36.4	28.7
Qualified—both good and bad	7.2	4.5	4.1	9.5	6.0	11.1
No opinion	8.0	17.7	7.0	7.6	7.2	4.9
All respondents	5000	445	1420	1825	795	515
1971						
Bad	43.7%	30.9%	41.0%	44.6%	47.9%	53.0%
Good	39.4	49.1	41.9	39.1	33.4	34.5
Qualified—both good and bad	6.9	4.5	5.0	7.6	8.4	9.0
No opinion	10.0	15.5	12.1	8.7	10.3	3.5
All respondents	5000	440	1430	1820	800	510
1970						
Bad	40.9%	33.6%	31.4%	46.0%	46.7%	48.3%
Good	38.0	43.4	43.5	34.9	35.4	32.0
Qualified—both good and bad	13.0	12.9	18.9	11.0	10.1	7.4
No opinion	8.1	10.1	6.2	8.1	7.8	12.3
All respondents	5000	495	1445	1745	843	472
1969						
Bad	33.9%	24.3%	26.9%	37.0%	39.5%	44.2%
Good	42.6	46.3	50.2	37.5	41.4	36.1
Qualified—both good and bad	7.1	4.7	6.4	7.9	7.3	8.3

	Total Canada	Maritimes	Que.	Ont.	Prairies	B.C.
No opinion	16.4	24.7	16.5	17.6	11.8	11.4
All respondents	5000	495	1445	1745	884	471

REASONS FOR BELIEVING U.S. OWNERSHIP OF CANADIAN COMPANIES IS BAD (1972).

Reasons	Total Canada	Maritimes	Que.	Ont.	Prairies	B.C.
1. Americans taking over our economy; Canada/Canadians should control their own business/economy	35.0%	30.6%	31.5%	40.0%	35.9%	29.5%
2. Profits/money leaves the country; doesn't benefit Canada; U.S. profits from our resources	29.0	41.3	35.4	19.8	31.9	29.8
3. We can do it ourselves/alone; should be more independent (not depend on U.S.)	12.4	11.3	13.0	11.4	13.0	13.3
4. Canadians take risk/initiative/invest in their own country; keep Canadian investments here	8.2	7.5	5.1	10.3	8.7	9.1
5. Discrimination; unequal trade; don't get a square deal; we pay more; manpower drain, etc.	3.5	2.5	3.1	4.4	3.0	3.2
6. Discourages Canadians; too much foreign interest (capital) in Canada (Canadians should have it)	2.5	2.5	1.8	3.0	2.5	2.8
7. Take jobs/business away from Canadians	6.3	3.1	9.4	6.6	2.5	5.6
8. Tend to "Americanize"/change/us/our methods; will lose our identity	4.4	1.3	5.5	4.2	2.7	6.3
9. Brings in undesirable (U.S.) unions; unions want wage parity with U.S.	.7	.6	.4	.6	1.7	.4
10. Miscellaneous or no particular reasons	3.0	3.2	2.0	3.7	2.7	3.6

REASONS FOR BELIEVING U.S. OWNERSHIP OF CANADIAN COMPANIES
IS GOOD (1972).

Reasons	Total Canada	Maritimes	Que.	Ont.	Prairies	B.C.
1. Creates more employment	44.9%	43.5%	49.1%	45.3%	38.1%	41.2%
2. Need outside investment for expansion/development of industry/resources	20.5	19.4	24.4	16.0	24.2	27.7
3. Canadians are not willing to invest (too cautious — need a push); if U.S. didn't do it, some other country would	13.3	7.5	11.3	14.8	15.6	17.6
4. Raises/expands the economy (better standard of living; helps Canada/Canadians)	13.3	14.5	10.9	15.1	13.9	11.5
5. Brings money into Canada — more money is circulated	6.6	9.1	4.0	6.1	7.6	13.5
6. Most of what we have now is due to American investing; our economy is based on U.S.; couldn't operate without U.S.	5.9	5.4	7.4	5.6	4.8	3.4
7. Creates a friendly relationship/co-operation; stabilizes; keeps us par with U.S.; help each other	1.5	2.7	1.3	2.1	.7	—
8. Better/more products; world market—more to export/trade	1.5	1.1	2.4	.6	1.7	2.0
9. Miscellaneous reasons	1.7	2.2	1.5	2.2	1.0	.7
10. No particular reason	1.9	4.3	1.5	1.3	3.1	.7

What do you think?

1. Which of the first four documents you read come closest to stating your views? Why?

2. (a) Where would you place yourself in the Star survey? Why?
   (b) Which reasons, cited in the Star survey, for believing that foreign investment is good or bad seem to you to be the most important? Why?
   (c) Explain the change in opinion from 1968 to 1972.
   (d) Account for any regional differences in opinion that you notice.

The Phenomenon of American Investment

How much foreign investment is there in Canada? How much of this investment has come from the United States? In which sectors of the Canadian economy is foreign investment concentrated and why?

Why has Canada been an attractive field for foreign investors? How has Canada become so heavily indebted to other nations, particularly the United States?

In reading the next few selections you will examine the extent and distribution pattern of U.S. investment as well as the reasons why Canada has attracted U.S. capital.

What implications do you think your findings have for the resolution of the issue of foreign investment in Canada?

1.   HOW MUCH OF CANADA IS FOREIGN-OWNED?

The figures given below, compiled under CALURA (Corporation and Labour Union Returns Act), show the percentage of foreign investment in Canada. Keep in mind that U.S. investors were responsible for 80 percent of all foreign investment in Canada.

Industry	% Canadian	% Foreign
Agriculture and Forests	94	6
Book Publishing	5	95
Chemical Products	12	82
Communications	99	1
Construction	85	15
Credit Agencies	57	43
Electrical Products	32	64
Financial Industry	87	13
Investment Companies	71	29
Machinery	26	72
Manufacturing	42	58
Mining	31	67
NHL Teams	14	86
Paper and Allied Products	60	40
Petroleum and Coal	1	99
Primary Metals	45	55
Public Utilities	81	19
Retail Trade	69	21
Rubber Products	6	93
Transportation	91	9
Transportation Equipment	12	87
Wholesale Trade	58	31

In addition, 37 percent of trade union members in Canada belonged to Canadian unions and 63 percent to American unions. Fifty-seven percent of all university teachers were Canadian while 43 percent were non-Canadians.

BREAKDOWN FIGURES ON FOREIGN INVESTMENT

| | *Country where control is held: 1968* | | | |
| | U.S. | Britain | Other countries | Canada |
		% of industry assets		
Agriculture, forestry, fishing, trapping	5.0	0.3	1.2	55.0
Mining	50.9	3.7	11.9	31.3
Manufacturing	42.7	6.9	8.7	38.4
Construction	8.9	4.1	0.9	68.2
Transportation Storage Communications Public utilities	6.0	0.5	2.7	26.7
Wholesale trade	19.3	7.0	5.2	57.7
Retail trade	17.0	3.8	0.4	56.9
Services	12.4	2.0	5.7	53.0
Finance	6.5	2.1	4.2	33.7
Total nonfinancial industries	29.1	4.7	6.4	40.8
Total all industries	18.4	3.5	5.4	37.4

INCREASE IN FOREIGN INVESTMENT 1965-1968

| | Total assets of all corporations $ million | | 50% or more foreign-owned % of all assets | | Less than 50% foreign-owned | |
	1968	1965	1968	1965	1968	1965
Agriculture, forestry, fishing, trapping	1,080.3	842.0	6.4	8.8	55.1	46.6
Mining	11,720.0	8,575.6	62.8	57.9	35.0	39.8
Manufacturing	42,163.0	32,876.4	58.1	55.4	38.6	40.1
Construction	5,199.4	3,591.0	13.8	9.9	68.3	68.7
Transportation	11,747.6	10,070.4	8.4	7.4	22.0	20.0
Storage	452.9	731.6	24.7	10.2	71.0	85.7
Communications	4,416.4	3,167.6	0.4	0.9	10.5	11.1
Public utilities	2,340.6	1,814.5	15.7	11.7	83.4	87.6
Wholesale trade	9,373.3	7,338.0	31.4	26.7	57.8	60.4
Retail trade	6,815.0	5,245.0	21.2	17.7	56.9	56.4
Services	4,841.8	3,346.1	19.7	12.5	53.4	52.2
Finance	89,764.1	67,296.6	12.6	11.3	33.8	34.3
Total nonfinancial industries	100,150.3	77,598.2	39.4	36.0	41.6	42.8
Total all industries	189,914.4	144,894.8	26.8	24.5	37.9	38.9

What do you think?

1. *How do you feel about the above figures? Why?*
2. *Which industries are controlled by foreigners and which ones by Canadians?*
3. *Give reasons why certain parts of the economy are dominated by foreign investment while other parts are almost completely under Canadian control. How important to the Canadian economy are the parts which are dominated by foreign investors? Why?*
4. *Why have Canadians retained control over public utilities, railways and financial institutions?*
5. *By how much did foreign investment increase between 1965 and 1968? Do you think this trend has continued? Do you think it will continue in the future? Why?*
6. *Which industries have shown the greatest increase in foreign investment? How can you account for this?*

2. WHY CANADA?

Irving Brecher and S. S. Reisman in their "Canada-U.S. Relations," a brief presented to 1968 Watkins Task Force on the Structure of Canadian Industry (Information Canada, 1968), argued that Canada is an attractive investment field.

The need for foreign capital and the willingness to borrow from abroad, however, are no assurance that such capital will be forthcoming. Nor, indeed, are the availability of rich resources and of great potential for growth any guarantee that foreign investors will come forward. Many countries are able to meet these conditions and yet have not been able to attract foreign capital in sufficient amounts.

There are other basic conditions which have to be satisfied. A central consideration in this regard is the "investment climate" of the capital-importing country. This embraces the broad economic, political, and social framework of institutions and attitudes, which have a profound impact on the confidence of foreign investors. A major factor in Canada's ability to attract and hold foreign capital has been this country's highly favourable investment environment. This has been in marked contrast with the situation in many other countries seeking foreign capital.

More specifically, Canada has had a long tradition of freedom for the flow of capital and income across its border. Canada has also had a long history of stable and orderly government. In addition, a skilled labour force and a highly developed educational system; an adequate transportation network and other social-capital facilities; reasonably stable economic and social conditions; a strong desire for material advancement; and positive encouragement by all levels of government — all of these factors have helped to make Canada an attractive outlet for private foreign capital. In this respect, therefore, no comparison can properly be made between Canadian experience and that of the less developed countries.

Other factors have also favoured Canada. Particularly important has been the similarity in political institutions, language and social customs with the main capital-exporting countries of the past century, namely, the United Kingdom and the United States; as well as Canadian proximity to the United States which has emerged as the predominant source of foreign capital. The effect of this on Canada's investment relations with that country merits special emphasis.

Canada finds itself next to the greatest industrial power in the world. The common geographic setting, the fact that resources are complementary to a degree, the nearness of the major population centres, the two-way flow of population, the similarity of industrial organization and language, the sharing of media of communication and entertainment — these and many related factors have quite naturally led to a substantial influx of industrial capital from the United States. Many American companies have come to regard their Canadian operations as simply an extension of their domestic market. Expansion into Canada was not as costly for these companies as expansion into other countries, given the similarity of tastes and standards of living. Indeed, over time the influx of United States firms itself has helped to shape some of the social and economic similarities. The same forces have encouraged the entry of Canadian firms into the United States market. The relative size of the two countries, and the different stages of industrial maturity, however, have naturally meant a much greater northward flow of capital.

What do you think?

1. *According to these authors, why has Canada attracted foreign investment, particularly investment from the U.S.? In your opinion which of the factors they cite are the most important? Why?*

2. *Can you suggest other factors, such as government policies or Canadian business attitudes, that have also contributed to making Canada a good investment opportunity? What are some of these other factors?*

3. *The U.S. has not always been the largest foreign investor in Canada. In 1913, for example, U.S. investment was 21 percent of total foreign investment while the U.K. was responsible for over 70 percent. How can you account for this shift?*

American Investment: Disadvantages

Several commentators have maintained that the real concern in the issue of American investment should not be national sovereignty, identity or independence, but whether or not American investment has hindered the development of an economy that is suitable for Canada's capacities and needs. This view stems from the contention of economic nationalists that U.S. investment, which has been encouraged by certain Canadian economic policies, has distorted and retarded the Canadian economy.

What harmful effects do economic nationalists attribute to Canada's "branch plant economy"? According to economic nationalists, what connection is there between U.S. investment and the unemployment rate? between U.S. investment and Canada's innovative abilities? Where does the money for further U.S. investment come from?

Economic nationalists raise these questions and many others. They claim that U.S. investment costs Canada a great deal. What are their arguments? Do you agree with them?

1.   CANADA'S INDEPENDENCE IS THREATENED

The Toronto Star *in its leading editorial October 23, 1972 highlighted the findings of the Gray Report. The Report was concerned with evaluating the effects of foreign investment in Canada.*

Today, more than any time in our 105 years as a nation, Canada's independence is threatened. Not by our enemies, but by our friends.

Steadily, peacefully and with the willing connivance of Canadians, investors from the United States have taken over our resource development and three-fifths of our manufacturing industry. Control of our economy — the very heart of independent action — is slipping out of our hands. The standards and attitudes of others have increasingly become our own. Our traditions and Canada's future are dissolving into the dynamic complex of economic, cultural and social forces below the border.

There may have been an excuse in the past for doing so little to resist this peaceful invasion, on the ground that its extent and implications were unknown. After all, it brought obvious benefits: capital that Canadians couldn't (or wouldn't) risk, new technology, industry, jobs.

What we failed to realize was that the capital investments would be recovered, many times over, in profits and interest flowing to foreign investors; that the imported technology would lock us into another country's patterns of experiment and invention, instead of making us create our own; that industry could be expanded, curtailed or shut down to suit the interests of outsiders, not Canadians; that the kind and number of jobs would likewise be decided by foreigners, with scant regard for Canadian needs or aspirations.

But there is no excuse for inaction now that the costs and drawbacks are known. They have been identified with growing clarity and precision by a dozen carefully researched studies over the past few years. And they point, in sum, to one ultimate, intolerable result: the loss of Canadian independence. Not only in economic and cultural matters, but finally in politics as well.

    *   *   *   *   *

The evidence of the erosion of our independence is all around us. It has been carefully documented in the Gray Report on foreign direct investment in Canada, a 2½-year study prepared by the Liberal Government itself. Perhaps it was because the Report was so explicit about the dangers, that the government was reluctant to publish it.

Already it is clear we have lost much of our capacity to pursue full employment and the kind of economic growth we want. The report identified American branch plants here as the conduits through which U.S. government law and policy flows into Canada. U.S. anti-trust laws may affect branch plant operations here, preventing mergers that might mean more efficient and economical production for the smaller Canadian market. And the U.S. to improve its balance of payments, may cause American firms to transfer funds from their Canadian subsidiaries, with harmful effects to investment and jobs in this country.

At this moment, American legislation is using tax incentives — in effect, export subsidies — to encourage U.S. firms to set up Domestic International Sales Corporations. This could lead to a shift of export production from branch plants here to parent companies in the U.S.

Even before the Gray Report, a federal task force, headed by economist Mel Watkins, reported that the intrusion of American law and policy into Canada was the most obvious way in which foreign ownership "erodes Canadian sovereignty and diminishes Canadian independence."

But it was the Gray Report studies that spelled out, page after page, how deeply American ownership had come to shape economic and cultural life in Canada.

American-owned parent firms put their own global interests ahead of Canada's concern for performance and jobs in branch plants here. It is the parent's interest that governs whether to open or close plants, allot research funds, develop export markets or borrow money to finance operations. As a result, the development of Canadian capacities and activities in these areas is stultified.

Canada has become heavily dependent on innovation and technology imported from the U.S. While helpful in keeping our economy modern, this second-hand pattern works against our chances of developing distinctive products for the world market.

Branch plants for which many important activities are done elsewhere by the parent company, "with the result that the development of Canadian capacities or activities in these areas is stultified." In the resource industries, this often means extracting raw materials and shipping them south of the border for processing, leaving Canadians in the old "hewers of wood and drawers of water" role. In manufacturing, it usually means that the parent companies hog research and development.

U.S. investment operating behind Canada's protective tariffs has created a miniature replica of the American economy, with too many firms and too many products, high-priced because their plants can't get the economies of large-scale production available in the 15-times-larger U.S. market. This "replica effect" is underlined in the Watkins Report and the report of the parliamentary External Affairs Committee chaired by Ian Wahn.

Many Canadians must go to the U.S. or abroad to gain top-level skills in management, research and technical know-how; then their developed talents are often lost to Canada. In that vast sector of our economy which is under foreign ownership or control they cannot, as Canadians, aspire to the highest jobs in their companies.

Foreign-controlled companies import a large and growing share of the goods and services they need from the U.S. This retards our manufacturing industries and leaves fewer opportunities for Canadians in such fields as advertising, public relations, management and investment counselling.

The return on U.S. investment—the $2 billion worth of interest, dividends, patent royalties and other services charges that flow out to the U.S. each year — threatens future trouble for Canada's balance of payments

To sum up, the major economic benefits of foreign ownership are ultimately reaped by the foreign owners. Canadians furnish the labour, much of the market, and more and more of the financing of foreign controlled firms in Canada. But without Canadian ownership, it is outsiders who in the end decide the distribution of benefits — in their own interest.

What is meant by?

"branch plant"
"anti-trust laws"
"sovereignty"

What do you think?

1. *"Control of our economy—the very heart of independent action— is slipping out of our hands."*

(a) *Do you agree that control of the economy is "the very heart of independent action"? Why?*

(b) *According to the findings of the Gray Report, how is this happening?*

(c) *What Canadian governmental or business policies do you think have contributed to this situation?*

2. *Explain what is meant by "the miniature-replica effect." How was it created? How does it influence the Canadian economy?*

3. *Words such as "stultified", "dependent", "retards" are prominent in this analysis. Explain why. According to the Gray Report how are these effects created?*

4. *"To sum up, the major economic benefits of foreign ownership are ultimately reaped by the foreign owners." Do you think this is an accurate assessment? Why or why not?*

2. LET US JOIN TOGETHER

This illustration is a reproduction of a poster by the Committee for an Independent Canada.

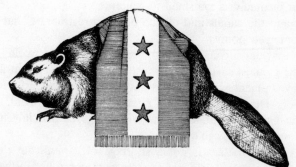

let's keep it Canadian

The survival of Canada as an independent nation is one of the most important issues facing Canadians today.

The time for mere talk is past; action is very urgently needed.

Let us join together in urging our elected representatives to commit themselves honestly and enthusiastically to Canadian independence.

COMITÉ POUR L'INDÉPENDANCE DU CANADA
COMMITTEE FOR AN INDEPENDENT CANADA

What do you think?

1. *How do you respond to this poster and why?*
2. *Why does the Committee for an Independent Canada feel that Canada's "survival as an independent nation" is at stake? Do you feel that this statement is supported in fact by the findings of the Gray Report? Why or why not?*

3.   CANADA DOES NOT NEED FOREIGN CAPITAL

Cy Gonick, an NDP member of the Manitoba legislature, wrote the following excerpt as part of an article, published in the Toronto Star, *October 23, 1970, attacking what he called the "myths" of foreign investment.*

1. *Canada needs foreign capital.* Without it we are doomed to a state of economic backwardness — a 30 percent drop in our standard of living Prime Minister Trudeau has said. This was true for the economy of the 19th century and the early 20th century. We had a narrow economic base, and our income was too small to generate the savings needed to build the railways and the canals and all the other infrastructure that go with a newly developing economy.

Now that our income is among the highest in the world — and we are among the greatest savers in the world — we can just about finance our economic development with our own savings, and to a very large degree we already do. Despite all the talk about foreign investment, almost all investment in Canada is financed out of savings earned in Canada. But much of this money is foreign owned.

Today our problem is not a shortage of capital, but that a great deal of the money earned in Canada is foreign controlled. When it is reinvested, it allows already existing foreign companies located in Canada to expand and to buy up Canadian companies. And we call that foreign investment.

We are at a stage now where we are being bought out by our own money. The actual foreign cash makes up only a small part — in 1968, less than 15 percent — of foreign investment in Canada. The rest of the foreign investment is done by reinvesting profits already earned in Canada, by depreciation allowances, by borrowing money from Canadian banks, and by grants and loans from provincial and federal governments.

Conclusion: There is no economic need for more takeovers, no economic need for more foreign investment. If we can maintain full use of Canada's national income, we can generate enough capital to serve our needs.

What do you think?

1. *According to Mr. Gonick, who foots the bill for foreign investment? How? Why?*
2. *Do you think that Canadian financial institutions and Canadian governments should refuse to lend money to foreign investors? Why or why not?*
3. *Do you think that Canadian investment circles are more likely to support U.S. ventures than Canadian ventures? Why?*
4. *What proportion of Canadian savings are invested in other countries? Should Canada regulate the export of Canadian capital? Why or why not?*

4.   EXPORT RAW MATERIALS, EXPORT JOBS

This selection is another excerpt from the Cy Gonick article which appeared in the Toronto Star, *October 23, 1970.*

2. *It is in Canada's interest to act as a resource base for the U.S.* That is where we are most productive. That's where we can make the most earnings.

What is ignored by this argument is that the export of raw material is in reality the export of Canadian jobs. Resource extraction provides fewer than 100,000 jobs in Canada, but the refinery and fabrication of those resources created millions of jobs in the U.S., Europe and Japan.

The announcement of the export of natural gas to the U.S. is only the latest example of our short-sightedness. In the short-run it creates jobs and profits; in the long-run it destroys our future. We now learn that the price of natural gas in the U.S. will almost double in the next six months. The U.S. is running out of raw materials; the costs are, therefore, rising. This put us at a distinct advantage — perhaps for the first time.

Conclusion: If we refrain from entering into resource export deals and instead fabricated our resources here, we could be using our growing cost advantage to win a major place for ourselves among the manufacturing nations of the world — with the jobs and the incomes that go with it.

What do you think?

1. *How much of the resource sector of our economy is controlled by foreigners? (see page 17)*
2. *Why does this investment make Canada a "resource base" for the United States?*
3. *According to Mr. Gonick, how does foreign investment in Cana-*

dian resources and a generous Canadian resource export policy
cost Canada jobs?
4. In your view would Canadian ownership of Canada's natural resources alter this situation? Why or why not?

5.   CANADA'S INNOVATION RECORD

Figures from the Gray Report show that Canada is lagging other
industrialized nations in technological innovation. The ranking was
derived by dividing the absolute values by the number of industrial
employees to correct for country size.

Country	Number of Industrial Employees (,000)	1. Location of 100 Significant Innovations since 1945 With USA Base 100	Rank
Belgium	1,645	20.6	5
Canada	2,428	0	10
France	7,940	8.5	8
Germany	12,385	38.3	4
Italy	7,776	13.2	7
Japan	17,129	7.9	9
Netherlands	1,847	18.3	6
Sweden	1,535	88.4	2
U.K.	11,798	51.8	3
U.S.A.	25,063	100.0	1

What do you think?

1. (a) Do you think American investment is responsible for Canada's
       poor record in the field of technological innovation? Why?
   (b) What other reasons could be cited for Canada's poor showing?
2. The 1968 Watkins Report on the Structure of Canadian Industry
   observed that "power accrues to nations capable of technological
   leadership, and technical change is an important source of economic growth."
   (a) Is technological innovation crucial for economic development?
       Why or why not?
   (b) Is it to Canada's advantage to develop her own technological

abilities rather than importing inventions and technological developments from the U.S.? Why or why not?

6. THE EFFECTS OF THE MULTINATIONAL CORPORATION

Anthony Westell, in the Toronto Star *of February 18, 1971, discussed the power of the multinational corporation and its effects on the Canadian economy.*

So the debate on economic nationalism, although rising in volume and passion, is deeply confused. The problem is often discussed in terms of U.S. capital: How much do we need? How much should we admit? In what sectors of the economy? Under what terms? But this type of broad question can be more concealing than revealing.

What we are really concerned about is power. We want to ensure that we have the power to make our own national policies, as far as reasonable in an interdependent world. We fear that if too much of our economy is owned abroad, effective decisions over employment, investment, trade and even foreign policy will be made abroad in the head offices of giant corporations beyond our control.

So where do we find the decision-making power we want to control? In feudal times, ownership of land on which to grow food and make profits was power. With the industrial revolution, power passed to capitalists who owned the factories and mines which produced wealth.

Many nationalists still think in those terms: that if we control capital, we have power. But that is no longer true.

John Kenneth Galbraith, the economist, and others have demonstrated that in the modern world, ownership does not give the power to control the giant corporations which are among the most dynamic elements in our economy. The thousands of people who own shares in, for example General Motors, have no effective power to control the corporation's policies.

Power has passed from the owners into the hands of what Galbraith calls the technostructure: ". . . It extends from the most senior officials of the corporation to where it meets, at the other perimeter, the white and blue collar workers whose function is to conform more or less mechanically to instruction or routine. It embraces all who bring specialized knowledge, talent or experience to group decision-making. This, not the management, is the guiding intelligence — the brain — of the enterprise."

In other words, the decisions which concern us — how many people to employ, what factories to close and what new ones to build, what goods to export and where to sell them — are not made by the owners of capital, or even by boards of directors nominally elected by the owners. The decisions are made by a structure of specialists contributing information to the group — managers, accountants, technologists, production engineers, lawyers, salesmen and others.

This is where business power lies in the modern world, beyond the control of capital and, increasingly, of governments. If we want to safeguard Canadian sovereignity, control of the technostructure, and not simply of capital, is the real problem.

The technostructure is powerful precisely because it is a dynamic form of business organization. It succeeds because it is more efficient than older types of companies.

U.S. corporations gobble up Canadian companies, not just because they have more capital to invest, but because they are better able to make efficient use of resources.

The Economic Council of Canada put it this way in a recent report: "A feature of industrial organization and trade among advanced countries is the emergence of more and larger firms that have manufacturing operations, frequently on a specialized and integrated basis, in several countries.

"In general, such firms have significant competitive advantages arising from their ability to combine large amounts of capital, competent management, skilled professionals and advanced technology, and to move these to economic locations for production."

The multinational corporations already account for about 15 percent of the total production of the free world. They are growing so fast that the council says they may control half the total production by 1990.

This is the reality of foreign ownership in Canada. It is not simply a question of capital, but of management and technology to make the most efficient and profitable use of capital.

The recent report of the Senate's Special Committee on Science Policy suggested the same thing from a different angle when it quoted with approval a statement by a British cabinet minister that the organization of science is the central source of power for our generation, comparable with the ownership of industry and land in times past.

In other words, power is the result of harnessing science to industry in the most productive way, and this is achieved in giant corporations by the technostructure of experts.

Operating in several countries, they often control the process of production from taking the raw materials from the ground to refining to manufacturing and retailing, avoiding the normal disciplines of the commercial market, setting trade patterns by selling goods from one subsidiary to another across international borders, shifting profits to get the best tax deal, and moving vast sums of capital and teams of highly skilled personnel.

The influence of the corporations is pervasive also in other and more subtle ways.

They produce the *organization man,* the employee who identifies strongly with his company image and accepts its goals as defined by head office. If the employee is in Canada, he is thus importing the values of U.S. society.

By creating demand for their products, corporations also tend to reproduce abroad the U.S.-type of consumer economy, with all that implies in wasteful use of resources, pollution of the environment and emphasis on private pleasure rather than social service.

The giant corporations which move into Canada, or expand their operations here by taking over Canadian firms, thus bring us all the advantages of efficient use of technology — but at the price of encroaching on national sovereignty and values.

What do you think?

1. *"If we want to safeguard sovereignty, control of the technostructure and not simply of capital, is the real problem."* Explain what the author means by this statement.
2. Does the existence of the multinational corporation make the issue of foreign ownership outdated? Why or why not?
3. (a) What economic benefits are derived from the operation of multinational corporations?
   (b) What economic disadvantages are derived from the operation of the multinational corporation?
   (c) How can we enjoy the benefits while minimizing the disadvantages?
4. According to Mr. Westell, how can the multinational corporation be accused of distorting the Canadian economy? Is Mr. Westell correct? Why or why not?

American Investment: Advantages

The defenders of U.S. investment in Canada see the rising tide of economic nationalism in this country as an often emotional and unrealistic assessment of the U.S. influence in Canada. They claim that far from hurting the Canadian economy, U.S. investment is vital to its further development; and that the reaction against further investment is not based on economic considerations but on the old Canadian reaction of anti-Americanism for the sake of anti-Americanism.

What would the curtailment of U.S. investment do to Canada's economic development? its standard of living? its manufacturing and resource industries? its unemployment rate? What would be the result if Canada could no longer draw on the technological know-how and innovations of American parent corporations? What would happen to Canada's export markets? to its tax revenues? to the industries which support and service U.S. subsidiaries? What would be the effect on the underdeveloped regions of Canada?

How strong do you think the continentalist argument is? Does it present an effective case against economic nationalism? How much attention sholud the continentalist argument be given when planning Canada's economic future?

1.   COSTS OF ECONOMIC INDEPENDENCE

Robert W. Bonner, Vice-Chairman of the MacMillan Bloedel Company, spoke on June 24, 1971 to the Ontario Conference on Economic and Cultural Nationalism. The following is an excerpt from Mr. Bonner's address.

I am convinced that Canada today is a freer, stronger, more independent nation than she would have been if she had listened to and accepted the arguments of economic nationalism, which have thundered from her press and podiums for generations. If all the dire warnings about foreign capital domination had had any relevance to the true state of our affairs, the country would have passed out of existence years ago.

Instead, having maintained one of the world's most accessible economies in terms of outside investment, Canada is in full possession of her sovereignty, probably more independent of outside influences than she has ever been.

Canada has taken independent initiatives with respect to her NATO commitments, her relations with the Soviet Union and China, her concern for Arctic pollution and the freeing of the Canadian dollar.

Canada has chosen to stand aside from the American involvement in south-east Asia.

How could all such self-assertion have taken place, except for the fact that the nationality of capital invested here is not a real factor in the exercise of Canadian sovereignty or Canadian independence.

*   *   *   *   *

[*Mr. Bonner also argues that foreign investment, contrary to the thinking of economic nationalists, is not detrimental, but beneficial to the Canadian economy.*]

The real test of a company as help or hindrance to Canada's future rather lies in answers to these questions:

1. Is the company organized to be an optimum contributor to the Gross National Product?
2. Is the company a growing provider of jobs for Canadians?
3. Is the company a reliable and responsible taxpayer at local, provincial and national levels?
4. Is the company willing and able to reach public policy objectives?
5. Is the company profitable without special concessions by way of public assistance?

Clearly, many Canadian companies would not meet all these tests. Many foreign-owned companies do.

If Canadian companies are nevertheless to be favoured, this may be nationalism and a case may be made for such favoritism. But, we should be frank with ourselves and admit that nationalism, at that point, ceases to be economic.

*   *   *   *   *

Much of the debate favouring economic nationalism seems to take place out of sight of current realities. The realities are these, to name but a few.

Canada's labour force is growing at a rate 50 percent faster than the general growth rate of the national population, and the trend can be expected to continue through the decade. No other western nation faces a population explosion in its labour force of this magnitude and the alarming aspect of it, to me, is that few people in positions of responsibility seem to appreciate the unique gravity of this problem.

No matter how successful we may be in framing policies to cope with current unemployment, our efforts are often cancelled out by the month-to-month addition of thousands of young Canadians to the labour force — 2½ million of them in this decade. These people are not unwelcome visitors; they are Canadian citizens fully entitled to share the nation's wealth. Many of them are uncommonly well-educated, eager to contribute to their nation's future. High unemployment amongst them is an incalculable waste. Still, I see no evidence that we have hit upon a policy to initiate a growth rate sufficient to create gainful employment for this vast pool of talent.

A debate on the pros and cons of foreign ownership and Canadian nationalism is almost totally irrelevant to this problem.

We would need an annual real growth rate of about 9 percent over the next two years in order to approach anything like full employment. After that, we would need a 6 percent annual growth rate in order to provide work for our youthful labour force through the balance of the decade. As you know, the current performance is about 3½ percent in real terms and rarely exceeds 6 percent. What are we to conclude from these figures except that our economy needs very large new pools of capital, whether or not some may approve of its source.

By 1975 it will cost between $66,000 and $70,000 in capital to create one new job. In that same year, some 375,000 people will join the labour force and the capital requirement to provide the necessary jobs for that group alone will be some $26 billion, or double the amount we were able to generate in the middle of the last decade. If risk capital on that scale were available solely from Canadian sources, it would be a fine thing; but under the circumstances of the seventies, capital of this magnitude from domestic sources only is most unlikely.

One of those circumstances critical to this period is Canada's cultural commitment to personal freedom whereby we cannot, as authoritarian countries can, force our citizens to save or to invest in domestic enterprises.

Given the shortfall of capital in the past, are we now to legislate into existence an entirely new community of Canadian shareholders?

One prediction I have seen is that national savings will be from $1.3 to $2 billion short of our financial requirements in 1975. Individual Canadians on average save 6 percent of their incomes, voluntarily. The fact that we choose to spend the bulk of our incomes on a comparatively high standard of living, rather than postpone consumption, is some indication to me that we as a nation are not willing to forego bread in favour of a rather nebulous concept of economic independence.

Thus, if we are wholeheartedly and effectively to embrace economic nationalism, it seems clear that Canadian spending habits will have to bend in favour of a broader-than-historical investment in Canadian equities. Public measures will have to be devised —

(a) encouraging or compelling substantially greater Canadian savings:

(b) encouraging or compelling investment in equities rather than in debt securities;

(c) encouraging or compelling Canadian investment rather than foreign;

(d) discouraging or forbidding sales of Canadian assets or equities to non-Canadians;

(e) discouraging or forbidding foreign capital's entry into Canada;

(f) substantially increasing the numbers of Canadian shareholders;

(g) thrusting a very broad role upon the CDC (Canadian Development Corporation).

If we decide to depart from a free capital policy only for so-called industries of the future, some of these measures will have to be employed.

If we decide to "buy back the country", most — I think all — of these measures become mandatory.

We shall be at that point in an almost totally managed economy.

Bureaucrats, not businessmen, will be seen to run the private sector.

What economic independence we do not thereby achieve, we will no doubt have thrust upon us by a flight of funds, especially those from the United States.

It is not a course I recommend.

This is an age in which man is growing cabbages in space. It is an age in which only the agile survive intense international competition. It is an age that demands openness, flexibility and the maximum exchange of ideas, data and capital.

It certainly is not an age for moats. Indeed, they have long ago ceased to be effective.

Canada should be encouraging the development of an international community of thought in which business decisions can be made multinationally. Free capital movements are part of that community, and it is precisely the kind of community in which Canada could thrive.

By allowing capital to move freely across our borders we do more for Canada's independence than by throwing up nationalistic barriers to investment because new capital bolsters our economic strength and it is that strength which helps assure our national survival. It also permits us to spend as we grow.

I am no advocate of economic dependency and I have never maintained that it is a good thing for Canadian capital to lie idle while others take the risk and the profits, or losses. But Canadian capital is not idle; it is simply insufficient to keep our people fully employed at standards of living desired by our people and at the same time competitive internationally, unless we choose to regiment ourselves and conscript our savings in a way which I find personally abhorrent.

*   *   *   *   *

The argument for a policy of growing nationalism is weakened by the failure of the economic nationalists to demonstrate that Canada's political sovereignty has been or is threatened by her open economy.

They talk about monies going abroad without mentioning Canadian dividends coming home.

They do not show us how our lives would be different if we suddenly closed our borders to outside investment. They make no assessment of foreign reaction. They seldom mention that we would certainly be poorer by withdrawing in this fashion from the world.

What do you think?

1. *"How could all such self-assertion have taken place except for the fact that the nationality of capital invested here is not a real factor in the exercise of Canadian sovereignty or Canadian independence."*
   (a) *Do you feel that foreign investment threatens Canadian sovereignty or independence? Explain why or why not?*
   (b) *Do you think Mr. Bonner offers an effective rebuttal to those who feel that foreign investment threatens sovereignty or independence? Why?*
2. Explain why Mr. Bonner argues that a restriction on foreign investment and favours to Canadian companies is nationalism, but not "economic" nationalism.
3. What arguments does Mr. Bonner present to defend his position? Outline these arguments under:
   (a) Canada's independence   (b) economic efficiency
   (c) job-creation   (d) free enterprise system
   (e) internationalism   (f) national survival
   How would the economic nationalism argument you have read attempt to answer Mr. Bonner? Where in your view would it be effective, if at all? Where would it be ineffective? In both cases, explain why.
4. Has Mr. Bonner influenced your own views concerning the benefits and dangers of foreign investment? If so, how and why?

2. THE BENEFITS OF FOREIGN INVESTMENT

Mr. Gordon Archibald, president of the Maritime Telegraph and Telephone Company, speaking to a conference in Toronto, pleaded for continued U.S. investment in Canada. His remarks were recorded in the Globe and Mail, *October 8, 1972.*

A vigorous plea for the benefits of continued foreign investment in Canada was made yesterday by Gordon Archibald of Halifax, chairman and president of Maritime Telegraph and Telephone Co. Ltd.

Businessmen must rally to convince others who oppose foreign investment on emotional and nationalistic grounds, said Mr. Archibald, past president of the Canadian Chamber of Commerce, in a speech for a Conference Board in Canada panel at the Royal York Hotel.

"Few if any practical businessmen oppose foreign investment, particularly in our resource industries," he said. "It would be fine if Canadians could control all companies doing business in Canada, but this is not practical.

"Until we can, let us be thankful we have a wealthy neighbour whose citizens have the resources and are willing to invest in areas where we Canadians—even when funds are available—are not so inclined to invest our money."

". . . It would be fine, too, if we could process our resources in Canada and sell the finished product locally and abroad. Where it is practical, this should be done in the interest of more employment for Canadians in the short term, and to develop more diversified trading capacity in the long run. Here again it is not always practical to do this and until it is (we should) accept the other option of moving raw materials for processing outside the country."

*   *   *   *   *

"It is my belief that we are 'out in front' and foreign investment has played an important part in placing us in a winning position," he said, noting briefly that those problems presented by foreign investment must be solved by government and business in continuing consultation, in order to continue the benefits.

He linked rapid growth and expansion of the Canadian economy, development of resources and manufacturing with high inflow of foreign capital into Canada.

"Canada has clearly benefited by both a strengthening and a deepening of our economy, by a stimulation of population growth (one million people in the western provinces are there only because of foreign investment), and, of course, by the attraction of related services and secondary industries."

*   *   *   *   *

The Committee for an Independent Canada's charge that Canada is being "bled" is questionable indeed, he said. Its claim of a net outflow of $2.6 billion in a 10-year comparison of subsidiary payments to U.S. parents with new U.S. investment money coming into Canada, is meaningless and misleading, he added.

The basic inflow-outflow comparison ignores the overall economic gains resulting from the foreign investment itself, in the form of various taxes and reinvested profits; the creation of exports, substitutes for imports, and other beneficial effects to the balance of payments, he said.

"If we are looking at a 10-year record of $2.6 billion outflow back to the United States, we must also multiply this by three to look at the kind of money being generated in taxation and new investment within our borders. This is quite apart from the millions of U.S. dollars annually flowing into Canada."

Warning against the "serious danger" of adopting "any kind of nationalism or simple protection for domestic competitors," or "desperation measures to save Canada from an imaginary self-induced situation," Mr. Archibald deplored the lack of a clear policy, either for an open economy or otherwise, to deal with direct foreign investment.

What do you think?

1. *How has foreign investment put Canada "out in front", according to Mr. Archibald? Evaluate his arguments.*
2. *What practical problems are there in having all Canadian resources processed in Canada? Can they be overcome? If so, how?*
3. *How does Mr. Archibald rebut the argument of the Committee for an Independent Canada (CIC) that Canada is being "bled"? How effective do you find his rebuttal?*
4. *Why does Mr. Archibald argue that Canada's situation is "imaginary" and "self-induced"? How accurate is this assessment?*

3. A REGIONAL VIEWPOINT

Mr. Stephen Weyman, president of the Atlantic Provinces Economic Council, presented a brief to the Commons Standing Committee on Finance, Trade and Economic Affairs on June 13, 1971. The committee was discussing the proposed government policy on foreign take-overs of Canadian firms.

Both public opinion and observable fact make the foreign investment issue substantially different in the Atlantic Provinces from, say, in southern Ontario. This should be fully considered before any legislation is passed.

The Atlantic Provinces tend to regard foreign investment as being any investment that comes from outside the Atlantic region; that is, we have come to make no distinction between investment that comes from central Canada, the United States or other foreign countries, regarding it all somehow as foreign.

Mr. Marchand, the Minister of Regional Economic Expansion and Mr. Stanfield, the Leader of the Opposition, have expressed the views of most Maritimers on the matter. Asked to restrict DREE grants to Canadian-owned corporations, Mr. Marchand said:

I do not want to make economic philosophy on the backs of underdeveloped regions.

Mr. Stanfield put it this way:

For those living in the Gaspé peninsula, on the North Shore, in the Maritimes and elsewhere in Canada, it is of little import whether the company's director is from Detroit, Boston or Toronto.

To be blunt, it seems as if certain segments of opinion in central Canada, having achieved the benefits of industrialization for themselves, now wish the Atlantic Provinces to forego the industrialization they never had in the interest of maintaining an ill-defined Canadian economic independence.

We realize that many Canadians from coast to coast are legitimately concerned that the political independence of the country cannot be maintained if economic control is lost. We also recognize that no Canadian government could remain oblivious to the pressure our present government has been under in recent years to "do something." Our fear in the Atlantic region is that in doing something, this government and future ones will be pushed into taking evermore stringent measures without understanding their economic impact on our region.

If we are to believe our provincial premiers, and to trust in our own faith in the future of Atlantic Canada, we are on the verge of an economic breakthrough. Major oil and gas discoveries are tantalizingly close. New world trading and shipping patterns hold out great promise for us. The potential of our deep-water ports is just beginning to be realized. Fundy tidal power is no longer just a dream but a real possibility. The seas and seabeds around us abound in wealth that is awaiting to be exploited — intelligently exploited.

But we will need capital — and those intangibles that come with capital: entrepreneurship, technological innovation and managerial excellence — in amounts that are currently beyond our regional and national capacity to generate.

Last year, the Atlantic Development Council presented its 10-year development strategy for the Atlantic region to Mr. Marchand. In it, the Atlantic Development Council said that if unemployment in our region was to be reduced to a rate of 4 percent by 1981, 170,000 new jobs would have to be created, 50,000 in manufacturing, and our friends from the Chamber of Commerce have made the same quote. Capital investment of about $25 billion would be needed. Of this amount, Mr. Marchand indicated that in the order of 15 percent to 20 percent could be expected to come from government sources. This would leave as much as $20 billion to come from the private sector. The obvious question: is private investment of this magnitude possible if foreign investment is discouraged?

*   *   *   *   *

An industrial strategy should attempt to reconcile regional development policy with national development policy, to take the former out of its socio-political context and make it an integral part of a national industrial plan.

Until this is done, until we receive some answers to the questions about the sources of capital we need, the Atlantic provinces are going to have to fight a delaying action against the rising forces of economic nationalism. We hope Mr. Pepin will get on with the job. We would like to participate in it.

*   *   *   *   *

Mr. Otto (Liberal M.P. for York East): Mr. Chairman, I was looking at the brief on page 2 at the top:

. . . we tend not to make any distinction between investment that comes from Central Canada, the United States or other foreign countries, . . .

And on page 5, at the bottom of the first paragraph:

. . . feel that it will have very little effect on our region, given the common attitude that any investment from outside the region is "foreign".

Does this truly reflect the attitude of the Council or of the people of the Maritimes that we in central Canada or in the West are foreigners?

Mr. Weyman: I think we purposely put these words in our brief, Mr. Chairman, to reflect some thoughts that many members of our board of governors share, and I might say that several other governors share, and I might say that several other governors of APEC saw these remarks that Mr. Flemming and I have worked on. This bill before you, before the Parliament, regarding foreign ownership we think starts in the heartland of Canada, had its origins there far more than in the Atlantic area and perhaps relates to the influence of our great neighbours to the south more in the centre of Canada than it does in our area. Our exposure to the United States and our feeling of more independence and more identity as an independent area from the United States I think is a stronger feeling in the Atlantic area than in central Canada. I think it is fair to say that a lot of Maritimers, a lot of Atlantic people, a lot of New Brunswick people where I come from, feel that we have seen more central Canadian people buy out Maritime firms and close them down than other people from other parts of the world, the United States and elsewhere. When they buy out Maritime firms, they tend to keep them going and perhaps expand them.

. . . I feel that many of us have sometimes felt that we have been better off when it has been a non-Canadian purchaser. That is correct, I did say that, but I do not feel that we are not Canadians and do not want to be involved in the industrial development of our country. However, we do not want to be, if you like, always branch plants of Ontario industries.

What do you think?

1. (a) Why do you think the Atlantic Provinces "make no distinction between investment that comes from central Canada, the United States or other foreign countries, regarding it all somehow as foreign"?
   (b) Explain what Mr. Weyman means by "Ontario branch plants." Does central Canada exert the same kind of control over the Atlantic Provinces as the U.S. exerts over central Canada? Why?
2. (a) Do you feel that the so-called regions of Canada enjoy a feeling of more independence and more identity as an independent area from the United States than does central Canada? If so, why?
   (b) Is the issue of foreign investment a central Canadian issue? Why does Mr. Weyman think so? Do you agree? Why?
   (c) To what extent is Mr. Weyman's argument supported by the Star figures on page 13?
3. (a) What economic problems faced by the Atlantic Provinces are not shared by central Canada? What other areas in Canada face similar problems?
   (b) To what extent can foreign investment assist in alleviating these problems and why?
4. Does the problem of regional economic disparity reveal a weakness in the economic nationalism argument? How would an economic nationalist answer Mr. Weyman? Do you think that economic nationalists have successfully attempted to deal with this problem of regional economic disparity? Support your view.

4.   THE MYTH OF CANADIAN INDEPENDENCE

Douglas C. Greenwood of Barrie, Ontario, criticized the claims of economic nationalists in a Letter to the Editor in the Globe and Mail, February 28, 1972.

A great deal is heard nowadays about Canadian independence. Plans to restrict the investment of foreign capital in Canada are being prepared by the federal government. And an attitude of antagonism to both U.S. and European enterprise in Canada exists in two major political parties.

All this is based on an illogical belief that Canada is somehow being cheated and that we can supply our own development capital, thus guaranteeing control of our country while at the same time growing richer. All such thinking becomes a multiple myth if we expect to maintain our present standard of living and development. A small nation of twenty-one million people can, generally speaking, keep company with the technological and creative giants of today only as a consumer and domestic producer, never as an innovator.

Virtually every single product (and many, many services) that we take for granted in Canada, have their origin outside this country. Even the snowmobile, could never have been developed and produced without the necessary materials, components and machine tools, all of which were originally researched and developed in either the United States or Europe. And this goes for most other products that might seem to be entirely Canadian. Everything, from finery to contemporary philosophies, comes to us almost entirely from original innovations motivated and supported by the vitality of a mass-market free enterprise that, today, can occur only in vastly populated industrial countries such as Europe and the United States.

With regard to all this, the head of Ogilvy and Mather Inc., a large U.S. advertising agency, said in Washington recently that we should stop being so nationalistic when the world is moving to greater international and interdependent socio-economic co-operation. "It is time that Canada's leaders made it clear to those whose votes they seek that the price of isolation from the United States is poverty. It happens to be true," he warned.

I think it is vital for Canadians to realize just what the country is heading for if legislatory powers are lured by the myth of Canadian independence; it comes with the barbed hook of, at best, a complete political break-away of our wealthier and more productive provinces or, at worst, an agrarian existence under a Cuban-like despotism.

What do you think?

1. (a) Why does Mr. Greenwood feel that Canadian independence is a myth?
   (b) Explain why you think Mr. Greenwood's case against economic nationalism is effective or not.

2. Evaluate Mr. Greenwood's contention that the wealthier and more productive provinces of Canada would separate if the economic nationalists won substantial legislature concessions. Why do you think he feels the way he does? Would Mr. Weyman (page 36) agree with him? Why?

3. (a) Explain what Mr. Greenwood means by an "agrarian existence under a Cuban-like despotism." What criticism is implied here of economic nationalism and economic nationalists? Is Mr. Greenwood correct? Support your answer.

(b) Evaluate the merits of this type of argument. What strengths does it have. What weaknesses?

Canadian Policy

Concern over U.S. investment has been evident in Canada for some time, particularly since the mid-1950s, when the Royal Commission on Canada's Economic Prospects, headed by Walter Gordon, spelled out in detail the magnitude and possible dangers of U.S. investment. Since that time there have been several other government inquiries on the same theme.

What has been the response of Canadian governments, federal and provincial, to the findings of these reports? What policies have been instituted? Are they adequate?

1. CANADIAN POLICY ON FOREIGN INVESTMENT

This selection consists of extracts from the 1968 Watkins Task Force Report on Foreign Ownership and the Structure of Canadian Industry (Information Canada, 1968).

While there has been concern among Canadians for some time about foreign, especially American, ownership and control of Canadian industry, it has, in general, been the policy of all levels of Canadian government not only to permit, but to actively encourage, foreign investment.

Although Canadians have been anxious to maintain political independence, they have also wanted to maintain a high standard of living and develop the country's natural resources.

Unlike France, the United Kingdom and Japan there is no formal screening for foreign investment and no governmental agency with which a foreign investor must consult prior to undertaking direct investment. While this absence reflects, compared to most countries in the world, a particularly liberal policy toward foreign direct investment, it does not mean that Canadian policy has been non-existent. In particular, the Canadian government has discouraged foreign ownership or control of certain key sectors and industries: American control of railways in the post-Confederation period; airlines, bus lines, and radio stations in the 1920s and 1930s; television stations and insurance companies in the 1950s; and newspapers and banks in the 1960s. Canadian ownership and control have been ensured by the setting up of Crown corporations, as in the cases of Air Canada and the Canadian Broadcasting Corporation.

The substantial increase in foreign direct investment since 1950 has resulted in a number of specific policy steps. The Canadian tax structure has been altered in various ways to encourage foreign investors to do things deemed consistent with the Canadian interest. The balance of payments implications of foreign investment have received considerable attention. Incidents of American extraterritoriality and the issuing of American guidelines to direct investment firms have created much apprehension and some new policy initiatives, of which the most notable is Canadian guidelines for foreign owned firms. No systematic overall policy has emerged, however, and Canadian policy remains one of the most liberal in the world.

A clear Canadian policy at the level of the federal government has taken shape over the past decade to maintain Canadian ownership and control of federally-incorporated financial institutions, while the pre-existing policy of maintaining Canadian ownership and control of the media of communication has been strengthened. In general, this reflects the Canadian commitment, a liberal policy towards foreign investment notwithstanding, to protect Canadian business in these key sectors of the economy and the society. The rationale transcends narrowly economic considerations. Communications media lie at the heart of the techno-structure of modern societies. Canadian ownership and control facilitate the expression of Canadian points of view. Financial institutions, because of their pervasiveness and their potential as bases for influence and control, constitute the commanding heights of the economy. Canadian ownership and control facilitate the exercise of Canadian economic policies. The key sector commitment, and its variant, the key firm commitment, have not been extended, however, by the development of any policy instruments to deal with foreign take-overs outside these sectors.

Canadian policy toward foreign investment has been piecemeal and gradual, and apparently more so than policies pursued elsewhere. In some part, this is the result of the Canadian federal system. Jurisdiction over subsidiaries lies, to some extent, with the provinces, and provincial governments have generally not distinguished between residents and non-residents of Canada in their policies on investment. More generally, Canadian policy has been consistent with a favourable attitude on the part of Canadian governments at all levels toward foreigners who wish to invest in Canada. This attitude has deep roots in Canada, and is unlikely to change significantly.

What do you think?

1. *Outline the existing controls on foreign investment suggested by this extract. Summarize the types of policies Canadian govern-*

ments have adopted towards certain sectors of the economy. Do you agree or disagree with the philosophy behind these policies? Why? Do you feel these policies are adequate? Why or why not?

2. *(a) According to this extract, what is the basic weakness in Canadian policy towards foreign investment? How could this weakness be remedied?*

 (b) In your view is it better for governments to attempt to establish broad policies to meet all situations or to produce specific legislation to solve specific problems? Why? What advantages and disadvantages can you see in both approaches?

3. *Does the Canadian federal system make it extremely difficult for federal and provincial governments to deal with the problem of foreign investment? Why?*

2. THE CANADA DEVELOPMENT CORPORATION

Liberal Finance Minister Edgar Benson introduced on January 25, 1971 legislation to set up the Canada Development Corporation. Jack Cahill, a Toronto Star reporter, wrote the following article for that paper on January 26, 1971.

The Canada Development Corporation, with an eventual $2 billion to spend and a mandate to develop and maintain Canadian industry, will be in operation before the end of this year, Finance Minister Edgar Benson said last night. He made the prediction after he introduced in the Commons a long-promised bill to set up the corporation as a holding and investment corporation — it would be Canada's biggest — in which the Canadian public will eventually buy most of the shares at $5 each.

Benson described the corporation as a private profit-making enterprise in which the government would hold a minimum 10 percent interest. It would not, he said, make any attempt to "buy Canada back" from foreign investors, nor act as a buyer of last resort to prevent sales of Canadian industries to foreign owners. "Rather," he said, "the corporation will be forward-looking. It will provide a huge pool of capital for investment in Canadian industries and no doubt do much to help keep in Canadian hands companies which might in future fall into foreign ownership."

The aim of the goverment is that the corporation will become a vast and profitable investment company, paying dividends to its common shareholders according to company policy and the level of its profits. Holders of preferred shares would get a fixed dividend and have first call on profits. Shares would ultimately be listed and traded on stock exchanges.

A statement by the finance department said that the corporation "will act in the broad area in which the national interest and the profit motive are compatible." Asked what the corporation would do in areas where the two were not compatible, Benson emphasized that the government intended the corporation to make a profit. For instance, he said, the corporation would not be allowed to invest in Air Canada or Canadian National Railways because they were not strictly commercial enterprises and if the corporation was to make an investment "it must be a good investment."

He said he believed the bill would be given second reading — approval in principle — within a few weeks and that the corporation would be fully organized by the end of the current session of Parliament.

Preferred shares would be used in some instances as part of deals involved in the purchase of equity in companies, Benson said. The corporation could make short-term investments, get involved in joint ventures with other groups, lend money, issue guarantees and invest in businesses operating outside Canada. Benson said the corporation would begin by buying "at a fair and reasonable cost" the government's interests in Polymer Corporation Ltd., Eldorado Nuclear Ltd., Panarctic Oils Ltd., and Northern Transportation Co. Ltd. The government's assets in these four companies are estimated to be worth about $300 million. After that, Benson said, the corporation will assume significant equity positions, generally worth more than $1,000,000, with its investments in Canadian companies. "Whether its investments are made independently or in concert with other corporations, they will aim at ensuring Canadian control," he said.

The government's move was welcomed by former finance minister Walter Gordon, an ardent Canadian economic nationalist, who first advocated the idea of a Canadian Development Corporation in 1963, when he was finance minister. Conservative Opposition Leader Robert Stanfield said he had "no ideological opposition" to the proposal. But new Democratic Party Leader T. C. Douglas described it as a "sellout to big business" and vowed that his party would fight the bill all the way through the parliamentary process. Douglas objected to the idea that the corporation would take over a number of successful government-owned enterprises — "owned by all the people of Canada" — and turn them over to the corporation "which will be 90 percent owned by private enterprise."

Benson's bill would set up a corporation which would have:

—$1 billion in authorized capital, consisting of 200 million voting shares to be issued eventually to the public at no par value but a probable issue price of $5 a share.

—$1 billion worth of preference shares at a price to be determined. They might be voting or non-voting shares.

—A board of 18 to 21 directors, who must be Canadian citizens and the majority of whom must be residents of Canada.

—Shareholders who must be either Canadian citizens or residents of Canada, although non-voting preferred shares may be held by others.

—No individual or group of associated shareholders with more than 3 percent (worth $60 million) of the outstanding shares of the corporation.

—A minimum of 10 percent government interest in the corporation.

Benson said the basic idea of the corporation he proposed was to "help develop and maintain strong Canadian-controlled and Canadian-managed corporations in the private sector; and to provide greater opportunities for Canadians to invest and participate in the economic development of Canada.

"The corporation will help shape and secure future Canadian development," he said. "It will be a large-scale source of capital to create major new enterprise. It will join others in acquiring and rationalizing existing companies where competitiveness may be improved by merger, amalgamation or other corporate arrangements. In helping to bring these changes, it will reduce the risks of an undesirable degree of foreign control of the enterprises concerned."

But Benson emphasized that the corporation would not "become a tool of government" and that it would only attempt to prevent the sale to foreign interests of Canadian companies that were profitable and viable.

*   *   *   *   *

Benson said he did not believe that the basic concept of the corporation had been changed since Gordon first proposed it in 1963. "I don't think the idea of the CDC ever was to buy Canada back," he said.

What do you think?

1. What is the purpose of the Canada Development Corporation?
2. (a) Why did Mr. Benson emphasize that the CDC would not "buy Canada back"?
   (b) Should that function be part of the CDC's role? Why or why not?
3. How effective do you think an institution like the CDC is for:
   (a) Canadian economic development?
   (b) Dealing with the problem of U.S. investment? Why?

3. A CHRONOLOGY OF CANADIAN POLICY

The committee for an Independent Canada prepared this brief outline chronicling Canadian policy on the foreign ownership issue.

1957—Walter Gordon's *Royal Commission on Canada's Economic Pros-*

pects first officially posed the question of foreign ownership as an issue requiring government policy decisions and intervention.

1959—*The National Energy Board Act* gave the board regulatory power over all stages of production, movement, sale or export of energy and sources of energy, wherever Parliament has jurisdiction, including the Territories, and over inter-provincial and international oil and gas pipelines and electric power lines. This control includes the licensing of construction, standards of construction and operation and regulation of rates.

There is as yet no strategic power to block foreign takeovers in the energy industry. U.S. firms own almost 100 percent of our petroleum refineries and control most of the pipeline industry.

1962—*Corporations and Labour Unions Returns Act* (CALURA) empowered the government to collect financial and other information on the affairs of corporations and labour unions carrying on activities in Canada. Such information was considered necessary to evaluate the extent and effect of non-resident ownership and control of corporations in Canada and the extent and effects of the association of Canadians with international unions.

Information gathered by CALURA is classed as non-confidential and confidential. The first category which includes date and purpose of the incorporation of the business, name of officers and directors and ownership of share capital is available for each firm to any person who makes application for it. The second class of information covering assets, sales, projects and payments to non-residents is presented in statistical form each year, but does not disclose any data for individual firms. Though subject to a considerable time lag, the annual reports of the minister under the Act remain the best source of information on the extent and trends of non-resident ownership of the economy.

1963—Walter Gordon's first budget of the new Liberal government headed by Lester Pearson included the strongest measures ever brought to bear on the U.S. takeover of Canadian business corporations. A 30 per cent tax was to be levied on the value of shares of Canadian firms listed on stock exchanges sold to non-resident corporations or individuals. To further encourage Canadian ownership, the 15 percent withholding tax on dividends paid to non-residents was to be reduced to 10 percent for companies whose shares were at least a quarter Canadian owned, and increased to 20 percent for firms with a lower proportion of domestic ownership. Gordon also proposed a faster rate of depreciation to companies with the requisite 25 percent Canadian ownership.

A few days later on June 19, after severe pressure from the financial community had been brought to bear on him, Gordon announced the withdrawal of the take-over tax.

While Walter Gordon's direct attack on foreign ownership did not succeed his 1963 budget aroused national concern to the point where the government finally did act to protect key sectors of the economy such as the financial institutions, communications, and transportation. Amendments to the Bank Act, the insurance, loan and trust companies acts limited the proportion of shares in these concerns by non-residents to no more than 25 percent and at least three-quarters of the directors must be Canadian citizens resident in Canada.

More recently, Cabinet direction to the CRTC has resulted in the repatriation of several hundred million dollars of assets in the broadcasting industry.

Even the long-awaited Canada Development Corporation had its basis in the finance minister's controversial budget.

1968—*Foreign Ownership and the Structure of Canadian Industry* (the Watkins Report) updated the research and made a number of new recommendations:

1. A Special agency to coordinate policies concerning the multinational enterprise by means of the following functions:
    (a) collecting and disseminating information necessary for the surveillance of foreign-owned firms;
    (b) examining licensing agreements and facilitating the import of technology with minimum restrictions on its use.
    (c) facilitating export promotion.
    (d) initiating international cooperation with respect to the multinational firm in such matters as investment guarantees, harmonization of anti-trust policies, and international charters, and
    (e) exercising public surveillance over foreign-owned subsidiaries.
2. Establishment of a government export trade agency to ensure that export orders are filled when they conform with Canadian law and Canadian foreign policy.
3. Creation of a Canadian Development Corporation to act as a large holding company with entrepreneurial and management functions to assume a leadership role in Canada's business community.
4. Distribution by large corporations, including foreign-owned subsidiaries, of their shares to Canadians, thereby increasing the supply of Canadian equities.

1970—*Commons Standing Committee on External Affairs and National Defence* (the Wahn Report) produced a long list of recommendations reflecting growing public concern over the extent of foreign ownership, including

1. Constant review and strengthening of the Winters guidelines;
2. Support for the Watkins objectives and conclusions;
3. Multilateral tariff reductions and arrangements for specialization and mergers of Canadian firms, especially in "high technology" industries;
4. Growth of merchant banking facilities, that is to say, of Canadian financial institutions with entrepreneurial ability;
5. Restrictions on non-residents borrowing in Canada for expansion of subsidiaries or establishment of new enterprises;
6. Support for a CDC structured as a large building company with entrepreneurial and management functions, but not as a "buy-back" agency or mutual fund;
7. A Canadian ownership and Control bureau similar to the Watkins Reports special agency, but with power to block takeovers in key sectors;
8. Recovery of control over our resources industry;
9. Distribution of at least 51 percent of voting shares of subsidiaries to Canadians, over a reasonable period of time;

1971—*Canadian Forum Version of the Gray Report.*

Three broad strategies for dealing with foreign investment were examined in the Report, although the first of these was recommended:

1. The introduction of a screening process, i.e. a government agency with the power to negotiate for better performance from foreign direct investors (e.g. further processing), and with the power to block investment that does not make a net contribution to the Canadian economy or that does not accord with the objectives of the government;
2. the delineation of further "key sectors" in which foreign ownership would be regulated;
3. the introduction of across-the-board ownership rules, (e.g. 51 percent Canadian ownership) and other structural changes relating to the use of Canadian managers and directors.

Under (2) the "key sector" approach, some sectors of the economy should be reserved for Canadian control if practicable ways are found for administering them. The "key sector" approach was regarded as more costly to the economy than the screening process, but it could be used as a supplement to the screening process.

The approach requiring 51 percent Canadian ownership was rejected as being too costly and not in itself a guarantee of efficiency.

The major recommendation is for a new screening agency and this is discussed under a number of different headings.

1973—*Foreign Investment Review Act.*

In January, 1973, the federal government introduced Bill C-132 in the House of Commons. Cited as the *Foreign Investment Review Act,* the new legislation would establish an agency to examine and assess proposals for foreign takeovers and the entry of new foreign direct investment, including the expansion of existing foreign-controlled corporations into 'unrelated' fields. After receiving the report of the Foreign Investment Review Agency, the federal cabinet would either accept or reject the individual application under discussion.

The first part of the bill would make subject to review foreign takeovers of firms valued at more than $250,000 or with annual gross revenues of more than $3 million. The requirement for screening would apply to the takeover of both Canadian-controlled and foreign-controlled companies operating in Canada.

The second part of the bill provides for the screening of new foreign direct investment, including the expansion of established foreign-controlled corporations into "unrelated" activities. The bill does not define what is a related or an "unrelated" business. The government will establish the criteria either by guidelines or in regulations under the new act.

The bill provides that the second part dealing with new investments be proclaimed separately. The Minister of Industry, Trade and Commerce has stated that the screening of new businesses established with foreign capital would begin only after the provinces were consulted and "some experience" was gained in operating the takeover review process. The bill does not empower the review agency to screen the expansion of the existing operations of established foreign-controlled companies, even though growth in the sector accounts for a large percentage of the increase in foreign ownership.

Other Legislation.

1. The government intends to introduce shortly a bill to screen licensing agreements.

2. Legislation which would require the majority of directors of federally incorporated companies to be Canadians will be introduced by March.

What do you think?

1. List the steps taken by the federal government since the 1957 Gordon Report to deal with the issue of foreign investment. What

is your opinion of government policy so far in this matter? Why?
2. Explain why many of the recommendations made by the various government-sponsored inquiries have not been acted upon.
3. Compare the recommendations of these government reports. Have they become more, or less, sweeping over the years? Why?
4. How has public opinion influenced government action in this issue? Do you feel that government policy has reflected or run counter to the public opinion? Why?

Proposals

Just as there has been little unanimity on the question of the advantages and disadvantages of U.S. investment in Canada, there has been little unanimity on a possible solution for the problem.

The proposals have crossed a wide spectrum, from a call for outright nationalization of Canadian resources and industries to a plea for outright continental integration of the Canadian and U.S. economies. Myriad proposals have, of course fallen somewhere between these two extremes.

This section provides the opportunity for you to examine and evaluate some of the proposals being made: nationalization, continental integration, the "key-sector" approach, the "screening" agency, the buying up of foreign-owned and foreign-controlled firms, the channelling of Canadian capital into Canadian investment opportunities, better corporate behaviour by U.S. firms, as well as a proposal calling for a complete restructuring of the Canadian economy.

In your view, which proposal, if any, is the most suitable for furthering Canada's best interests? Why?

1. AN INDEPENDENT SOCIALIST CANADA

The following document advocating an "Independent Socialist Canada as a solution to the problem of U.S. investment is from the 1969 Waffle Manifesto. The "Waffle" was an ultra-nationalist left-wing faction of the NDP whose most vocal spokesman was Professor Melville Watkins of the 1968 Watkins Report on the Structure of Canadian Industry.

The Manifesto was presented to the national convention of the New Democratic Party in October 1969 where it was defeated by the more moderate sections of the party. What has happened to the Waffle since that time?

The most urgent issue for Canadians is the very survival of Canada. Anxiety is pervasive and the goal of greater economic independence receives widespread support. But economic independence without socialism is a sham, and neither are meaningful without true participatory democracy.

The major threat to Canadian survival today is American control of the Canadian economy. The major issue of our times is not national unity but national survival, and the fundamental threat is external, not internal.

American corporate capitalism is the dominant factor shaping Canadian society. In Canada, American economic control operates through the formidable medium of the multi-national corporation. The Canadian corporate elite has opted for a junior partnership with these American enterprises. Canada has been reduced to a resource base and consumer market within the American empire.

    *   *   *   *   *

Canadian development is distorted by a corporate capitalist economy. Corporate investment creates and fosters superfluous individual consumption at the expense of social needs. Corporate decision-making concentrates investment in a few major urban areas which become increasingly uninhabitable while the rest of the country sinks into underdevelopment.

The criterion that the most profitable pursuits are the most important ones causes the neglect of activities whose value cannot be measured by the standard of profitability. It is not accidental that housing, education, medical care and public transportation are inadequately provided for by the present social system.

The problem of regional disparities is rooted in the profit orientation of capitalism. The social costs of stagnant areas are irrelevant to the corporations. For Canada the problem is compounded by the reduction of Canada to the position of an economic colony of the United States. The foreign capitalist has even less concern for balanced development of the country than the Canadian capitalist with roots in a particular region.

An independence movement based on substituting Canadian capitalists for American capitalists, or on public policy to make foreign corporations behave as if they were Canadian corporations, cannot be our final objective. There is not now an independent Canadian capitalism and any lingering pretensions on the part of Canadian business men to independence lack credibility. Without a strong national capitalist class behind them, Canadian governments, Liberal and Conservative, have functioned in the interests of international and particularly American capitalism, and have lacked the will to pursue even a modest strategy of economic independence.

Capitalism must be replaced by socialism, by national planning of investment and by the public ownership of the means of production in the interests of the Canadian people as a whole. Canadian nationalism is a relevant force on which to build to the extent that it is anti-imperialist. On the road to socialism, such aspirations for independence must be taken into account. For to pursue independence seriously is to make visible the necessity of socialism in Canada.

What do you think?

1. Discuss the following:
   (a) "The major threat to Canadian survival today is American control of the Canadian economy."
   (b) "American corporate capitalism is the dominant factor shaping Canadian society."
2. (a) Why does the Waffle Manifesto insist that public ownership is the only way to guarantee Canadian independence?
   (b) Evaluate the critique of Canada's capitalist class contained in the Manifesto.
3. What are the strengths and weaknesses of the arguments in the Manifesto? What are your attitudes to the ways in which the arguments are presented? Why?
4. (a) What areas of the Canadian economy are presently under public ownership? Do you consider public ownership a Canadian "tradition"? Why?
   (b) Is there a difference between the public ownership advocated by the Manifesto and the public ownership already in Canada? Explain.
   (c) How would the supporters of the Manifesto propose to introduce public ownership? What would be the benefits and the costs?
   (d) What is your opinion of public ownership in general or as an instrument for Canadian independence?
5. Would the nationalization of foreign-owned industries influence Canada's position as a member of the international trading community? Why?

2. INTEGRATION: RISKY BUT FAVOURABLE

The suggestion that Canada and the U.S. should integrate their economies is a polar opposite to the Waffle's position on the issue of U.S. investment. This action would involve free trade (or an approximation): no tariffs, or very few tariff barriers between the two countries. It might also include industry-by-industry agreements such as the one presently contained in the Auto Pact. Debate over this suggestion has been heated.

*Dian Cohen, an economist who writes for the Toronto Star, ex-
amined the option of integration and concluded that it would favour
Canada. Ms. Cohen's article appeared in the October 2, 1971 issue
of the paper.*

What would happen to Canada if we opted for closer—or total—economic
integration and the U.S. accepted? What would happen to our industries?
What would happen to our jobs?

For the sake of argument, let's assume we chose a degree of economic integration that lets us snuggle up to the U.S. as close as we can,
without losing our status as a politically independent, sovereign nation.

Eric Kierans, the Liberal's renegade, a cabinet minister, has always favored free trade in manufacturing, but when asked yesterday how
he felt about economic integration he said: "Emotionally, I'm dead set
against it." Is there a contradiction here? Perhaps. A great many Canadians fear that closer economic ties with the U.S. would result in an expansion of the Canadian resource industries and a contraction in Canadian
manufacturing. We all know by now, thanks to Kierans, that resource
industries don't create jobs. Manufacturing industries do.

Free trade theory itself is at the root of the fear that there would
be a loss of jobs—and even of population—if we tied in more closely with
the U.S. The reasoning goes like this: Since Canada has more accessible
natural resources than other countries, it will specialize in producing raw
materials and primary goods rather than highly manufactured products.

Specific examples, however, are hard to come by.

Bruce Wilkinson, a University of Alberta economist, says that
more than anything else, the U.S. tariff discourages more Canadian exports
to the U.S. The next most dampening factor is the Canadian tariff which
protects Canadian operations so that they don't have to be efficient. Implication: Eliminate the tariffs and watch efficiency and exports soar.

It is obvious that in the event of closer economic integration with
the U.S. there would have to be large and costly changes in the structure of
Canadian industry. It is obvious, too, that there would probably be stress
periods of additional unemployment and retraining during the transitional
phase. Some industries would fold. Others would become increasingly
specialized. Most studies indicate, however, that the transitional costs
would be relatively short-term, and once borne would be over with for all
time.

W. E. Haviland, N. S. Takacsy, and E. M. Cape, in a study of the
pulp and paper industry, point out that pulp and newsprint are already
being produced in Canada, under internationally competitive conditions.
Their study concluded that under free trade conditions Eastern Canadian
producers could successfully specialize in sanitary tissues, cardboard, and
fine papers. Cape said yesterday that "Canada has the advantage of more

and better wood than the U.S. We have the greatest amount of experience and technology for making machinery for the pulp and paper industry. We are as close to New York and Chicago as any of our potential competitors. If our share of the market in these other papers was the same as it is in newsprint, those sectors would be 10 to 15 times bigger than they are now."

On the other hand, economists David Bond and Ronald Wonnacott looked at the Canadian furniture industry and concluded that, with free trade, most of it would simply disappear. According to their study, Canadian furniture couldn't meet the import competition nor could it get into the U.S. market.

*   *   *   *   *

The Wonnacotts' conclusions seem to be echoed by all the other experts who have studied in detail the implications of economic integration.

- The advantages of free trade access to larger markets would be much more significant for Canadian than for American producers.
- Canadians would not, with economic integration, became hewers of wood and drawers of water.
- Adjustment difficulties should not be exaggerated. Canada's small size makes it unnecessary for Canadians to compete with Americans all along the line. It is necessary only that they compete successfully in the production of a relatively limited number of products.

Paradoxically, Canada might become more dependent yet less vulnerable. Specifically, Canada woud be ensuring through such a treaty that U.S. tariffs would not be raised against Canadian exports, and this possibility is one of the major present sources of Canadian vulnerability.

What is meant by?

"primary industry"
"competitive advantage"

What do you think?

1. *Explain in your own words the argument behind the proposal for Canada's closer integration with the U.S.*
2. *Eric Kierans is a free trader. Yet "emotionally" he is opposed to the removal of tariff barriers. Explain this contradiction. Do you agree with Mr. Kierans? Why or why not?*

3. INTEGRATION WOULD DOOM CANADA

Peter C. Newman, editor of Maclean's Magazine and a founder of the Committee for an Independent Canada, argued in an article in the October 9, 1971 edition of the Toronto Star *that economic integration with the U.S. would be disastrous for Canada. Do you agree?*

The advocates of this option claim that economic union with the U.S. would ensure a much more efficient allocation of Canadian resources: that we would, both as a nation and as individuals, become richer as our living standard reached that of the U.S. They believe that such an arrangement would give Canadian industry the once chance to obtain what it has never had: access to a huge consumer market.

It's an alluring prospect, all right. But it won't work.

*   *   *   *   *

There is little proof that a common market would deliver the benefits claimed by its proponents—and considerable evidence that it would produce some disastrous effects they aren't even discussing. But because it's an option that Canadians must now consider seriously and may eventually even have to vote on, it's essential to understand what's involved:

The establishment of a North American common market would mean the gradual dismantling of the tariffs on the $28 billion worth of goods that flow across the 49th parallel every year. It is a commerce that constitutes the world's largest trading partnership. Historically, our tariffs have been considered the legitimate price of Canadian independence; the economy's only protection against unlimited competition from the industrial giant south of the border. At the same time, the nature of the U.S. tariff structure has been at least partially responsible for the Canadian economy's concentration on raw material extraction. American tariffs rise according to the degree of processing. The tariff on cod, for example, jumps 30 percent when it's shipped in the form of fish sticks instead of frozen blocks.

A common market with the U.S. and the totally unimpeded access to our resources such an arrangement would allow, might well mean, as its advocates claim, an unprecedented resources boom. The trouble is that primary extractive industries don't create jobs. The spectacular resource boom of the 1950s failed to provide any base for expanding employment opportunities. Despite the billions of dollars invested in new mines, pulp mills, smelting and oil wells, by 1960 all of these industries were employing only 4 percent of the labor force, 1 percent less than in 1950.

Canada's most pressing economic problem is that we have the fastest growing labour force in the world. Dr. Sylvia Ostry of the Economic Council of Canada has predicted that 2,600,000 new jobs will have to be found in the 1970s merely to absorb the influx of new job seekers. That's the equivalent of 22,000 new jobs a month during the next 10 years. Only such labour-intensive activities as manufacturing could even begin to produce jobs in those numbers.

At the heart of the argument put forward by the proponents of a common market with the U.S. is their conviction that our factories would obtain the advantages of large-scale production and gain access to the huge consumer markets of the U.S. It would give them the kind of quantum leap in customers they couldn't hope to reach without at least another century of Canadian population growth.

There are four main flaws in this simplistic notion:

1. At the same time as our industries would gain access to the U.S. market, American manufacturers would be swamping us with their goods, which would start with a competitive edge over our own products because of the built-in price advantages of their longer production runs.

2. The disadvantaged regions of Canada would be no better off than before. It would be mainly the factories of Ontario's Golden Horseshoe that could be successfully integrated into the American economy. Most of the industrial expansion started after the establishment of a Common Market would take place south of the border, through the extension of production runs in American factories. Of the many factors that go into the production of any item, only two—marginally lower wages and proximity to raw materials—might favour a few Canadian locations.

3. A study for the Royal Commission on Canada's Economic prospects by D. H. Fullerton and H. A. Hampson showed that the average costs of manufacturing in Canada run about 36 percent higher than in the U.S. And an Economic Council investigation of the same problem concluded that the capital invested for each Canadian employed in manufacturing is 40 percent greater than in the U.S. These are disadvantages that no common market arrangement could overcome.

4. Nearly two-thirds of the factories that do operate in Canada are now American owned. In fact, more than 90 percent of Canadian plants important enough to have more than 5,000 names on their payrolls are owned by the outsiders. Under a common market, it's highly doubtful that American plants would be allowed to compete with their parent firms. The classical doctrine of free trade implies that business transactions are carried on by independent companies in different countries at arms length. But in this era of multinational corporations, it would be a pure illusion to imagine that most of the subsidiaries operating here would become anything but feeder plants for head office operations.

*   *   *   *   *

A U.S. Cabinet Task Force, headed by George P. Shultz, Nixon's labour secretary, last year called for the development "of common or harmonized United States-Canadian policies with respect to pipelines and other modes of transportation, access to natural gas, and other related energy matters."

To Americans, the idea of treating North Americans as a single entity is hardly startling, since they tend to think of us as an economic adjunct anyway. But to Canadians, such an arrangement would have serious political implications. Could two nations of such disparate population and power realistically concern themselves with "continentalization," or would the outcome of such an agreement bound to end up as something closer to "Americanization"?

Any tariff-free arrangement would place severe limitations on independent Canadian action in every area of domestic concern. Eliminating the 50-cents-per-ton tariff on U.S. coal coming into Ontario, for example, would not satisfy the conditions of free trade, unless the $6-per-ton subvention on Nova Scotia coal sold in Ontario was also eliminated. Already, as a condition of removing the 10 percent surcharge, the Americans are demanding prior consultation with Ottawa in cases of provincial or federal industrial development programs. In other words, if a Canadian factory is granted a low interest loan or a special tax write-off that might make it more competitive in the export market. Washington would have to approve the scheme.

The removal of U.S.-Canadian tariffs inevitably would be followed by "harmonization" of the two countries' monetary fiscal and social policies. Common institutions for dealing with pollution and other social problems, common securities regulations, common anti-trust laws, and a common currency would follow. Eventually, pressures would come or the removal of all boundaries and the establishment of common citizenships. It would be the end of the "Canadian dream".

What do you think?

1. *What are Mr. Newman's economic arguments against economic integration? Has he effectively answered the arguments in Ms. Cohen's article (page 52)? Why or why not?*

2. *What is Mr. Newman's "nationalist" argument? Do you agree with him? Why or why not? Do you feel that Canadians who favour economic integration could agree with Mr. Newman? Why or why not?*

3. *"Historically, the tariff has been considered the legitimate price of Canadian independence." What has been the "price" of the tariff? What have been the benefits? Would you favour the removal of tariff barriers between Canada and the U.S.? Why or why not?*

4. INTEGRATION: TWO CASES

The following case studies, taken from the Toronto Star of October 21, 1971, examine the possible impact of integration on two Canadian workers. How do the arguments presented by Ms. Cohen and Mr. Newman explain the possible effect integration would have on them?

FOR RAY, INTEGRATION WOULD MEAN A RAISE

Canadians bought more than $5,000,000 worth of Dominion Luggage last year in stores from Halifax to Vancouver. But a shopper in Buffalo will get nothing but a blank stare from the sales clerk if he asks to see a Dominion suitcase, overnight case or bag. That's because a 20 percent U.S. tariff keeps almost all Dominion luggage north of the border.

Complete economic integration with the U.S. would mean more jobs at Dominion's 200-man North York plant, Robert Slan, president of the company, predicts. Sales in the giant U.S. market could also mean higher wages for employees like foreman Ray Fusco, who joined Dominion 22 years ago when it was a tiny 12-man shop. "There would certainly be much more prosperity all around," Slan says, "and this could be passed on to employees." Slan admits his employees don't make as much money as their counterparts in the U.S., "We've been thinking about the U.S. market," Slan says. "But this tariff has taken us out of the picture. We can't compete."

Dominion luggage has been displayed at several U.S. trade shows "and we are constantly being told that our workmanship is far superior to U.S. products," Slan says. "But we're trapped." Less than 2 percent of Dominion's sales last year were in the U.S. The 10 percent surcharge recently imposed by the U.S. will probably dry up even that little trickle. Complete economic integration "really makes sense," Slan says. "After all, we are very closely tied already and we all live on the same continent."

If the trade barriers suddenly crumbled, there would be an initial period of confusion. "We would probably be forced to specialize . . . not carry as many items," Slan says, pointing out that Dominion now manufactures 330 different products. "We have so many items because we serve an entire Canadian market," Slan says. "If we specialize, we can gear up for much longer runs which would be more economical as we sell fewer items but in a much larger market."

FOR ANITA . . . UNEMPLOYMENT

Complete integration of the Canadian and United States economies would mean personal disaster for Mrs. Anita Antoni, a women's dress finisher in the Spadina Avenue garment district. Her boss, Abraham

Michaelov, says he would be forced to close his small shop, throwing 35 workers out of jobs, if he had to compete on even terms with U.S. clothing companies. Mrs. Antoni's husband, a cloth cutter for a larger garment manufacturer, would stand to lose his job, too.

The jobs of the Antoni family are secure now because of the protection of a high Canadian tariff on finished garments coming into Canada from the U.S. American made woven fibre dresses, like the ones Mrs. Antoni makes, are hit with a 22 percent tariff and an additional 12 percent federal sales tax. The tariff goes as high as 27 percent on some knitted items. Meanwhile, the U.S. imposes a similar tariff on Canadian garments. A woven fibre dress exported to the U.S. would be subject to a 17 percent tariff and, now, an additional 10 percent surcharge. Both tariffs—the U.S. and Canadian—means there is very little clothing exporting done between the countries. And for small shops like Michaelov's Michele Manufacturing, that guarantees economic survival. "If suddenly the big U.S. clothing companies started bringing their dresses here we would be wiped out," Michaelov says. "There is just not any way we could compete. We are a small shop and our costs for making dresses are higher than what the U.S. companies have to pay."

There are dozens of small garment manufacturers employing hundreds of workers in the Metro area. Most are geared for short production runs to serve the limited Canadian market. Michaelov, for example, had only $200,000 in sales last year. This year, Michaelov has salesmen canvassing in the west and hopes to sell a little more.

"We are not what you would call big business," Michaelov says. "It costs us more to produce a dress because we are a small shop." The U.S. companies, because they produce thousands of copies of a single dress, can cut their costs, he explains. "I came to Canada three and a half years ago from Israel," says Michaelov. "I can do okay here. But if this integration thing ever came about there would be nothing else to call it but disaster."

What do you think?

1. Explain why the removal of Canada-U.S. customs tariff would benefit Dominion Luggage but ruin Mr. Michaelov?

2. Why is specialization a more economical and efficient form of production? How do you think the economy would be affected by increased specialization in manufacturing?

3. How would those who favour economic integration justify the effect of this policy on people like Anita? Is this justification adequate? Why or why not?

5. THE SCREENING CONCEPT

Lying somewhere between the two poles of nationalization and continental integration is the suggestion that a screening agency be created to inspect and regulate foreign investment.

This selection is an excerpt from the Financial Post *interview with Professor Abraham Rotstein, published February 20, 1971.*

The screening agency suggestion has been called the "middle way." How can you account for this?

The debate over Canada's ownership problems already is lengthy, somewhat hostile and, so far, inconclusive.

Recently a newer approach, some would call it a middle way, has started to be advocated. Less dramatic than many earlier recommendations, its strength may lie in its ability to reconcile warring factions.

Among the backers of this approach is Abraham Rotstein. As associate professor of economics at the University of Toronto, his interests fan out in several directions. He is managing editor of *Canadian Forum,* the left-leaning monthly magazine for opinion and the arts, chairman of Praxis Corp., an organization seeking social reforms, and a founding member of the Committee for an Independent Canada.

He discusses his personal views on "the middle way" with FP's Paul Gibson.

FP: Concern over foreign ownership is mounting in Canada. What's been wrong with our policy to date?

Rotstein: We've followed a carte blanche policy toward foreign investment. Except for restrictions on the takeover of financial institutions and our media, we have made a virtue of the massive American expansion into our country. Canadian passivity has been fostered by an ideology of laissez-faire and a faith in the necessarily benevolent consequences of the operation of the free market.

F.P.: Some have argued that the best way to regain control over the Canadian economy is through nationalization of both foreign-owned and Canadian-controlled companies. The banks and other financial institutions sometimes are named as targets. Do you agree with such an approach?

Rotstein: It would mean taking on the opposition of the strongest remaining sector of the Canadian business class. In my view, it's far more important to do the possible straight way, rather than take the long way round which is much more difficult and doubtful. In practical terms, I think this comes down to regulation rather than nationalization.

F.P.: How would you decide which particular areas need regulating?

Rotstein: We must begin by knowing a great deal more about the operations of foreign-owned companies. I don't mean simply the official statistics. We must know about their licensing agreements, their royalty payments, their management fees and the way in which they divide up world markets in terms of exports.

F.P.: What would you do with such information?

Rotstein: Test it against various criteria in regard to the national interest.

For example, is the excessive drain of funds through management fees and royalties a method of tax evasion? Is the restriction on exports through these marketing arrangements harmful to Canadian employment? We would certainly want to look at employment policies.

F.P.: In effect, you are urging the creation of a government agency to control foreign subsidiaries in Canada. How wide a role should it have and to whom should it report?

Rotstein: I would see it set up as a separate government department, but it could come under the Department of Industry. I think it might follow some of the broad lines developed in the Watkins and Wahn reports. By and large, it should be the agency with which new foreign investment should deal in the first instance.

F.P.: Your policy, then, is one of regulation rather than nationalization?

Rotstein: I don't think the crucial question is who owns the title to a company. It's what the company is doing, how it operates. Is it doing things in the national interest?

F.P.: Doesn't ownership of title decide all the subsequent functional factors?

Rotstein: If you believe in the classical rights of property, that ownership of title means the right to decide everything, then, of course, you've got to go after title. In the modern economy, we've come a long way from that belief. We believe public interest can be expressed in various ways through controlling some of the operations and some of the functions. Regulation is a very old approach. All I am really suggesting is that it be extended.

F.P.: You are suggesting, then, that the decision-making power on licensing, marketing and the other points you've mentioned should be taken away from the owning management and be placed in the hands of a public agency.

Rotstein: Essentially it's a matter of guidelines—of developing our guidelines and having an agency prepared to apply them in specific instances, and making exceptions where these are necessary.

F.P.: Isn't there a danger your regulation of business will lead to greater bureaucracy?

Rotstein: There are various possible results, and nobody can guarantee the outcome. But it seems to me that business itself in the larger corporations is not free of bureaucracy. Some of our most bureaucratized institutions are the large corporations and they are not always the most efficient ones.

What do you think?

1. *Describe what is meant by a screening agency? Why is it referred to as the middle way?*
2. *(a) What powers would be given to a screening agency by Professor Rotstein?*
   (b) Do you feel these powers are adequate for regulating U.S. investment and controlling its influence? Why or why not?
   (c) Do you feel that the bureaucratic involvement implicit in the screening idea would be harmful to the Canadian economy? Why or why not?
3. *What questions might a screening agency ask a foreign firm contemplating the takeover of a Canadian company? Why?*

6. CANADIAN OWNERSHIP IS VITAL

Would a screening agency be adequate for dealing with U.S. investment? The Toronto Star, in an editorial on March 15, 1971, argued that control of foreign firms through regulations and guidelines alone is not enough, that Canadian ownership of resources and industry must be a primary goal. Do you agree?

A battle is reportedly going on behind the scenes in the federal cabinet on the issue of foreign ownership of Canadian industry and what Canada should do about it. This argument may account, among other things, for the long delay in the appearance of the cabinet-level study which is being prepared under the supervision of Revenue Minister Herb Gray.

There are apparently two schools of thought on the subject. The first holds that it is not really of crucial importance how much of Canadian industry is owned by American or other foreign interests, so long as the firms involved are under effective supervision by the government. Members of this school put their faith in regulations and guidelines designed to ensure that foreign-controlled companies operate in accordance with Canadian national policy—or as the popular phrase puts it, that they "act like good corporate citizens."

The second school argues that this is not enough; that it is essential to check the flood of foreign takeovers and increase Canadian ownership.

In our opinion, this second school takes the more realistic view of the problem. The "control" group underestimates the difficulty of regulating a giant multinational concern once it is firmly established in Canada.

It is easy for a government department to make sure that such a concern pays its taxes or that it complies with minimum wage laws and similar statutes. But it is a different matter when the officials try to supervise internal corporate management and policy. Here the relevant facts are not all written down in the balance sheets. Many of them are known only to a few insiders in the board of directors and the top executive posts, and these men may not be at all forthcoming with what, to them, is a foreign government.

For instance, a complaint sometimes made against Canadian subsidiaries of U.S. corporations is that they do not go after export sales for their products as a Canadian firm would; that they are unwilling to compete with the parent company in overseas markets or to trade at all with countries on the U.S. government's blacklist, like Cuba or China.

The federal government may issue directives requiring companies in this position to mount a more vigorous sales campaign abroad. The XYZ Company (Canada) may promise to comply, and go through the motions most convincingly, sending out salesmen with great fanfare, entering exhibits at international fairs and so forth. But only the insiders will know how genuine these efforts really were—how many promising sales opportunities were quietly ignored so as not to tread on the toes of the parent XYZ Company in the United States.

That is why it is so important to emphasize Canadian ownership— to retain it at its present level, and as far as possible to regain it where it has been lost. A sound policy should include, as a bare minimum, the establishment of a review board to sit in judgment on future takeovers and permit only those that are considered to serve the national interest—for example, by bringing in needed capital and technology that wouldn't be available otherwise—and barring those that bring only a change in control.

Canadian share ownership and Canadian membership on the board of directors are the surest ways of influencing a company's policy where it is made—on the inside. Ottawa's program on foreign investment should firmly promote both.

What do you think?

1. Describe and account for the Star's position on the screening idea.
2. How would Professor Rotstein answer the Star's "ownership" argument? With whom do you agree and why?
3. What percentage of the voting stock of a large corporation assures control? The Star has suggested (Nov. 13, 1971) 50 or 51 percent Canadian ownership. Is this enough to ensure Canadian control? Why or why not?

4. *What is the difference between the ownership advocated by the Star and by the Waffle group? Account for this difference.*

7. A SELECTIVE APPROACH TO CANADIAN OWNERSHIP

Prime Minister Pierre Trudeau does not feel that blanket Canadian ownership of Canadian resources and industry is necessary. Rather, Trudeau proposed a selective approach to the retention and/or retrieval of Canadian ownership. Why? Trudeau's remarks were quoted in Time, *March 30, 1970.*

I think the art will not be to try and remain distinct from the Americans in all things but to choose those areas in which we think our values are superior. We can't expect, without becoming much poorer, to control all of our economy. What we can do is make an effort to control those economic or financial institutions which are of greater importance in the free development of this society. This Government isn't trying to buy back Canada—to use that cliché. Its trying to make sure that we control that small number of institutions which have greater impact on our development as an individual society, and for the future, that we divert our savings, our hard-earned investments more and more to areas which are areas of future potential greatness for Canada rather than try and spread our ownership or our investments all across the board.

We don't want to put a tariff on culture, or a barrier on brains or on capital or technology just because it comes from the U.S.A. Very often it is better than what we have and we should take it. But, in cases where it is not better we should defend ourselves against it.

What do you think?

1. (a) *What is a "key sector"? What key sectors does Canada still control?*
   (b) *Is Mr. Trudeau advocating, among other things, a "key sector" approach? Why?*
   (c) *What advantages and disadvantages can you see in a "key sector" approach?*
   (d) *Could such approach be feasible or useful without using a screening process to determine what sectors of the Canadian economy should be owned or controlled? Why?*
2. *"We don't want to put a tariff on culture or a barrier on brains or on capital or technology just because it comes from the U.S.A. Very often it is better than we have and we should take it. But in cases where it is not better we should defend ourselves against it."*

(a) *Do you agree? Why or why not?*

(b) *Who should decide what is foreign but desirable as opposed to what is foreign but undesirable?*

(c) *How can Canadians defend themselves against what is foreign and undesirable?*

8.   REROUTE CANADIAN CAPITAL

Does the solution lie in curbing foreign investment or in encouraging Canadians to invest more in their own economy? John S. Moir and D. M. L. Farr gave their views in The Canadian Experience *(Toronto: McGraw-Hill Ryerson, 1969).*

The plain fact is that Canada has benefited enormously, all through her history, from the influx of foreign capital. With the capital have also come skills, technological know-how and access to foreign markets that could not otherwise have been obtained. Without the large capital inflow from abroad Canada's industrial expansion and living standards would not approach their present levels. To attempt to discriminate against United States investment in Canada, as Walter Gordon, the Liberal Party finance minister, did in his first budget in 1963, is a dangerous manoeuvre that can lead to unfortunate consequences. Such a policy is discriminatory because it singles out one country for attention; it is economically unsound because it disturbs a natural movement of economic forces; it is risky because it invites retaliation. Persisted in, discrimination could discourage American investors in Canada, reduce the flow of American capital, and slow down the rate of Canadian economic growth. Such a policy could also poison Canadian-American relations for many years. Few Canadians would be prepared to face all these possible consequences.

The solution to the problem would seem to lie not through discriminatory regulations applied to foreign investment, but through encouraging Canadians to invest more of their own funds in the growing sectors of their economy. Life insurance companies, with tremendous assets at their disposal, clearly should place more than the 5 percent they now do in the common stock of Canadian companies. Over the years the volume of savings by Canadians has steadily increased, both in relation to the national output of Canada and in relationship to total investment. Canadian investment in the United States is valued at over $8 billion, a larger investment on a per capita basis than that of America in Canada. The comparative scale of the two economies inevitably determines that the impact of the one on the other is bound to be spectacular. Yet the Canadian economy is growing stronger and achieving a better balance every year. In the long run these trends may help to reduce Canada's economic dependence on the United States.

What do you think?

1. Evaluate the authors' arguments opposing any discriminatory policy toward U.S. investment.
2. (a) Why do Canadians not invest more money in Canada?
   (b) Does federal government policy encourage Canadians to invest in their own country? If so, how?
3. Should there be government restriction on Canadian investment abroad? Why or why not?
4. To what extent, in your view, would the authors' proposal contribute to resolving what you feel are the problems, if any, posed by U.S. investment in Canada? Why

9. A NEW INDUSTRIAL STRATEGY

Are the proposals which you have encountered so far sufficient to solve the problem, or should they be regarded as partial measures which must be incorporated into a larger scheme to be really effective? Why have some commentators agreed that Canada must restructure and revitalize its entire economy to regain its economic independence?

The policy advocated by these people is usually referred to as a "new industrial strategy." Generally, this involves switching from an economy based on resource exploitation to one based more on manufacturing and service industries. The measures proposed to make this switch vary.

The following section, which broadly outlines the thrust of a "new industrial strategy", is taken from a special issue of International Perspective, a Department of External Affairs publication, entitled "Canada-U.S. Relations: Options for the Future." The article by External Affairs Minister Mitchell Sharp, was released in August, 1972.

How does the "new industrial strategy" relate to the other proposals you have seen? Can it accomplish economic restructuring without creating economic dislocation? What opposition might it encounter and why?

The basic aim of the [third] option would be, over time, to lessen the vulnerability of the Canadian economy to external factors, including, in particular, the impact of the United States and, in the process, to strengthen our capacity to advance basic Canadian goals and develop a more confident sense of national identity. If it is to be successfully pursued, the approach implicit in this option would clearly have to be carried over into other areas of national endeavour and supported by appropriate policies. But the main thrust of the option would be towards the development of a balanced and efficient economy to be achieved by means of a deliberate, comprehensive and long-term strategy.

The accent of the option is on Canada. It tries to come to grips with one of the unanswered questions that runs through so much of the Canada-U.S. relationship, and which is what kind of Canada it is that Canadians actually want. It is thus in no sense an anti-American option. On the contrary, it is the one option of all those presented that recognizes that, in the final analysis, it may be for the Canadian physician to heal himself.

The option is subject to two qualifications. "Over time" recognizes that the full benefits will take time to materialize, but that a conscious and deliberate effort will be required to put and maintain the Canadian economy on such a course. "To lessen" acknowledges that there are limits to the process because it is unrealistic to think that any economy, however structured, let alone Canada's, can be made substantially immune to developments in the world around us in an era of growing interdependence.

The option is one that can have validity on most assumptions about the external environment. A basically multilateral environment, of course, in which trade is governed by the most-favoured-nation principle, would enhance its chances of success. But it would not be invalidated by other premises. That is because the option relates basically to the Canadian economy in such a way as to make it more rational and more efficient as a basis for Canada's trade abroad.

The present may be an auspicious time for embarking on this option. Our trading position is strong. We are regarded as a stable and affluent country with a significant market and much to offer to our global customers in the way of resources and other products. Our balance of payments has been improving in relative terms. We are no longer as dependent on large capital inflows as we once were. A new round of comprehensive trade negotiations is in prospect during 1973. Above all, there is a greater sense of urgency within Canada and greater recognition abroad of Canada's right to chart its own economic course.

The option assumes that the basic nature of our economy will continue unchanged. That is to say that, given the existing ratio of resources to population, Canada will continue to have to depend for a large proportion of its national wealth on the ability to export goods and services to external markets on secure terms of access. The object is essentially to create a sounder, less vulnerable economic base for competing in the domestic and world markets and deliberately to broaden the spectrum of markets in which Canadians can and will compete.

In terms of policy, it would be necessary to encourage the specialization and rationalization of production and the emergence of strong

Canadian-controlled firms. It is sometimes argued that a market of the size of Canada's may not provide an adequate base for the economies of scale that are a basic ingredient of international efficiency. The argument is valid only up to a point. The scale of efficiency is different for different industries and there is no reason why a market of 22 million people with relatively high incomes should prove inadequate for many industries which are not the most complex or capital-intensive.

The close co-operation of government, business and labour would be essential through all phases of the implementation of such an industrial strategy. So would government efforts to provide a climate conducive to the expansion of Canadian entrepreneurial activity. It may be desirable, and possible, in the process to foster the development of large, efficient multinationally-operating Canadian firms that could effectively compete in world markets. It may also be possible, as a consequence of greater efficiencies, for Canadian firms to meet a higher proportion of the domestic requirement for goods and services. But that would be a natural result of the enhanced level of competitiveness which the option is designed to promote; it is not in the spirit of the option to foster import substitution as an end in itself with all the risks that would entail of carrying us beyond the margins of efficiency.

The option has been variously described as involving a deliberate, comprehensive and long-term strategy. It is bound to be long term because some substantial recasting of economic structures may be involved. It is comprehensive in the sense that it will entail the mutually-reinforcing use and adaptation of a wide variety of policy instruments. Fiscal policy, monetary policy, the tariff, the rules of competition, government procurement, foreign investment regulations, science policy may all have to be brought to bear on the objectives associated with this option. The choice and combination of policy instruments will depend on the precise goals to be attained. The implications, costs and benefits of the option will vary accordingly.

In saying that the strategy must be deliberate, it is accepted that it must involve some degree of planning, indicative or otherwise, and that there must be at least a modicum of consistency in applying it. One implication of the conception of deliberateness is that the strategy may have to entail a somewhat greater measure of government involvement than has been the case in the past. The whole issue of government involvement, however, needs to be kept in proper perspective. The government is now and will continue to be involved in the operation of the economy in a substantial way. This is a function of the responsibility which the Canadian Government shares with other sovereign governments for ensuring the well-being and prosperity of its citizens in a context of social justice. A wide variety of policy instruments and incentives is already being deployed to that end, largely with the support and often at the instance of those who are more directly concerned with the running of different segments of the economy. It is not expected that the pursuit of this particular option will radically alter the relationship between government and the business community, even if the government were to concern itself more closely with the direction in which the economy was evolving.

Much the same considerations apply to the relationship between the federal and provincial jurisdictions. It is true that, in the diverse circumstances that are bound to prevail in a country like Canada, the task of aggregating the national interest is not always easy. There may be a problem, therefore, in achieving the kind of broad consensus on objectives, priorities and instrumentalities on which the successful pursuit of anything on the lines of the present option is likely to hinge. Part of the problem may derive from a divergent assessment of short-term interests. In terms of longer-range goals, it is much less apparent why federal and provincial interests should not be largely compatible or why the elaboration of this option should not enhance and enlarge the opportunities for co-operation with the provinces. Indeed, there are many areas, such as the upgrading of Canada's natural resource exports, where the implications of this option are likely to coincide closely with provincial objectives.

What do you think?

1. *Explain why Mr. Sharp feels that a new industrial strategy is not a case of anti-Americanism but of the Canadian physician healing himself. How do you think economic nationalists would react to this statement? Why?*

2. *(a) Do you think that some or all of the proposals you have examined in this section would be useful as specific measures to encourage a new industrial strategy? If so, explain how tariff reduction, nationalization, a screening agency, retrieval of Canadian ownership, a key sector approach, the re-channelling of Canadian capital could contribute to a new industrial strategy, if at all?*

   (b) Refer to the CIC's chronology of government policy on page 45. What recommendations made by the Gordon, Watkins, Wahn and Gray reports could be used as a part of such a strategy? Why?

4. *What would be the reaction of the following to the implementation of an industrial growth policy?*
   (a) Canadian business circles
   (b) provincial government
   (c) Canadian trade unionists
   (d) ecologists
   (e) U.S. business
   (f) U.S. government

(g) economic nationalists and their opponents
In each case explain why.

5. What would be the advantages of the strategy for:
   (a) Canadian trade
   (b) Canadian manufacturing
   (c) Canada's job market
   (d) Canada's economic stability
   (e) Canadian independence
   (f) Canada's resource industries?

6. How important are the possible disadvantages of such a strategy?
   (a) increased government intervention
   (b) dislocation of Canadian economy
   (c) danger of U.S. retaliation
   (d) bad side effects of increased industrialization
   In your opinion, do the advantages outweigh the disadvantages
   or vice-versa. Why?

10. INDUSTRIALIZATION WOULD RUIN CANADA

Columnist Dennis Braithwaite argued in an article in the Toronto
Telegram, *September 10, 1970, that increased industrialization would
destroy Canada's calm, safety and comfort by transforming it into
a mini-U.S.*

Well, what's wrong with being a hewer of wood and a drawer of
water? Isn't it this very condition of our economy that makes Canada a
comfortable, safe and relatively calm place to live?

Independence from the United States, either in Melville Watkins' or
Walter Gordon's version, envisages the development of our manufacturing
industries to a level not even dreamed of today. Instead of sending our ore
and our oil and potash, our lumber, fish, grain and all the rest, to the U.S.
for processing, we would do the job ourselves, thereby transforming this
backward land into a modern industrial giant.

Perhaps it would all come true, though I think the economic odds
are against it. But what would we lose in the process? Aren't all the
problems tearing at the U.S. today, excepting only the racial one, a direct
consequence of her phenomenal technological and industrial development?

We are so used to thinking about the difficulties of living with a
giant, or in Trudeau's phrase, sleeping with an elephant, that we overlook
the considerable advantages of the arrangement. For our high standard of
living we have not had to pay the price that's been exacted from our

affluent neighbors. They see this, even if we don't and that's why so many are coming here to live.

If one thing's been demonstrated by the American Dream it is the fallacy of universal happiness through the production and destruction of material goods. A chicken in every pot may equal happiness, but two cars in every garage is only the beginning of the long slide into an engulfing neurosis of discontent. The "richest" nation in history is also the most desperate and the least loved.

We are the envy of the world for the very reason that we have, through pure luck, achieved an American standard of living without the American agony, or anyhow its worst manifestations. Our pollution is less than theirs, we have more room to move about in, vaster tracts of untouched land, much less crime and civil disorder. Nobody has reason to hate or fear us.

Our nationalists ask us to move from this state of undeserved well-being into a new industrial revolution that will be neither new nor revolutionary, but a borrowed thing, a stale piling on of more concrete and steel, more miles of superhighways, more jet ports, more and loftier smoking chimneys, more useless packages and broken bottles in our streams and ditches. For what purpose? Because it is our destiny to make Canada "great" and, more important, make Canada "ours."

Even assuming that we have the technological knack, the drive, the imagination and the historical motivation, at this late date, to do what the Americans have done, which I don't believe, would it be the right thing to do? Would it make any sense, would it be more than political opportunism or envy transformed into imitation of the thing envied?

The curse of men and of nations is they don't know when they are well off, or realize it too late. We may escape the curse, for another generation or two at least, by ignoring the nationalists' foolish and angry cries.

What do you think?

1. Do you agree with Mr. Braithwaite that Canada now is as pleasant a place to live as he seems to suggest? Why or why not? If you do not agree with Mr. Braithwaite, what problems faced by Canadians could be ameliorated by an industrial strategy?

2. (a) Is it fair for Mr. Braithwaite to suggest that Canada's economic nationalists would want to duplicate the American economy? Why or why not?

   (b) Is it possible for Canada to step up industrialization without imitating the U.S. economy? Defend your answer.

3. Is the object of the new industrial strategy to make Canada "great" or "ours"? Explain why or why not.

11.   HOW TO PACIFY CANADIAN NATIONALISM

How does U.S. business view the developing concern in Canada over U.S. investment? Does it feel that it is a Canadian problem alone, or do some American businessmen feel that U.S. firms themselves can help alleviate the problem?

The Toronto Star published on March 10, 1971, an article which first appeared in a U.S. business publication. The author proposed some guidelines for U.S. firms to follow in their Canadian operations.

Business International, a New York weekly newsletter circulated to multinational corporations, has published an article titled "Twelve Steps to Pacify Canadian Nationalism."

Business International advises its U.S. readers: "Corporations should devote time and resources to help allay the rising tide of nationalism in this key market."

The 12 steps it advocates "should be a fundamental part of every management's strategic tool kit, lest recent preliminary skirmishes develop into more serious confrontations."

Business International advocates that, compatible with profits, American companies operating in Canada:

—Develop exports to other countries;

—Process natural resources in Canada;

—Buy the maximum amounts of materials, components and services in Canada;

—Assure reasonable profits to their Canadian operations and taxes to Canadian authorities through proper pricing of goods and services sold to the parent company;

—Retain enough profits in Canada to assure growth of affiliates;

—Assure search and development work in Canada;

—Give the company Canadian management and directors;

—Offer shares to Canadian investors "or, possibly even better, encourage the Canadian public to own parent company shares;"

—Publish financial information—in English and French—even if not legally bound to do so;

—Pay more attention to the Canadian government's concern about pollution and the ecology;

—Support Canadian cultural, intellectual and social objectives;

—Treat Quebec as a distinct market within a market and use linguistic diplomacy.

What do you think?

1. To what extent would the implementation of these suggestions satisfy the grievances of those Canadians who are concerned about U.S. investment? Why?

2. (a) Are U.S. businesses in Canada likely to follow these guide- lines at present? Why or why not?
   (b) Under what circumstances do you think U.S. businesses might adhere to such guidelines? Why?

3. Do you feel that foreign investors have a moral obligation to follow such guidelines? Do such guidelines constitute an un- necessary and unfair intrusion on business operation? Defend your answer.

The Cultural Debate

What is resented in Canada about annexation to the United States is not annexation itself, but the feeling that Canada would dis- appear into a large entity without having anything of real distinc- tiveness to contribute to that identity; that, in short, if the United States did annex Canada it would notice nothing except an increase in natural resources.

Professor Northrop Frye, the distinguished University of Toronto English scholar, has written the above in his critical commentary on Canadian literature, *The Bush Garden* (Toronto: House of Anansi, 1971). The word annexation is a strong one and perhaps points to a threat that does not exist; but Frye has underlined a central theme in the debate over growing American influence in Canada: What is all the fuss about anyway? Does Canada have a distinctive culture of its own to preserve? Or has "Canadianness" already been absorbed by a U.S. identity and U.S. values?

If there are perceptible differences between the Canadian and U.S. societies, what are they? What are their origins? How important are they to Canadians? Are they threatened by U.S. influence and if so, to what extent? How can they be preserved? Should they be?

This section is divided into three parts. The first deals with the general question of whether Canada does have an identity quite distinct from that of the United States. The second is concerned with the relationship between the U.S. economic penetration and the U.S. cultural penetration of Canada. In the third part there are various documents regarding specific areas in Canadian life where the U.S. cultural influence is being felt, what is being done about it and what can be done about it.

1. MY QUEST FOR CULTURE

In the autumn of 1971, Henry Morgan, the American writer and broadcaster, moved to Toronto from New York. This column by Mr Morgan appeared in the Toronto Star on December 10, 1971.

If it is true that Americans are bent on destroying Canada's culture, this American is determined to stem the tide. I will help to save Canadian culture. As soon as I find out what it is.

I approached Marshall McLuhan, the celebrated discoverer of the Death of the Printed Word in Our Time.

"What is Canadian culture?" I asked him.

"Non-existent," he smirked.

"Is there an American culture?"

"Yes. It's in Harvard. I've been there."

Figuring, rightly, that I had the wrong man, I went to a cocktail party. I approached a girl whose measurements indicated that she had a large brain.

"What is Canadian culture?" I smiled.

"Oh, a dirty old American man," she glowed.

Figuring, rightly, that I had the right girl, we went on to discuss Eskimo carvings, filling in the Spadina and opening an account for her at Simpsons.

I asked my friend who runs the Buzz Buzz in my neighbourhood.

"Well, it's like a melting pot here," he said. "You get all kinds. That's why the town is finally getting off its keister."

Do Canadians wear funny suits? Do they smell odd? Is it something in the water? I've been here for about ten weeks now and the only difference I've found is that when you pick up a jar that says "peanut butter" the other side says "beurre d'arachides."

By sight I can't tell a guy from Moose Jaw from an Indianapolite, or whatever they call themselves. Everybody around here seems to speak the same language I do, and I can read the newspaper with no trouble whatsoever.

It's true that they don't play much ice hockey in Louisiana and there are no curling rinks in Miami Beach. But our scotch comes from Scotland and our coffee from Brazil.

We too, can pick up the phone and call China. It's just that we don't have anything to say.

Maybe culture is something they keep in a box at the Royal Ontario Museum (which is better than anything I've ever seen back home, by the way).

What it comes down to, ladies and gents, is that culture isn't something that can be weighed or thumped or pushed around. It's what you are inside. It's who you really are as you.

And Mr. Nixon can't give it to you. And he can't take it away.

What do you think?

1. *"Yes. It's in Harvard." Why did Mr. Morgan feel that he had the "wrong man"?*
2. *If culture is "what you are inside," and "who you really are as you," do you think that there is a Canadian culture that is separate and distinct from the U.S.? Defend your answer, being as specific as possible.*
3. *"And Mr. Nixon can't give it to you. And he can't take it away." Do you agree? Why or why not?*

2.   WHAT IS LEFT OF OUR CANADIAN IDENTITY?

In a Letter to the Editor in the Toronto Star, *November 2, 1971, Bruno C. Meingast of Mississauga, questioned the existence of a distinct Canadian culture.*

I would be the very last to wish Canada become part of the United States, since I feel Canadian. But are not all of us pushing daily hard enough to achieve just this? By lack of reason, by indolence, by lack of ambition and lack of a firm-handed leadership or at least by complacency?

We are constantly bemoaning and deploring the lack of and stressing constantly the necessity for a "Canadian image," a "Canadian identity," whatever that is. Yet, in reality, we copy the Americans in just about everything possible; we live and behave as they do. Just what, aside from natural resources and a beautiful but very neglected scenery, have we got to brag about that would entitle us to the claim of that Canadian identity?

Travelling south—except for the customs officials, a much livelier activity all around you, a much higher percentage of coloured people, restaurants mostly with a superior catering service as compared with ours, slightly more friendliness, often much lower prices—you would hardly be aware that you crossed the border into the United States. You couldn't make either side more American or more Canadian for that matter. The restaurants are stereotyped from Vancouver to Miami. The buildings may be somewhat larger and taller across the border but otherwise very similar. Provincial parks and private summer resorts are of the same green as ours, except that they are better organized, cleaner, and give you more for your money than their Canadian counterparts.

Furthermore, we watch American TV stations, simply because they are better than our own. We sing, listen to and play American tunes, since we have hardly any of our own. We eat American hamburgers and other foods by the ton at innumerable American chain outlets, simply because they are in every corner of the land.

We import American unions, American know-how, and American personnel to man key positions of Canadian-based American firms; we import draft dodgers, long-hairs and troublemakers. We import much of our clothing hand in hand with American fashions, besides precision tools and machinery which obviously cannot be produced here. What is now left of our Canadian image and/or identity?

What do you think?

1. *According to Mr. Meingast, is there such a thing as a Canadian identity, separate from an American identity? What evidence does he use to support his argument? What evidence can you offer either to support or refute his argument?*

2. *What impact is "American" culture having on other countries?" Is the Canadian experience unique? Why?*

3. *Why are Canadians preoccupied with the "identity" question? Because there isn't one? Because there is one, but it's threatened? Other reasons? Defend your position.*

4. *(a) Are all Canadians equally concerned about preserving a special Canadian identity? Are Maritimers more pro-Canadian than Albertans or Ontarians?*

   (b) Where in Canada is anti-Americanism and pro-Canadianism strongest? Be specific and support your argument with specific evidence.

   (c) What role do you feel French Canada plays in protecting the Canadian "identity" from U.S. influence? Why?

OPERATION YANKEEGOHOME

Duncan Macpherson takes a humorous look at an aroused Canadian nationalism.

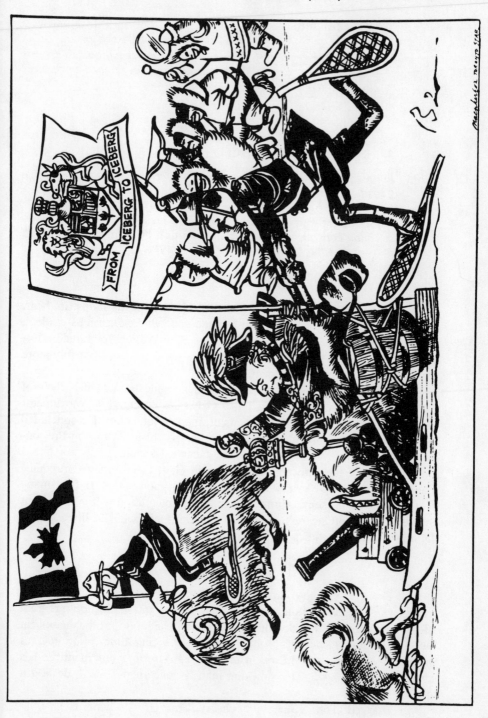

What do you think?

1. *Why did the cartoonist choose these particular symbols to express his ideas? What do you think he is saying about Canadian culture? Do you agree with him? Why or why not?*

4. IS THERE A DIFFERENCE?

Printed below are two articles which question the existence of a Canadian culture distinct from that of the U.S. The first selection is from Galt, U.S.A. *(Toronto: Maclean-Hunter, 1971), a book by journalist Robert Perry, published by* The Financial Post. *The second selection consists of excerpts from an article by Terrence Wills which appeared in the* Globe and Mail, *July 6, 1971.*

GALT, U.S.A.

By my count, Galt has a greater proportion of its industrial heart tissue under American control than Canada as a whole. Decisions made in the United States, in corporate board rooms or in Washington, could affect more than half of the industrial payroll of the small city, and possibly more than half its industrial assessment.

The same decisions could have wider implications in the whole of the Grand Valley, Ken Whittington, a Galt sales executive and a director of the Canadian Institute of Management, made a job count. He concluded that almost 85% of the industrial assets in the Kitchener-Waterloo-Preston-Hespeler-Galt complex were controlled outside Canada.

Most of the truly influential men in Galt, the company presidents like Harry Lee and the civic mandarins, see only good in this. In fact, many of them advocate some form of economic integration with the Great Republic. *Most* of the rest of the adult citizens of Galt just don't give a damn, or if they do, keep their own counsel.

       *   *   *   *   *

For Galt's blue-collar population the question of foreign control remains an 'egghead' issue, until a takeover or rationalization program affects employment. Ray de Souza, who covers the labor and business beat for the Evening Reporter, probably knows the Galt blue-collar man as well as anyone in town. "Erosion of culture? Asserting our identity? His pay cheque: that's what the working man is concerned about," de Souza told me.

I asked Toni Kitchen, a cheery Galt girl studying English at McMaster University, what foreign control of industry in Galt meant to young adults. She didn't have to pause to think. She spoke, and three fellow students nodded in agreement.

"I don't think it affects us at all," she said. "I, for one, was not aware of it. And I'm indifferent to the situation. Even if it's 70%-80% [foreign control], it's too late to stop it, because it's employing our parents and us too. So it really doesn't bother me. It's *there*."

Galt was founded in 1816, and populated largely by immigrants from Scotland. They built a virtual replica of a Scottish shire in that part of the Valley. Diligent, God-fearing Pennsylvania Germans migrated Through the Valley to settle around what is now Kitchener-Waterloo. Two tiles of Canada's heralded cultural mosaic had been laid. A heritage had been bestowed upon the valley. If you want to find that heritage now, you'll have to dig deep—through an incredibly thick, persistent layer of American commercial culture.

Pa Cartwright, Frank Sinatra, Fords, Chevs, Coke, Pepsi, Jello, Kellogg's Corn Flakes, Bufferin, Esso, Gulf, Wrigley's, Kotex, the whole overwhelming flood of goods, ideas and values has so Americanized the valley that sometimes to a visitor the heritage seems like a harmless myth. It's there, I suppose, literally and figuratively hidden, hidden behind the billboards and burger stands.

* * * * *

In Galt, the universal popular culture, the basic lifestyle to which youngsters conform and new immigrants aspire, has been designed, manufactured and promulgated in the United States. I asked Toni Kitchen, the McMaster student and her friend Jan Sandaj, who's studying mathematics at the University of Waterloo, how young adults reacted to what amounts to voluntary cultural annexation.

"I realize that we are influenced," the girl said, "but I don't see why it matters. I just don't see. So what? I accept it the way it is. So what?

"A lot of the fads in Canada are fads because they're fads in the United States. For example, snook boots: square-toed boots. They're getting popular here because they're popular in New York State. That's the only reason. A lot of Canadians don't like them, but they're wearing them just because the Americans are wearing them," Sandaj added.

* * * * *

When they're superimposed on a city like that, the trappings of Americanization sometimes seem as absurd as a vision of Laura Secord doing a topless go-go number. (Strings of faded plastic pennants flicker in the wind over a used car lot. Sure, guy, they're an eyesore, but like you *gotta* have pennants to sell used cars. Who'd buy a used car, forfright'ssake, if you didn't have pennants?)

On Hespeler Road, a main artery between city limits and down-town, Galt has started to develop a Strip: five lanes of roadway edged with outskirt sprawl a hodgepodge, a sampler of the delights of affluence Greasy spoons—motels—service stations—muffler shop—restaurants—truck repair—auto suppliers—car dealers. It has a long way to go to catch up with the blatant overpowering, almost hilarious ugliness of Strips in central New Jersey, Long Island and California. But give it time.

*   *   *   *   *

A significant number of Newfoundlanders have migrated to Galt to find jobs bringing with them one of the few remaining distinct cultural tiles of the old Canadian mosaic. They have an unfamiliar, freewheeling, no-man-owns-me style and a lilting manner of speech. In Americanized Galt, more attuned to the melting pot than the mosaic, the Newfoundland-ers met unexpected hostility and alienation. The irony is, a teacher (who has heard all the cruel Newfie jokes in class) told me, "that there's probably more resentment of immigrants from other parts of Canada than there is against American economic ownership and decision making authority."

Galt is a small American city: highly industrialized, prosperous, work-oriented, ambitious; hewing to middle-American standards of success, status and progress; dedicated largely to the traditional American proposi-tion that if it sells, it's good. And about half of its most influential business-men report to American masters.

Galt U.S.A., exists in the sovereign dominion of Canada by invita-tion, not by invasion. It could of course, be many towns in Canada, large or small, east or west. History didn't confine to southern Ontario the attitudes and pressures that Americanized Galt. So to understand even a little about the 'American presence' in Galt is also to understand something about the Canadian character, about the nature of Canada itself. . . .

IS THERE A NORTH AMERICAN MAN?

If one considers the majority of the continent, is there a North American Man? Some of the many immigrants to the United States from Canada see themselves as just that. They do not see themselves as Canadian-Americans the way immigrants from Mexico call themselves and are called Mexican-Americans; in fact there is no such term as Canadian-Americans because Canadians in the United States are just about indis-tinguishable from native Americans. Yet these immigrants say they do not feel really American or, any longer, really Canadian. This is why some of them feel more like North American Men.

"Because there are just no major differences between a Canadian and an American," said Dr. Alastair Macdonald, who was born in Windsor.

Sitting in his office in a Los Angeles suburb, he said: "Business is organized pretty much here as it is there. Churches. Schools. We are all North American. That is the concept we have to accept."

Monty Hall, who was born in Winnipeg, has made a good deal of money on *Let's Make a Deal,* a TV game show he originated and for which he is master of ceremonies. "I don't consider myself a Canadian living in the United States, nor do I feel like an American," he said. "I do feel like a North American. I travel this continent quite a bit. I make personal appearances all over the United States now, and I have been in many parts of Canada, and the people may talk a little differently in their speech patterns, and they may have strange politics in certain areas where they have been inbred, but the average person is identical, really. The person who lives in Winnipeg, and in Vancouver, and in Orange County, California, or Memphis, Tennessee, has much in common, so much so that when I made a personal appearance in Memphis recently, the head of the advertising council there, was a Canadian. Even with a Southern drawl, he came from Winnipeg originally. And they are all so basically the same."

Dr. Walace Sterling, Toronto-born former president of Stanford University: "One could go at this in different ways: Manners, morals, attitudes. I think, in terms of attitudes, yes, there is a North American Man, and in a certain way I would include French Canadians. Their attitude can be more sharply differentiated as a North American Man, I should think, but I think there is sort of a North American attitude: simple things: I think we are a more free-wheeling. We get on a first-name basis more readily despite differences, sometimes considerable differences in age."

Sitting beside the pool of the San Diego home of her Montreal-born father, Leo Anfossi, listening to her parents and other immigrants talk about a North American Man, Janet Anfossi, a bright young woman, interjected quietly: "Isn't culture the key we're looking for? There is the term Mexican-American because there is a Mexican culture that is different from the American. Is there a Canadian culture that is different? No. It is just a quirk of fate that there is a border there.

[*Mr. Wills goes on to examine this cultural sameness more closely.*]

Is Canada Ottawa-born mimic Rich Little impersonating President Richard Nixon? Is Canada Paul Anka, Giselle Mackenzie, Lloyd Bochner, Percy Faith, Art Linkletter, Mort Sahl, Mack Sennett, or William Shatner? All were born in Canada and made it big adding to American culture. Like all immigrants they fitted into the American culture effortlessly; they found no difficulty expressing themselves with the American culture. How distinct then from the American culture can be the Canadian culture in which they were raised? What then do they think of Canada's efforts to develop a culture distinct from the American?

to manage a subsidiary for its American owners. He's very much at home in Galt. In fact, he finds more cultural differences between various regions of the United States than he does between Ontario and the northern states. A significant number of Newfoundlanders have migrated to Galt to find jobs bringing with them one of the few remaining distinct cultural tiles of the old Canadian mosaic. They have an unfamiliar, freewheeling, no-man-owns-me style and a lilting manner of speech. In Americanized Galt, more attuned to the melting pot than the mosaic, the Newfoundlanders met unexpected hostility and alienation. The irony is, a teacher (who has heard all the cruel Newfie jokes in class) told me, "that there's probably more resentment of immigrants from other parts of Canada than there is against American economic ownership and decision making authority."

Galt is a small American city: highly industrialized, prosperous, work-oriented, ambitious; hewing to middle-American standards of success, status and progress; dedicated largely to the traditional American proposition that if it sells, it's good. And about half of its most influential businessmen report to American masters.

Galt U.S.A., exists in the sovereign dominion of Canada by invitation, not by invasion. It could of course, be many towns in Canada, large or small, east or west. History didn't confine to southern Ontario the attitudes and pressures that Americanized Galt. So to understand even a little about the 'American presence' in Galt is also to understand something about the Canadian character, about the nature of Canada itself. . . .

What do you think?

1. How do you think Mr. Perry defines "culture"? Compare his conception of culture with those of Professor Galbraith and the authors of the Gray Report (pages 88 and 89). Evaluate his definition. What do you think of it?

2. (a) According to Mr. Perry how has American investment influenced Canadian culture in Galt? How do you think this happened?

   (b) What reasons might Mr. Perry give for the Newfoundlanders' retention of a distinctive cultural style? Are the Newfoundlanders proof for Mr. Weyman's (page 36) assertion that the problems posed by foreign investment are experienced only in central Canada? Why?

3. (a) Explain why the people of Galt do not care too much about the issue of Canadian nationalism. How typical do you think this attitude is?

   (b) If residents of Galt are typical of Canada, who is making all the fuss about American investment and why?

5. THE ROLE OF FRENCH CANADA

The preliminary Report for the Royal Commission on Bilingualism and Biculturalism (Information Canada, 1965) discussed, among other things, the relationship between the Quebec problem and the growing influence of the United States.

A number of participants expressed a strong desire for personal and national independence on the one hand, while on the other hand they emphasize the existing cultural and economic dependence on the United States. Likewise, for many, the desire for independence was tempered by a lively awareness of the greater economic development and higher standard of living across the border.

The principal concern of those who raised this question at our meetings centred on the manner in which the tremendous disproportion in population, wealth and power between the two countries threatens Canada's survival as an independent state, and gives new significance to the concept of equal partnership. There were several ways in which this interrelationship was discussed by participants.

First, many of those who viewed any form of union or dependence on the United States as undesirable, regarded the bicultural and bilingual nature of Canadian society as the major—if not the only—distinguishing feature which would keep Canada independent. This point of view, heard frequently, was most often put forward, as in Windsor, in the form of a warning that, "We must all be interested in Canadian culture for I fear if we are not, we Canadians could soon be engulfed and drowned by the American culture." In London, one man clearly stated his support of biculturalism as a bulwark against the merging of Canada with the United States when he said, "Equal rights across the country for both cultures and both languages—this will be a terrific barrier to being swallowed up by the large state to the south, which may be very friendly, but which can take many little things that we want and (things) that we are prepared to pay a dividend to keep." This man, like many others, saw biculturalism as the only safeguard against cultural annexation, and he went on to say: "I do not think we have a chance of keeping [Canada independent] unless we do develop something which will clearly distinguish it culturally from that mass reservoir. We are going to be sucked in with or without any pressure from them. We have to become a bicultural and bilingual nation completely from coast to coast."

* * * * *

Some Canadians, who did not see union or a close relationship with the United States as desirable, still considered that economic realities increasingly dictate that the primary language in Canada must be English. This opinion was expressed by both French-speaking and English-speaking Canadians, although they usually derived different conclusions from it. In Saskatoon a man stated that, "As time goes on there will be fewer and fewer people who will be purely French-speaking and more and more people will be English-speaking. Quebec is not only a part of Canada, it is also a part of the North American economy and there is a tide flowing that economically will force them to become increasingly industrialized in that province and to have a knowledge, and a good knowledge, of the language of commerce. That language of commerce. I think we'll have to admit, will be English in the North American economy."

The idea of North American economic necessity and linguistic pressure being a barrier to equal partnership was also voiced by French Canadians. Thus in Chicoutimi: "How necessary is English?" you may ask me now. We must not forget that we live among 200 million English-speaking people. It would be utopian to imagine that those who live in the region of the Saguenay or in the Province of Quebec can restrict themselves to their mother tongue when they live on the North American continent." A participant in Rimouski also emphasized the language pressure stemming from Quebec's position in the North American economy, pointing out that, "It is not because we have English-speaking people in Confederation that we have to speak English, it's because we have the neighbours to the south, the United States."

*   *   *   *   *

American proximity was seen by some English-speaking Canadians, especially in Western Canada, as one of the prime reasons against accepting biculturalism and bilingualism as a great issue in Canada, and dealing with it in the light of the concept of equal partnership. The major contemporary problem for Canada, they felt, was rather the question of north-south economic and social relationships, and the weakening of east-west ties. In the case of British Columbia, for example, the Commission had the feeling that many B.C. citizens thought of themselves as belonging socially, economically and culturally to the Canadian-American Pacific Coast region, and were thus indifferent to the concerns of distant French Canada.

*   *   *   *   *

The imposing model of the "melting pot" to the south was often in the back of people's minds as they discussed the question of unity, as against a duality or even a multiplicity of cultures. The "success" of the American experiment was presented by some as evidence of the futility of cultural duality in Canada, as in Kingston where a man affirmed, "What is going to happen here, regardless of what we say or what we think, is the same thing that happened in the United States—the old melting pot theory." However, a Halifax citizen took a different view, stating, "A nation with two cultures is original. The Americans have a melting pot culture and have done a darned good job of it! . . . But I think we should try something different."

The Commission on occasion also received a strong impression that the over-powering presence of the U.S. obscures the sense of national identity and responsibility among Canadians. The link with the larger country was seen both as a peril and a protection. Very few audiences seemed willing to decide whether to resist the peril or embrace the protection.

What is meant by?

"melting pot"
"cultural duality"

What do you think?

1. (a) Outline the arguments for and against the retention of bi-lingualism in Canada as a way to resist "Americanization."
   (b) From what parts of Canada would you expect the "for" arguments to come? The "against" arguments? Why?
2. (a) Do you feel that a national identity is needed to offset "Americanization"? Why?
   (b) If you feel that Canadian national identity is needed would bilingualism and biculturalism help in achieving such a goal? Why?
3. (a) To what extent is Canada a melting pot?
   (b) To what extent is the U.S. a "mosaic"?
   (c) How does the example of the U.S. "melting pot" influence English-Canadian attitudes towards Quebec, if at all?
4. Do French Canadians have more, or less, to fear from the U.S cultural influence in Canada? Explain why.

6.   CANADIAN CULTURE OR CANADIAN SITUATION?

Robert Adolph, an American professor teaching at York University, defines what he considers to be the basic differences between Canada and the U.S. Professor Adolph's remarks appeared in his article "Reflections of a New Canadian," Canadian Dimension, October-November, 1970.

Canada, because it has never quite made up its mind as to what form its national existence shall take, is not difficult to adjust to. In a passive, almost "feminine" way Canada, uncertain of its role, has admitted all influences, even when they have come to exploit her. Yet Americans must understand the differences. One should distinguish—if I, an outsider, may be allowed to contribute another crumb to your identity question—between *culture* and *situation,* both of which form identity. Between a Torontonian and, say, a Bostonian there is, culturally, only a "regional nuance," as someone says in *The New Romans.* I suspect Professor Mathews and I am sure Professor Grant would disagree here, discerning a distinctively Canadian, even English-Canadian, life style surviving from your counter-revolutionary origins in the teeth of Life, Walt Disney, Huntley-Brinkley, and waves of immigrants. Indeed, for many Americans Canada is a gentler, politer, less demonic and more reserved society. Nevertheless, I think there is a far greater difference culturally between a Bostonian and an Alabaman, or between any black and any white American, than between a Bostonian and someone from Toronto. Official mythologies to the contrary, America too is a mosaic, not a melting pot.

It is the *situation* of the Torontonian that is different from *any* American's and it is here, if anywhere, that your identity exists. The Torontonian lives in a more peaceful land. He need not worry about the draft for him or his children. In fact, his country has a long tradition of resistance to conscription, and now shelters more recent refugees from military service than any other nation in the world. A much smaller percentage of his taxes is spent on "defence." A sizeable fraction of his city is not in a quasi-revolutionary state. If he is concerned about his nation at all, he worries about things Americans hardly ever think about, mostly having to do ultimately with national identity: foreign take-overs, regional disparities, unfair tariffs, bilingualism, Quebec separating, and indeed, the entire country, whose organization he cautiously calls a Confederation, breaking up and dissolving.

Dissolving is a Canadian theme. In Canada civilization itself melts away into endless tracts of land. You are more aware of geography here. Much more than in the United States, which east of Denver and on the Pacific coast now seems an immense suburban subdivision. To live in Canada is to be aware of boundless tracts of wildly beautiful land and water with which, simply because they are in the same geographical expression—Canada—even the smog-breathing Torontonian must be in some sort of relation.

And yet—a thoroughly Canadian paradox, unknown in the present American experience—this huge *land* of yours is a small *nation.* Living in a small nation, especially one split into isolated regions, is existentially as well as economically different than living in a big one. To an American, Canada is a much clubbier place. This makes for a certain stuffiness and groupy, in-grown quality to life and institutions here, a state of affairs documented in *The Vertical Mosaic* by John Porter. But it also means that MP's are much more accessible than American congressmen. Unless I am sentimentalizing or simply ignorant, a more genuinely political existence is possible here. A very few well-organized people can do more here than in the States. I suspect that these conditions are true of smaller societies in general, especially those which have come under the British influence. Partly from this same clubbiness, partly, I would imagine, from a shortage of educational facilities, there is a lack, compared to the United States, of professional expertise in many fields. Yet it is easier here for an inspired amateur to make it, once he has gotten into the club, though the financial rewards will be less.

Perhaps the differing cultural results of the American and Canadian situations can be seen in what the two nations put on their most important document, the dollar bill. Where the arrogant Yanks inscribe on their currency national heroes and monuments or mystical symbols of power and authority—eyes out of pyramids and fierce eagles with bolts of lighting in their talons—you unpretentious Canadians prefer to adorn yours with prairies and telephone poles (doubtless symbolic of your McLuhanesque pre-occupation with communication over long distances and across language barriers), moose, sailboats, rodents, and the Queen, who doesn't even live here.

Finally, if you will again forgive me, an outsider, for telling you what you are like, there is your emotional life. Here I speak as one having authority, for at York I teach a course on ideas of love in the Western world from Plato to Leonard Cohen. Ontario, perhaps because of the lingering remnants of its preposterous liquor and censorship laws, has a reputation as one of the last citadels of puritanism on the continent, but I find little evidence of this at least among the young people of the province, and I have met many of them. There is no reason in the Canadian *situation* why your attitudes should differ from the Americans. In the larger scale, Toronto strikes all Canadians as unloving and frenzied; in fact, my impression is that resentment of Toronto is one of the few things that unites this country. I and many other Americans, however, find Hogtown more relaxed, cosmopolitan, and easygoing than any American city except perhaps San Francisco. My impressions of Montreal and Vancouver were similar.

Perhaps poverty, pollution, crime, racism, and repression will make a tolerable urban life impossible in Canada, too. But for at least this moment in history Canada—even the English Canada so often labelled dull and stodgy—is becoming increasingly attractive to those few Americans who know anything about you at all. Simply by going about your business in your situation you are living in a world that is getting to be different from the American model. Toronto now is more unlike Buffalo, Detroit, or

Cleveland than it was ten years ago. Situation—the accidents of history—may eventually create a Canadian culture which, while not the older Canada whose passing has been lamented by Professor Grant, could be something more distinctive and worthwhile than a "regional nuance" of American culture.

What is meant by?

"regional nuance"
"existentially"

What do you think?

1. *Explain what Professor Adolph means by "culture" and "situation". Why does he contend that Canada does not have a particularly distinct culture? Why does he argue that Canada has a distinct "situation"?*
2. *(a) According to Professor Adolph, how and why does Canada differ from the United States?*
   (b) Do you agree with his analysis? Why?
   (c) How important are these differences to you—that is, if you think they exist?
3. *Professor Adolph feels that Canadians, by going about their business in their situation, are living in a world that is getting to be different from the U.S. model. Why do you think Professor Adolph feels this is happening? Do you agree with him? Why or why not?*
4. *If Canada's situation is the source of her "identity," how is Canada threatened by Americanization, if at all?*
5. *How have Professor Adolph's remarks influenced, if at all, your feelings about:*
   (a) the views of Henry Morgan (page 74)?
   (b) the existence of a distinct Canadian culture?

7. ECONOMIC AUTONOMY UNIMPORTANT

Mavor Moore, general director of the St. Lawrence Centre for the Arts, tells of an interview with Canadian expatriate John Kenneth Galbraith. The source for the document is The 1968 Couchiching Conference Papers.

When Galbraith was asked: "Should Canadians be concerned more about cultural domination by the United States or about economic domination?" Galbraith replied: "This is an important question, and one which I think is very much misunderstood. In good Calvinist fashion, when Canadians talk about cultural autonomy, they really have economics in mind. They follow my friend, Walter Gordon, and talk about economic autonomy which on the whole is rather unimportant. It doesn't really exist any more anywhere in the world. The large industrial corporation, whether it's in the United States or Britain or Holland or Germany, or the Soviet Union, has a similar cultural impact. Were there an entirely separate Canadian corporation to make automobiles, the characteristics and manner of operation would be exactly like General Motors. If I were still a practising, as distinct from an advisory Canadian, I would be much more concerned about maintaining the cultural integrity of the broadcasting system and of making sure that Canada has an active independent theatre, book publishing industry, newspapers, magazines and schools of poets and painters." But his questioner pressed on: "Don't you think that Canada should make a determined effort to increase its stake in the Canadian economy?" And Galbraith replied: "I would say this is a very minor consideration as compared with increasing the Canadian stake in the things I've just mentioned. These are the things that count."

What do you think?

1. What do you think Professor Galbraith means when he uses the word "culture"? What do you think of this definition?
2. What is Professor Galbraith saying about the modern corporation? Is Canadian culture threatened specifically by American investment or rather by the general pattern of industrial, technological and economic development in today's world? Defend your view.

8.   U.S. INVESTMENT POSES A THREAT

The Gray Report (Information Canada, 1970) commented on the vulnerability of Canadian culture to the influences introduced by American investment. The author of the report claimed that the Canadian "branch plant mentality" is the result of "truncation", which occurs when decisions concerning the conduct of a business in Canada are made outside Canada.

DEFINING CULTURE

J. K. Galbraith (the Canadian-born American economist) has argued that Canadians should not worry about the concentrated U.S. ownership of Canadian business, but about maintaining the cultural integrity of the broadcasting system and making sure that Canada has an active, independent theatre, book publishing industry, newspapers, magazines and schools of poets and painters. This reflects a rather naive view of culture and nationhood.

There is no way of leaving the "economic" area to others, so that we can get on with the political, social and cultural concerns in our own way. There is no such compartmentalization in the real world.

When culture is understood in this broad sense, there can be little doubt that economic activity, as organized in the modern corporation, has a profound impact on culture, especially on the nature of the social, political and economic system, and the technology employed.

Having indicated the complex interrelationships within a culture, it is difficult to isolate and analyse the corporate impact, whether domestic or foreign, on culture. This is especially true in the case of Canada, since Canada is basically an open society and many influences have shaped Canadian culture and society.

It is difficult, for example, to distinguish those aspects of our cultural and social development which are the effects of general industrial, technological and economic development and those which are foreign or U.S. importations and infiltrations.

CANADIAN OPENNESS

It is equally difficult to disentangle the influence of foreign control of Canadian business from the impact of a common language, the mass media, political tradition similar in numerous respects, the use of the same books at universities and at public schools, imports, travel, common professional associations and trade unions, and close family and friendship links. Countries of similar cultures and per capita real income appear to be particularly susceptible to direct investment. While there are some important differences between Canadian and U.S. culture (the bilingual and bicultural character of Canada; the republican form of government in the U.S.; the tolerance in Canada of a greater role for governmental action, such as the CBC, the railroads, and Air Canada; distinctive Canadian institutions such as the co-operative movement on the Prairies, the Caisses Populaires in Quebec, and the existence of Socialist parties in Canada), the numerous and important cultural similarities facilitate direct investment.

A further factor which has facilitated foreign direct investment is that Canadians, by and large, are not very xenophobic. Canada has fewer national heroes and distinctive symbols than most other countries. Canadians seem to have less pride in their history and in their achievements.

LACK OF STRONG NATIONAL IDENTITY

While British, American or French history is, in a certain sense, part of our own history, it is studied more assiduously than Canadian history. The reasons for this are very complex, but in part Canadian diffidence towards nationhood appears to arise out of Canada's colonial past. In more recent times, Canada's proximity to the dynamic and powerful U.S. has induced a comparable feeling of dependence or inferiority.

The lack of a strong national identity and a distinctive culture tend to create, as outlined above, a vacuum and a greater receptivity to foreign influence and investment. The case of importing our culture from the U.K. or the U.S. reinforces this tendency by reducing the pressure on Canadians to develop their own cultural distinctiveness.

On this fertile ground foreign investment has a relatively easy task in shaping and influencing the Canadian environment. Looked at from the point of view of the U.S. investor, the openness and lack of cultural distinctiveness reduce the risk and cost of foreign investment since there is less need to adopt the product locally. Thus, foreign investment at one and the same time plays on cultural similarities and reduces the capacity for the distinctive development of national identity.

It is interesting to consider the situation of Quebec in the light of this analysis. Quebec has a distinctive culture, largely the result of different language and religious and educational institutions.

French Canadians by the large are taught French Canadian history. They know their heroes and their symbols. The government of Quebec is trying to retain and develop this culture through a number of policies, particularly those relating to language and education. These differences probably make Quebec a less attractive location for U.S. investment than Ontario.

It is, of course, very difficult to determine whether the higher rate of U.S. investment in Ontario is the result of cultural similarity or the more rapid rate of economic growth that they have enjoyed in recent years.

CULTURAL IMPACT OF TECHNOLOGY

Some of the less desirable aspects of what is often attributed to U.S. corporations should, in the opinion of some people, be attributed largely to the impact of modern technology. However, as pointed out above, it is for all practical purposes impossible to distinguish the impact of these two forces because they are almost always associated with each others.

Technology is developed in a particular milieu and tends to reflect certain other cultural values; for example, technology developed in the U.S. seems to place greater emphasis on rapid innovation and change and the satisfaction of peripheral wants, which often have to be created, than appears to be the case in Europe.

This seems to be especially true in manufacturing sectors

dominated by U.S. multinational companies. Compare the engineering and design and the rate of change in these two factors of a Chevrolet on the one hand and a Volkswagen or Volvo on the other.

This is not to say that Canada should opt out of technological society, but rather that if technology is in foreign hands it is likely that the use and adaptation of this technology to meet local cultural demands will be minimized. If technology is in Canadian hands, the chances are greater that its use will be adapted to the needs of the Canadian milieu.

CULTURAL IMPACT OF MARKETING CAPACITIES

The large investments required in the creation of new technologies and new products means that corporations must assure markets for them by spending vast amounts on advertising to create the wants and formulate the tastes, in the absence of which financial disaster could result.

The large investment required in the creation of new technologies and new products means that corporations must assure markets for them by spending vast amounts on advertising to create the existence of advertising spill-over. A "product image" often exists in Canada even before a dollar is spent on advertising here.

CULTURAL IMPACT OF TRUNCATION

Since a significant number of foreign controlled companies operating in Canada lack some of the decision-making powers and activities of a normal Canadian controlled business enterprise, their activities can be described as "truncated".

The exercise of vital entrepreneurial functions by the parent with the consequent truncation of entrepreneurial activities in the Canadian subsidiary has adverse effects, not only on Canadian economic development, but also on Canadian society in general. Truncation means less challenging jobs for the Canadian techno-structure which must frequently look to the U.S. for more challenging job opportunities. If you want to be on the 95th floor, with global horizons, you must go to New York; the highest one you can go to in Canada is the 54th floor.

But the effects of truncation go beyond reducing the number of challenging jobs for the Canadian techno-structure which must frequently and managers. The underdevelopment of the Canadian techno-structure has adverse social and cultural effects in that the "spill-over" benefits resulting from the interaction of these "brains" takes place not in Canada, but abroad.

Truncation also tends to engender a mentality of the second best with horizons and vision constantly centred on headquarters abroad. It represents a continuation of the colonial mentality described above. This attitude is manifested in many ways such as the preference for finishing a person's education by sending him to Oxford, Harvard, the London School of Economics or the Sorbonne.

It is manifested in the difficulty of recruiting top quality foreigners for business or our universities because of the general view that the best opportunities exist not in Canada, but abroad where parent companies and other centres of decision are located. The general effects of truncation are vividly summed up in the phrase "branch plant mentality."

However, the effects of truncation are not the only operative forces in this situation; the fact that Canadian society is quite elitist and that social mobility is more circumscribed in Canada means that Canadian society is not developing entrepreneurs at the same rate as occurs elsewhere. Social rigidity induces the expectation and mentality of working for others.

OTHER FACTORS

The U.S. manager who often accompanies U.S. direct investment in Canada also has a considerable cultural impact as a member of the business elite.

Having been born, educated and raised in the U.S., being familiar with the history, geography, and culture of that country, his impact is bound to reflect social and cultural values moulded in an American milieu. Often he brings with him a taste and preference for U.S. products and ways of doing things which go beyond the methods of doing business. His membership in American-based professional associations and clubs, his family and friendship links with the U.S., for example, will tend to reduce his identification with the Canadian community.

What is meant by?

"xenophobic"
"product innovation"
"multinational enterprise"
"entrepreneurial"
"techno-structure"

What do you think?

1. *How do you think the authors of the Gray Report defined "culture"? Give evidence. Compare their view of "culture" with that of Professor Galbraith. How does the difference in their definitions of culture account for their difference of opinion regarding the impact of U.S. investment on Canadian culture?*
2. *"Thus foreign investment at one and the same time plays on cultural similarities and reduces the capacity for the distinctive development of a national identity." Explain in your own words what*

this statement means. Why does the Gray Report reach this conclusion?

3. (a) Define what is meant by "truncation". According to the Gray
Report, what in Canadian society is truncated by American
investment?
   (b) Does culture develop from the material changes in a society
brought about by technological change? If so, how? Can decisions on technology significantly alter the way of life of
a people? How?

4. Is foreign investment possible without the risk of cultural penetration? Why? Is cultural penetration possible without foreign
investment?

5. Do you think that the Gray Report has effectively refuted Professor Galbraith's argument? Why or why not?

9.   U.S. MAGAZINES INUNDATE CANADA

The following is the testimony of Mr. Simon Bédard, Vice-President
of Actualité—before the Senate of Canada, Proceedings of the Special Committee on Mass Media, February 19, 1970.

Mr. Bédard: In addition to this, in the Province of Quebec, there
are some 200 or 300 American and English magazines on the newsstands.
Even though there are some English-language magazines in the Quebec
newsstands, at least they are Canadian. But when one is flooded by American magazines, when one is deluged by sensational magazines, detective,
sex magazines and so forth, when we watch our children go up to a news-
stand to purchase *Playboy* and similar magazines, when we attempt to
offer them educational magazines (magazines which will make them respectable citizens),—what do we get? We get rubbish.

A magazine is published in Quebec called *Vie et Carriére*. It is a
magazine aimed at young people, a magazine of general interest. It is a
magazine which has been in existence for five years and which was founded
ten years ago. Yet it has never succeeded in making ends meet although it
has tried everything. Everything has been attempted both with regard to
presentation and content. Why has it failed? Because we do not have the
means of reaching young people, because young people are inundated
with junk.

Mr. Fortier: With regard to the control you suggest, if I understand correctly, you make no distinction between the magazine originating
from the United States and the magazine from France. You state that there
should be uniform restrictions?

Mr. Bédard: Yes. Whether French, English, Spanish or Greek.
We should have some control. After all, we in Canada are not children.

We are able to write, we are even capable of presenting agreeable products.

Mr. Brouillé: Does this . . .

Mr. Bureau: It is quite normal that such magazines should be found just about everywhere, in hotel newsstands, and so forth; a certain quantity should be allowed to enter for the benefit of American tourists. However, to allow them to take over the Quebec market, the Canadian market, I feel, is quite abnormal.

Mr. Brouillé: For my part, I would say that we must not deprive ourselves of something which can enrich, something which comes from outside; after all, there are countries greater than ours which have something beneficial to contribute. We must enrich ourselves with the finest which the human mind can produce but we must not allow ourselves to be destroyed or swamped with just anything. When we reach this point, everything good we have is in danger of disappearing, of being buried. I feel that . . .

Mr. Bureau: Here again, Mr. Fortier, I am going to give you an example. The other day you had *Saturday Night,* a well presented magazine. You have *Maclean's* which is a fine English-language magazine. When the New York advertising agencies purchase advertising space in *Life,* let us say, they will be reaching some 150,000 persons—I do not have the exact figures—in English-speaking Canada. For General Motors, Chrysler, for large international companies, what sort of market can *Saturday Night* represent? When they purchase a page of advertising in *Life* magazine, they know that they are reaching 350,000 to 400,000 readers including persons in both English and French Canada. This sort of thing is harmful to our colleague, *Saturday Night* magazine.

Mr. Fortier: What worried me a little is the control you suggest over the free flow of information on the pretext that a given magazine is not as good as yours. This is more or less what you are saying although I do admit that your magazine is excellent.

Mr. Bédard: Mr. Fortier, it is impossible for us to inundate our American friends; however, you will agree that they can destroy us. Given this fact, we can be realistic enough to say that we want to be friends, that we are desirous of free exchange. However, when it is a question of culture, of the education of our population however, we wish to retain a certain control; we are not Americans, we are Canadians.

What do you think?

1. How important is advertising revenue to the survival of a magazine? What advantages do U.S. magazines have over Canadian magazines in this respect? What can be done to help Canadian magazines survive?

2. What magazines do you read most frequently? How many of these are published in the U.S.?

3. What Canadian magazines do you read on a regular basis? How many Canadian magazines can you name?

4. Obtain copies of Time *and* Reader's Digest *in both their Canadian and U.S. editions. Compare the content of the magazines for their respective months. What differences are there between the Canadian and American editions?*

10.   UNDERGROUND PRESS: AN AMERICAN PHENOMENON?

The Senate of Canada Special Committee on Mass Media heard, on March 10, 1970, the testimony of Mr. D. W. Anderson, editor of the Winnipeg underground newspaper Omphalos.

The Chairman: I wonder if I could go back to Mr. Anderson for something he said and perhaps put this question to you.

I am going to read a quotation from the story which was written on the underground press in a recent issue of "Canadian Dimension." It is an article by Richard Dahrin on the "Underground Press in Canada."

Before reading the quotation, let me make my own position pretty clear. I am a nationalist. I don't make any bones about that. Now, Dahrin is talking about the *Georgia Straight:*

Although relatively few of its readers are Americans-in-exile, and Americans contribute hardly at all to its existence, the *Straight* is still plugged into the U.S. Westcoast scene, and just like the rest of us, it is much less familiar with the comparatively weak, uncreative underground culture in the rest of Canada. Jerry Rubin and Allen Ginsberg and Herbert Marcuse, when they came to Vancouver were treated, in the *Straight* like visiting nuncios. Underground is American.

You made the point as to the vitality of the underground press in the United States—and I think you indicated—perhaps you didn't—that the underground press in Canada is a phenomenon which has been imported from the United States; so, what is the position of the underground press in Canada, vis-a-vis nationalism, and vis-a-vis the whole American thing?

Mr. Anderson: Well, nationalism is—let me put it this way; I am not a nationalist, and I don't apologise for it. I think that nationalism is one of those profound notions that's undergone a fantastic change in the last little while, just as so many other notions have undergone fantastic change.

What I mean to say is that perhaps a few years ago, it was acceptable to talk about nations and countries, but it's no longer acceptable to me at any rate, and I think probably it is true of most of the people involved in the underground press.

There is only one political reality and that is the American empire, and we are part of it.

The Chairman: Are you happy about that?

Mr. Anderson: Oh, on the contrary. I am very dissatisfied with it, but the point is that to be a Canadian nationalist—80 percent of our economy is owned by American corporations; for example, when even Prime Minister Trudeau admits that about 15 percent—I think that's the figure he quoted; he said our foreign policy was probably in the area of 10 percent to 15 percent where we can do something; in other words, we at *Omphalos*—We simply don't care about discussing national products.

The Chairman: You just throw up your hands?

Mr. Anderson: No, we think, to quote Che Guevara, "If you are going to go for the beast, you have to go for the belly of the beast," and the truth of the matter is we are out of the American empire and we are anti-imperialist.

What do you think?

1. (a) *What is the "underground press"?*
   (b) *Who reads it? How influential is it?*
2. *Are there any "distinctively Canadian" examples of underground newspapers?*
3. (a) *Discuss Mr. Anderson's position on nationalism. What do you think of it and why?*
   (b) *Do Mr. Anderson's views on nationalism support Mr. Laxer's argument (page 108) about the Canadian radical movement? Explain.*

11.   SING OUR OWN SONGS, DREAM OUR OWN DREAMS

The following are extracts from the testimony of Mr. Pierre Berton, author and TV host, before the Senate of Canada Proceedings of the Special Committee on Mass Media, March 25, 1970.

Finally, in the area of broadcasting I really want to support the proposals of the CRTC which as you know is that programming should be 60 percent Canadian content on television and even more important that the prime time or prime hours when most people are viewing, I think 50 percent of that has to be—two hours out of four have to be Canadian and that on radio 30 percent of the music played has to be Canadian in some way, even if it is only Lorne Greene, who holds Canadian citizenship, recording a new record on the set of Bonanza.

I want to go on in this area because the CRTC has finally got a philosophy in broadcasting and I think the thing that has been wrong in broadcasting in this country is that the philosophy we have had has been an American philosophy—not a Canadian philosophy—a philosophy that sees that broadcasting is an arm of the marketplace.

Now, I don't think that public broadcasting in this country should be concerned at any point with ratings or with revenue or with sales or with commercials. I think it is a scandal that the sales department of the CBC can now pre-empt any program on the air if they want to. They have the right to pre-empt the programs. Not the program department but the sales department is in control. Surely the purpose of public broadcasting in Canada is to strengthen national sentiment, to hold the country together. That's what it was started for—it's one in a long progression of rather awkward and expensive but necessary devices which go back to the days of the canals and the inter-colonial railroads and the CPR and it worked up to the telegraph lines and the pipe lines and the airlines and finally the radio and TV network.

It is kind of a marriage between the public and private sector to make the country workable. To create a national idiom, a national mythology to interpret Canada to Canadians; to tell us who we are, where we came from and where we are going. This is the job of the television network and the public sector, and we will not do that—we can't achieve that with a fifth re-run of *I Love Lucy* or its equivalent; nor even with the excellent U.S. public affairs programmes, as necessary as those are. We have to sing our own songs and we have to create our own heroes, dream our own dreams or we won't have a country at all.

What do you think?

1. Why does Mr. Berton support the CRTC (Canadian Radio and Television Commission) regulation requiring 50 percent Canadian content on prime-time TV for Canadian stations? What do you think of this regulation and why? What is the CRTC's role in Canada?

2. (a) What function does Mr. Berton see public broadcasting fulfilling? What historical precedents does he cite for this sort of public activity?

   (b) Do you agree with Mr. Berton on this function of public broadcasting? Why? Can you think of any dangers? Explain.

3. Is there a "Canadian sound" in popular music? Which are your favourite pop music groups? How many of these are Canadian? Which are your favourite TV programmes? How many of these are Canadian? What values, if any, do you feel are conveyed to you via TV, radio and records?

12. PUBLISHING CRUCIAL TO CANADIANISM

In its first interim report, The Ontario Royal Commission on Book Publishing emphasized the importance of an indigenous Canadian publishing industry and recommended government support for publishers.

It has been apparent from the outset of the Commission's inquiry at the beginning of January that Canadian book publishing is an industry which is of major importance in creating that sense of identity, political, historical, and cultural, which is Canadianism. Moreover, English-language book publishing in this country is preponderantly an Ontario industry, and this province therefore has a special responsibility to nurture and encourage it.

A striking consequence follows from the fact that on the one hand the contribution to the gross national product made by book publishing is relatively unimportant while on the other its cultural importance to the nation is substantial. Not only does every fluctuation in the economic health of publishing thus bear on the Canadian public interest, but even minimal degrees of help or hindrance to the industry can have an important impact on our national well-being. For the same reason, adverse business factors can be offset by public assistance at much less expense in the book industry than in other depressed areas of the economy. That the development of the book publishing industry can be stimulated, effectively and properly, by carefully planned economic assistance has long been recognized elsewhere, and we are of the opinion that situations may arise in our own book industry which justify similar assistance from the Province of Ontario, acting alone or in concert with federal agencies. We further believe that such a situation has arisen recently and that it is of such importance and urgency that it requires special consideration at this early stage in the work of the Commission.

The situation to which we refer is that of the proposed sale of McClelland and Stewart Limited, one of Ontario's and Canada's major Canadian owned book publishing firms.

The president and principal shareholder of McClelland and Stewart Limited, Mr. Jack McClelland, recently announced his intention to sell his shares in that company because of its and his inability to raise sufficient capital to continue in business. In his announcement Mr. McClelland also indicated that he might sell to foreign interests. He has recently notified the Commission that he has opened negotiations with American sources.

*   *   *   *   *

The Commission concurs with these statements [that McClelland and Stewart needed fresh capital to survive] and is of the view that such additional funds could not be obtained in Canada without the assistance of Government. Messrs. Clarkson, Gordon and Company have advised us that the requirement is approximately $1,000,000.

McClelland and Stewart represents an accumulated creative momentum in original Canadian publishing which could not quickly be replaced by other Canadian publishing enterprises should its program terminate or be sharply curtailed. We recognize the fact that part of the firm's present difficulties must be explained by the very scope of the program it has mounted, but that program is itself a national asset worthy of all reasonable public encouragement and support. The Commission is of the opinion that such encouragement and support, subject to prudent safeguards, should be offered at this time. In short, we believe it to be in the public interest that McClelland and Stewart should be preserved from bankruptcy if at all possible, and furthermore that it should not be permitted to be transferred to foreign ownership.

What do you think?

1. *How does book publishing contribute to the creation of a sense of identity? Why do you think the Commissioners felt that only if publishing in Canada is Canadian-owned will this sense of identity be genuinely Canadian? Do you agree with them? Why?*
2. *(a) What survival problems do you think a Canadian publisher faces in a U.S.-dominated industry? (See statistics, page 16.)*
   (b) Can Canadians be accused of failing to support a Canadian publishing industry? If so, why?
3. *The Commissioners' recommendation was followed. McClelland and Stewart received $1 million loan from the Ontario government.*
   (a) What are the advantages and disadvantages of governments subsidizing cultural industries such as publishing and film-making? On the whole do you feel that the advantages outweigh the disadvantages? Why or why not?
   (b) Is government support of cultural institutions a Canadian tradition? If so, explain why. Cite some examples.
   (c) What other methods can you suggest for expanding Canadian influence in cultural areas?

13. PUBLISHING: DOES OWNERSHIP MATTER?

William Darnell, of the U.S.-owned publishing firm of McGraw-Hill Ryerson, wrote the following in Quill and Quire. According to Darnell, if the reader's interests were kept in mind it really does not matter if publishing firms are Canadian or American owned.

I am concerned and frustrated by some of the current controversy and publicity that surrounds the Canadian publishing industry. There seems to be a concerted and deliberate attempt to polarize this complex industry—to divide it into two camps, the good guys and the bad guys, on the basis of a single criterion—ownership. I do not believe that ownership alone is a valid criterion for assessing the worth of Canadian publishing. I have the feeling that to accomplish their ends some of the more intemperate spokesmen for nationalism have resorted to the worst kind of chauvinism and have conveniently disregarded facts while appealing to thoughtless emotionalism.

The worth of our publishing industry depends only on how well it serves the consumer, the student who wants information, the reader who wants pleasure, and on how well it serves the writer—the Canadian author who needs an outlet for his creativity.

What does a consumer want from the publishing industry? He wants the industry to provide ready and convenient access to books and materials from all parts of the world, and he wants it to be the source of Canadian materials that reflect properly the Canadian scene and Canadian culture. The Canadian publishing industry, regardless of ownership, has for a long time done a pretty good job in meeting these objectives. The wholly or partially owned subsidiaries of British or U.S. companies provided books from their parent and sister organizations and at the same time most of them embarked on their own independent indigenous publishing programs. The Canadian-owned publishers served as agents for foreign publishers and produced Canadian materials.

What then has created the so-called crisis in Canadian publishing? The nub of the problem seems to be that the foreign-owned publishers have been more successful than the Canadian-owned publishers. There is nothing sinister about this. Generally, the foreign-owned firms have been better managed. The Canadians who run them have been chosen for their ability and they are retained only if they demonstrate competence. Too many Canadian-owned firms have been family affairs where management is by inheritance and not ability, or where management is by the owner and thus subject to no review. Also, many Canadian-owned firms are too small to be successful. Unfortunately, the publishing industry is an easy one to get into. It does not require large amounts of capital, or equipment, or staff; and because everyone has read a book, he feels that he is competent to be a publisher. As a consequence, the industry always has a group of marginal operators who are doomed to failure for lack of adequate resources. This situation is not unique, but somehow seems a virtue in publishing.

How well has the Canadian writer been served by the publishing industry? One of the most disturbing aspects of the current clamour is that it would have you believe that only a few Canadian-owned houses have ever published Canadian writers. Nothing could be farther from the truth.

An examination of *Canadian Books In Print* shows who has done the lion's share of publishing Canadian books. Good Canadian authors have not gone unpublished. There has always been intense competition for Canadian manuscripts, both in the educational and trade fields. Last year McGraw-Hill Ryerson published 115 Canadian titles and would have gladly published 515, if they could have found suitable manuscripts. One of the factors contributing to the trouble in the publishing industry is that a lot of books that were not worth publishing were published. If the current demand for handouts is met, taxpayers will subsidize a lot of bad books.

We should be more concerned about the real "gut" issues of publishing. How well is the Canadian reader being served by his publisher and how well is the writer being served by his publisher? Let us not be diverted by the ownership of the facilities.

What do you think?

1. (a) What cultural roles does Mr. Darnell outline for the foreign-owned and Canadian-owned publisher alike?
   (b) If you feel that these roles are being fulfilled, would you agree with Mr. Darnell concerning the irrelevancy of American ownership? Why or why not?
2. What reasons does he cite for the weakness of Canadian publishers? Do you agree or disagree? Can you think of other reasons?

14.   CANADIANIZING THE ADMAN

Mr. Jerry Goodis, president of Goodis, Goldberg and Soren Ltd., a Toronto advertising agency, discussed the effect of advertising in the shaping of Canadian culture in his book, Have I Ever Lied to You Before? *(Toronto: McClelland and Stewart, 1972).*

But I have arrived at two convictions that do seem to me relevant to the way I make my living.

The first conviction is that our media have got to change. And I mean fundamentally change—because the basic fact about print and broadcast media in this country is that they are paid for by advertising and that this system isn't working well enough by half.

I know I am biting the hand that feeds me; well, I've been accused of doing it often enough before now. But communication is vital to us—as participants in a democratic society, as Canadians, as humans. And somehow the media must be altered, or amplified or supplemented so that all groups have access to some outlet for their legitimate points of view, their beefs, their needs, their fears and their truths.

The premise is this: it would be hard to find a more persistent chronicler than advertising of the value system, with all the contradictions and imperfections, of any society. Even yesterday's revered prophet, Marshall McLuhan, is on to this.

This is just a simple truth. There is scarcely an ad or a commercial that does not imply an assumption or a judgment about life and people, and particularly about the enviable life and the desirable people: value assumptions; value judgments. We care a lot about hygiene and cleanliness? It shows in the ads. We worship youth? It shows in the ads. We despise certain groups? They are mysteriously absent from the ads. There is confusion about family roles? Father is allowed to appear a boob in the ads? *We care about Canada?*

Well?

I don't suggest we hamhandedly incorporate shots of the Peace Tower, Niagara Falls or Ookpiks rampant on a field of beavers. I simply suggest we stop copying American advertising. I suggest we try to find our own Canadian style of advertising. I suggest we bootleg our cultural assumptions into our commercials instead of theirs.

We don't want racial intolerance here? We should be the leaders in policing our advertising for the careless racial slur. I am bitterly ashamed the Coffee Crisp commercial with its cheap stage-Mexican joke should have been made in Canada.

We abhor violence? Then we don't make commercials like the Tareyton one that subtly link black eyes with masculinity.

We believe in courtesy as a way of life? Then we don't show people poking into someone else's medicine chest. We don't show children interrupting their parents with dental reports.

We think materialism isn't everything? Then we start looking for ways to say it, even in our advertising. Especially in our advertising. Even while selling goods we try to say a man's worth in this country doesn't depend on his possessions.

And maybe also we try to do advertising so excellent and so endearing that the next time I visit a Grade 5 class it's a Canadian ad they recognize and not an American one. Let's give them a little Canadian content to stimulate their Canadian mentality a little.

What do you think?

1. *Why do you think Mr. Goodis feels that the media must change fundamentally? Why does he deplore the fact that they are supported by advertising?*

2. *In what ways do you think the present system, where advertising supports the media, endangers Canadian culture? What are the alternatives?*

3. *If advertising reflects and influences a society's values, cite some*

ads you have seen which are not in your opinion "Canadian"
Write an ad which reflects Canadian values.

15.   CANADA A CO-OPERATIVE VICTIM

J. A. S. Evans in his article "Living with the Giant: Falling in Line,"
(Commentator, May 1970) remarks that often Canadians support the
Americanizing tendency in the cultural area.

Or let us look at another area where Canadians have a stake in "Americanization", and defend that stake with vigour. Private television in Canada is very profitable business. The total operating profit of the private televisions stations in 1968 was 17.5 million dollars, according to Frank Peers, author of one of the essays in this group. Last year, their profit was 17 million dollars. I got this statistic from CTV President Murray Chercover, who cited it in a press conference a few weeks ago, when he was in Ottawa to protest the new CRTC regulations governing Canadian content in broadcasting. (Admittedly, what Mr. Chercover said, as reported in the Toronto *Globe and Mail,* was "only $17 million", but since this profit represents nearly one-sixth of the total operating revenue of the private stations, the qualification "only" seems misplaced.) Incidentally, the operating revenue of the private stations is higher than that of the publicly-owned CBC. Yet, in 1968, all 17 private TV stations in Ontario spent 1,100,000 dollars on artists' and talent fees, which is less than the amount spent by one private French-language station in Montreal, CFTM. Even so, the private stations in Ontario do better than those in British Columbia. In 1967, all seven private TV stations in that province spent a total of 4,445 dollars on talent fees.

The justification for this minimal effort on the part of the private broadcasters is the article of belief that Canadians cannot produce good programmes, that every Canadian knows this deep in his heart or his liver, or wherever he knows such things, and that when an American programme is available on TV no red-blooded Canadian will watch a Canadian one, hockey games excepted. Actually, Canadian-made programmes can attract large audiences. The dramatic series, *Quentin Durgens, M.P.* had an audience of over two million each week. But no evidence to the contrary seems to disturb the private broadcasters' fixed belief in the inferiority of Canadians.

What is disturbing about all this is that the private broadcasters seem to have genuinely convinced themselves that Canadians are, by definition, incapable of producing programmes which other Canadians will watch. To be sure, U.S.-made programmes can be had at a very reasonable price. But I suspect that what the broadcasters really like about these imports is that they come neatly labelled with audience-ratings. The broadcasters do not have to take a chance. They don't have to exercise their own judgment and decide whether a programme is bad or good. They need not be venturesome.

Now this is what I should call a client mentality, which waits for its patrons to provide it with opinions.

The point of all this is that if Canada is a victim of American imperialism, she is a cooperative victim. The most serious danger to Canada comes from Canadians themselves, who fall too readily into a client relationship.

What do you think?

1. *According to Mr. Evans why do private broadcasters tend to use American programming?*
2. *What other sectors of Canadian business or finance could be accused of supporting the "American stake"?*
3. *Compare Mr. Evans' views with those expressed in the Gray Report. How important is the "client mentality" in explaining Canada's willingness to be Americanized? Can you think of ways to combat this mentality?*
4. *Does Mr. Evans' argument change your response to question 4 on page 75 (Henry Morgan)? Why?*

16.   GIVE CANADIAN FILMS A CHANCE

Below is an editorial from the Toronto Star, *June 26, 1972, dealing with the Canadian feature film industry.*

Over the last five years or so, Canada has developed a small but active movie industry, which has produced about 100 feature-length films. They are of varying quality—good, bad and indifferent—but the best of them—such as *Mon Oncle Antoine* and *Goin' Down the Road*—have won international acclaim and have been commercial successes wherever they were shown.

Yet, as *Star* columnist Alexander Ross has noted, most Canadians outside the big cities never get a chance to see these pictures. Our screens are full of foreign shows, and Canadian productions only rarely reach the screen.

The reason for this lies primarily in the distribution system. The two main theatre chains across the country are, in one case, American-owned and in the other, British. Of the distribution companies, too, 80 percent are foreign owned. The decision as to what films Canadians see are made for the most part outside the country, and by people who have an interest in pushing foreign shows.

Faced with a similar situation in radio and TV, the federal government has devised a quota system to ensure that an adequate proportion of the material broadcast was of Canadian origin. Yet the impact of the movies on our culture is almost equal to that of broadcasting. It is surely time to apply similar measures in this field to make sure that the fare provided on our screens includes a proportion of Canadian films.

The Canadian quota imposed on theatres need not be a large one, since our movie industry is small by international standards. But it should be large enough to make sure that audiences in every part of Canada get a chance to see Canadian films.

There's a jurisdictional problem here. While the federal government has clear authority to legislate on broadcasting, the provinces have traditionally controlled movie theatre licensing and film censorship. Ottawa should try to persuade the provinces to establish a reasonable Canadian quota for movies; and the persuasion can be backed by its undoubted authority, as master of Canada's international trade, to restrict the entry of foreign films.

What do you think?

1. Do you feel that films can reflect a national identity? If you do, give examples of well-known films which seem to reflect the country of their origin.
2. Can you think of a recent U.S. made film which does not reflect Canadian culture or values? Explain why you feel it does not. Would you say that this is true of all U.S.-made films?
3. Evaluate the proposals given in this editorial for the development of the Canadian film industry.

17.   U.S. PROFESSORS IMPORT U.S. VALUES

Henry Beissel, associate professor of English at Sir George Williams University in Manitoba, suggests that U.S. professors pose a threat to the teaching of a Canadian "perspective" at university. Mr. Beissel's article appeared in the Toronto Star, April 5-6, 1971.

In 1969 we hired 3,087 university teachers. According to official Manpower and Immigration estimates, 2,398 or 77 percent of these were non-Canadians, 1,040 coming from the U.S. and 500 from the U.K. This represents an overall increase of 10 percent in the hiring of foreigners over 1968. At this rate we shall be hiring only non-Canadians in 1972.

*   *   *   *   *

The fact that by far the largest contingent, namely 44.4 percent of all non-Canadians hired in 1969, were from the U.S. has to do partly with physical propinquity, and partly with the fact that Americans, generally speaking, are more pushy than Canadians. Where they have moved into departments they have often proved to be Trojan horses opening the gates for a veritable flood of fellow-Americans, sometimes from the same state and college.

One's most immediate response to the idea of introducing national-ist criteria into the operations of our universities is negative. We all share some notion that universities are concerned with "eternal human verities": the pursuit of truth and knowledge, after all, is universal. Even on reflection one might legitimately wonder what relevance citizenship has to the hiring of university faculty, or nationality to the curricula and the teaching of the arts and sciences. Indeed, many academics declare that both are irrelevant and that the only true criterion is excellence—and excellence (they claim) is international, global, well-nigh absolute.

Unfortunately many of my internationally minded colleagues, it seems, stop thinking at this juncture. Otherwise they would have asked themselves how it is that, if nationalism has no place in the university, all major countries in the Western world have legislation, built into immigra-tion laws or labor codes or employment policies, to control the hiring of foreign staff—and that consequently the universities in these countries do not employ any significant number of foreign nationals.

An important part of the answer is, I contend, that most civilized nations have recognized the crucial function of their universities in per-petuating and expanding, by critical analysis, interpretation and explora-tion, the values and traditions of their community. In other words, our liberal internationalists are laboring under grave misapprehensions about nationalism, academic excellence, and the "eternal human verities." Unless we clear our minds of the scholar's absolutism, Canada will soon have no more national identity than the state of Ohio.

*   *   *   *   *

I am not suggesting that taking out Canadian citizenship will change a man's temperament. But if it represents a serious commitment to the country it will change his perspectives. And perspectives are im-portant, less important in the natural sciences, but crucial in the arts where so much is subjective. Take history, for example. Since the past cannot be totally reconstructed (not that it would make much difference if it could be), you start with bits and pieces, say of a particular period. If it is fairly recent history and your material has not already been rigorously and blindly decimated by chance, you must make your own selection from a mass of available material. That selection can only be guided by your own personal

bias which, however educated and refined, remains a bias. Then you interpret the pieces you have chosen as evidence, i.e., you put them together
like a jigsaw puzzle. But they were not pieces in a jigsaw puzzle, and if
they fit it is because you have made them fit a picture you created from
your values and perspectives and commitments, and that likely existed
in your mind before you even started your research.

This is a somewhat simplified account of the work of a historian,
but it is true in its essentials. I am not suggesting that because of this, historical research or the teaching of history are worthless. Quite on the
contrary; everything depends on what kind of jigsaw puzzle we choose to
make of the bits and pieces of our world, because by that puzzle we shall
live, love, think, and die. There is not much room for objectivity in history,
and it makes a significant difference whether a student is reared on a reading of history predicated on the values and assumptions of U.S. society or
on those prevalent in Canada. The same is generally true of the other
disciplines in the arts.

What do you think?

1. Why do you think that there is such a large proportion of U.S.
   academics at Canadian universities?
2. Do American professors threaten to undermine Canadian culture?
   Why? What advantages to Canadian culture are there in having
   foreign academics?
3. Do you agree with Dr. Beissel's position or that of his "inter-
   nationally-minded colleagues"? Why? In your answer outline the
   case of both sides of the controversy.

18.   THE AMERICAN STYLE IN POLITICS

*James Laxer, who ran for the leadership of the federal NDP, de-
scribed the American influence on the Canadian New Left in his
article "The Student Movement and Canadian Independence." The
article appeared in* Canadian Dimension, *August-September 1969.*

The failure of the Canadian New Left has been that its American
perspectives have made it insensitive to the demands of a socialist struggle
in a dependent country. The New Left has been blind to the process
needed to achieve an alliance with potentially radical social forces in
Canada. It has placed its own unique life-style ahead of the general interests of the Canadian left. Some will object that New Leftists are now vitally
concerned with achieving an alliance with the working class. Of course
they are. The critical question is whether they are prepared to adapt their
political methods and priorities enough to make such an alliance possible.

To date the Canadian New Left has not been willing to make such adjustments and one reason for this has been the powerful impact of American radicalism on the development of the Canadian movement.

Along with the perspective of American radicalism have come specific political issues as well. The Canadian New Left has spent much effort on questions which are marginal to Canada—the race question or the draft—and when it has addressed itself to broader questions such as Vietnam, its demands for a Canadian response to the war have not generally been central to its campaign.

A case in point was the many Vietnam actions on Dow Chemicals Ltd., which does not make napalm in Canada, and which is far from central to Canada's contribution of strategic material to the war. A particularly ludicrous demonstration took place at the University of Toronto in the fall of 1967. One girl carried a sign which read "We ain't going to go" (a black anti-draft slogan), while spokesmen for the demonstration, several of whom were American, harangued a crowd of engineers who responded by chanting "Yankee go home."

*　*　*　*　*

The American orientation of the Canadian New Left has been entirely understandable. It has stemmed from the general Americanization of this country and from the accompanying malaise of Canadian politics.

The American youth movement has had a wide influence on the life-style and culture of young people in many parts of the world—not least in Canada.

Unfortunately, the cultural rebellion of the young in Canada has been far less suitable as the basis of a radical political movement than it was in the United States. The identification of middle-class Canadians at second hand with a culture heavily based on that of American blacks does not place Canadian youth in touch with a potentially revolutionary force in their society. Rather, it tends to cut them off from traditionally radical sections of the Canadian population, whereas it has precisely the opposite political effect on the youth movement in the United States. In Canada, where a primary aim of the left should be the struggle against domination by the American Empire in order to achieve a meaningful independence, the orientation of the New Left has been singularly inappropriate.

What do you think?

1. *What is the New Left? Why could it be described as a cultural movement?*
2. *Why does Mr. Laxer feel that the Canadian New Left was a U.S. import? Do you agree with him? Support your answer with evidence.*

3. (a) *Does Mr. Laxer feel that the Americanism of the Canadian New Left was bad for Canada? Why?*

   (b) *What other American political examples has Canada borrowed? Why do you think they have been borrowed?*

   (c) *Do you feel that such borrowing benefits Canadian politics? Why?*

19. THE AMERICANIZATION OF HOCKEY

Mr. Bruce Kidd now teaches politics at the University of Toronto. A few years ago he was an outstanding world-class runner. He wrote the following article in Canadian Dimension *in July, 1969.*

Hockey is our national game. It is in our blood. An intensely physical contest waged over a frozen land, it reflects the struggles of our history and the demands of our environment. Every Canadian male has played it—so much so that it is our only genuine puberty rite; every Canadian female is familiar with its intricacies, and every Canadian community has scrimped and saved to raise a temple to its joys. Hockey has been the source of community pride and national units; if the CPR held the country together during the early years of Confederation, certainly Hockey Night in Canada has done so in recent years.

Yet hockey is no longer exclusively Canadian. Probably our most successful cultural export, it is played in virtually every part of the world where winter brings freezing temperatures. The Europeans have altered the rules and the style of the game to such an extent that it only faintly resembles our own: Canadian teams abroad have always found it difficult to adapt to European rules. And as Canadian hockey is being played to an increasingly larger U.S. audience, it appears to be acquiring more of the characteristics of the biggest American sports seller, football. With the export of hockey, Canada has lost its influence over the game. Today the American market, which is the biggest consumer of Canadian hockey, has the largest voice in the determination of the character of the game.

The Americanization of Canadian hockey is merely the logical outcome of the professionalization of the sport that occurred more than fifty years ago. Hockey is a sector of the entertainment industry and each professional team is essentially a branch of the same corporation. The success of each team is not measured in the league standings but in its profit and loss column, although the two are interconnected.

It should be no surprise to students of other multinational corporations that the actions of the National Hockey League, the body that controls all North American hockey, have shown little concern for particularly

Canadian interests. Ten of the twelve NHL owners, the men who rule the League, are Americans or American syndicates. The two Canadian groups that own NHL franchises have been more concerned with the maximization of profits than the furtherance of Canadian interests. It is no injustice to attribute to a man like Conn Smythe a paraphrased "What is good for the NHL is good for Canada."

Many of the major decisions of the NHL have run counter to what could be considered "Canadian interests." The most recent and highly publicized example is the refusal of the League to grant a franchise to the city of Vancouver, despite its virtual guarantee of a sell-out crowd for every game. The apparent reason: Vancouver cannot offer a sufficiently large television market.

Whatever the cause, it is extremely unfortunate that a major section of the country that has carefully nursed and bred hockey as a parent cares for a favourite son, is unable to watch hockey at its best. A larger television market is also the reason why the American CBS network has priority over the Canadian Broadcasting Corporation in the telecasting of NHL games. Weekend games are now scheduled to suit CBS and if there is a conflict, the Canadian network must be happy with second choice. Once again in the playoffs this spring Hockey Night in Canada was telecast Sunday afternoon.

But it is in its control of national amateur and community hockey that the American-dominated NHL Board of Governors has displayed its most serious indifference to Canadian interests. Since 1940, when, after a long and bitter rivalry for players, the Canadian Amateur Hockey Association completely surrendered its independence to the NHL, the professionals have tyrannized the amateur game.

A highly publicized consequence of professional domination of amateur hockey has been the fate of the Canadian National Team.

It is popularly held that Canada can never regain the world hockey championship with a team of amateurs, but must resign herself to the bottom of the league until we can be represented by the world's best players on the professional NHL teams. It may be the case that a team of players whose sole activity is playing hockey will always beat a team of players who only devote part of their time to the game, but if so, it has never been convincingly proven. The professional leagues have never given the National Team a chance.

If the National Team is ever to prosper, it must be able to invite all the top amateur players in the country to play for its teams. This the NHL has never allowed the National Team to do. Once again, the CAHA has acquiesced to the professionals' wishes.

In the 1967 NHL-CAHA agreement, the national association agreed that none of its teams (including the National Team) could "approach, negotiate, or discuss employment with an unsigned drafted player before October 21 in any playing year without prior consent" (of the NHL). The NHL players' draft is simply a gentleman's agreement between member clubs not to negotiate with a player "drafted" by another club. But an "unsigned drafted player" is still an amateur player. By this clause, the CAHA agreed not to discuss hockey with the most talented young players until two months after the National Team would begin its practices. In another clause, the two parties agreed:

> The NHL shall pay to the CAHA specific funds for the subsidization of amateur leagues and teams except the National Team.

Here the amateur association agreed not to use any of its player-development funds for the development of players for the National Team. And to finally restrict the National Team, the CAHA national executive recently voted that "Canada's National Team not recruit junior-age hockey players," a ruling that eliminates 10,770 registered junior players as potential candidates for the Team.

As the Hockey Study Committee concluded, "It is rather tragic to note that professional hockey is obviously concerned about competition from one CAHA amateur team (the National Team) whilst it enters into agreement with the CAHA to develop to the highest possible level literally thousands of amateur teams from Senior to Bantam to serve its own purposes."

At this stage, NHL opposition to the National Team is strictly financial: the Canadian NHL teams fear competition at the box office should the National Teams ever become successful and all professional teams fear the possible drain from what is now a private reserve of talent. The extent to which an element of American nationalism is part of the League's antagonism can only be determined in those future years when international hockey becomes open to the professionals. Will the American NHL owners allow their Canadian born players to play for the Canadian National Team? That really is the question.

What do you think?

1. According to Mr. Kidd why has hockey been Americanized? Has this process weakened the Canadian sense of identity? Why?

2. (a) Why, until 1972, did the NHL show so little enthusiasm in a "Team Canada?"

   (b) How and why was Team Canada formed for the Canada-Russia series in 1972? Does this action refute Mr. Kidd's argument about the NHL? Why or why not?

3. What role do you feel international sports can play in "nation-building"?

The Political Debate

How does the power and proximity of the United States affect Canada's political affairs? To what extent does the American economic presence influence Canada's domestic politics? Is Canada's foreign policy actually formulated in Ottawa or in Washington?

In the area of domestic politics this section will examine the problem of extraterritoriality (the application of U.S. laws to U.S. firms operating in Canada), the involvement of American-owned firms in Canadian elections, as well as the relationships between economic control and political independence.

In the area of foreign affairs, this section provides some documents dealing with the issues of whether Canada's foreign policy is determined in Washington and whether an "independent" foreign policy is possible or even desirable.

Domestic Affairs

Does U.S. involvement in Canadian economic life necessarily mean U.S. involvement in Canada's domestic political affairs?

What are the problems posed by "extraterritoriality"? Does U.S. legislation applied to American subsidiaries in Canada constitute a threat to Canada's political sovereignty?

Do U.S.-owned firms actually influence Canadian politics? Is there a danger that contributions made by American-owned firms to Canadian political parties will result in undue American pressure being put on provincial and federal governments? Are such dangers real or imaginary?

1. THE U.S. VOICE IN OUR POLITICAL ARENA

The Gray Report (Information Canada, 1971) examined the impact of U.S.-controlled firms on the political process and public policy formation in Canada.

THE IMPACT OF FOREIGN CONTROL ON THE POLITICAL PROCESS AND PUBLIC POLICY

A main difficulty in this task is in isolating the impact of the foreign controlled firm from the generally pervasive impact of American influence in Canada.

THE BEHAVIOUR OF FOREIGN-CONTROLLED PIRMS

Conceptually, it is possible to envisage a very wide range of methods through which foreign controlled firms might seek to influence the political system and policies of a host country. Several different degrees of possible intervention are considered below. The extent to which each is experienced in Canada is the question at issue.

A foreign-controlled firm may act as the political agent of its home government and seek to overthrow or to maintain in power the host government to help advance the policy objectives of its home government. Conversely, the foreign controlled business may solicit the support of its home government to overthrow or maintain the regime in the host country.

With respect to elections, the formal organizations of the business community do not generally give open collective support to any one political party. Thus, while particular firms or businessmen may publicly support a political party, or contribute to one or more parties, such organizations as the Canadian Manufacturers' Association, the Canadian Chamber of Commerce, the Canadian Textiles Institute and the Canadian Chemical Producers' Association do not normally do so. In other words, foreign-controlled firms obviously do not cloak their intervention in electoral politics by having the trade associations act on their behalf.

Second, no evidence is available that would suggest that the behavior of the individual foreign-controlled firm differs in any significant way from that of the domestically controlled business firm in election campaigns; for instance, in its pattern of contribution to parties.

Another way in which the foreign-controlled firm might influence the political process would be by responding to the directives or requests of its home government to influence host government public policy, e.g. if General Motors were to lobby the government of Canada to give more active support to U.S. policy in Viet Nam. In practice, while there might be isolated illustrations of such behavior, there is no evidence of this being a common activity.

A fourth method through which the foreign-controlled firm can influence the political process is through its capacity to obtain the support of its home government (a foreign government) to uphold its interests in Canada. In the generality, the right of a home government to make these kinds of representations to the government of a country in which one of its firms has established a subsidiary is accepted as legitimate.

For the most part, once again little evidence has been found that foreign-controlled firms have frequent recourse to such a method of protecting or advancing their interests. In part, this may be because there is little discrimination between foreign- and Canadian-controlled firms in Canadian law and public administration. And, of course, when a foreign government does seek to intervene on behalf of a subsidiary, it does not necessarily follow that it will be able to convince the host government to modify its position. The cases of the Mercantile Bank and Time-Reader's Digest are the two most obvious examples of foreign government pressure being brought to bear on the political process due to the fact that these firms were foreign controlled.

It is not a criticism of the individual foreign controlled firm to observe that it can at times serve as a vehicle for foreign corporate influence within the Canadian political system. However, there are around 8,000 such firms in Canada, almost 4,000 are U.S.-controlled and many of these are amongst Canada's largest firms. The cumulative impact of their normal political activities thus gives the U.S. corporate view a very important voice in the Canadian political arena. Accordingly, the views expressed by Canadian industry will be heavily influenced by U.S. business interests.

What do you think?

1. *"A main difficulty in this task is in isolating the impact of the foreign-controlled firm from the generally pervasive impact of American influence in Canada." Explain why there is this difficulty.*

2. *According to the Gray Report, in what ways can foreign-controlled firms influence the political process and public policy in Canada?*

3. *The Gray Report says that foreign firms have not intervened "actively" in Canada's political arena and yet concedes that foreign firms have a certain "cumulative impact" on the views expressed by Canadian industry. Explain how this cumulative impact is created and estimate its role in political decision-making in Canada. How significant is this impact? What view are these firms likely to express?*

4. *The Gray Report noted little difference between the political behaviour of foreign firms and domestic firms. Are you surprised by this? Why?*

   (a) *Do you consider this situation to be evidence of good corporate citizenship on the part of U.S. firms or of an identity of interest between U.S. and Canadian business communities? Give reasons for your answer.*

   (b) *Could the nationalist argument have any appeal to Canadian industry? Would and could U.S. business and government exert pressure to counter this appeal? How and why?*

5. *Would you favour legislation calling for the political parties to reveal all the sources of their campaign funds? Why? Would your point of view be influenced by the fact that these sources might be American-controlled firms? Why?*

2.   CANADA CAN'T WISH AWAY LEGAL IMPERIALISM

*The following selection was by Professor Mel Watkins, a leading
Canadian economic nationalist. Watkins was particularly concerned
about U.S. government regulations affecting the behaviour of U.S.-
owned firms in Canada. (Dave Godfrey, Mel Watkins, eds.: From
Gordon to Watkins to You [Toronto: New Press, 1970].)*

The multinational corporation is like the man who came to dinner.
You welcome him as a guest and then find that he's making the rules and
giving the orders for the household.

It doesn't have to work that way, but it *does* work that way because
most multinational corporations have American parent companies and
because the United States holds that their operations anywhere in the world
are subject to its laws and politics.

In effect, the U.S. infringes the sovereignty of the host country
where the American subsidiary is located.

As Jack Behrman, a former assistant secretary of commerce in the
Kennedy administration, observed in 1968: "These interferences could not
occur in the absence of the multinational enterprise; home governments
would simply not agree to concerted policies. They are faced with such
interference only because of the control gained by the U.S. government
through the existence of the multinational enterprise—headquartered in the
United States." He notes: "To some governments, it appears legitimate for
a foreign government to have power over their domestic corporations."

The experts—in international law and international economics—
label this practice "extraterritoriality." This tongue-twisting word in fact
means legal imperialism. And virtually without exception, the experts join
Mr. Behrman in deploring it.

The United States is not the home country for all the world's
multinational corporations—only for most of them—but it alone has taken
the hard line that its corporations abroad are subject to its jurisdiction. It
does so in three particular areas—anti-trust policy, East-West trade controls and balance-of-payments controls.

Canada, having more than its share of American ownership, is
particularly subject to infringements on its sovereignty through American
extraterritoriality. In his book *Choice for Canada*, Walter Gordon cited a
case in point: "Not very long ago, the Canadian government concluded
a wheat sale with Russia that involved the shipment of flour to Cuba. But
the three largest milling companies in Canada, all of which are subsidiaries
of American parent corporations, were prohibited under United States law
from making flour for Cuba." He thought this "a relatively unimportant
incident" but concluded: "It serves to demonstrate, however, how foreign

ownership can influence the day-to-day operation of the Canadian economy."

Two years later, my own report on foreign ownership took a hard look into the whole issue, so much so that Sidney Rolphe of Long Island University labelled the report "one of the purest *cris de coeur* against the excesses of American extraterritoriality." It came up with a set of concerted and tough proposals to protect the Canadian interest, including a government export trade agency to try to compel U.S. subsidiaries in Canada to fill orders from Communist countries, U.S. law notwithstanding.

Extraterritoriality was back in the news with the publication of a monograph by A. E. Safarian of the University of Toronto, one of the economists on the task force that prepared the Watkins Report. For Safarian, and even more so for the Canadian-American Committee—a Who's Who of Canadian and American businessmen and labour leaders—extraterritoriality is the problem posed for Canada by American ownership; not much else matters. In a preface to the monograph the committee manages to get surprisingly hot under the collar: "The committee states its support for the view developed in the study, namely, that extraterritoriality is the area in which the most serious Canadian-American conflicts have arisen and are most likely to arise and in which solutions most need to be found."

One does not have to believe that this is "the most serious" issue —it is not: The economic and political disintegration of Canada consequent on pervasive American economic penetration ranks higher . . . to laud a committee which is a lobby group for North American economic integration for taking a stand on something in the area. . . .

But what should be done? Solutions, after all, "need to be found." Would you believe : "In view of the enormous growth of U.S. direct investment in other countries we also urge that the United States government review comprehensively its practices relating to the extraterritorial application of its laws and regulations to the foreign activities of U.S. companies"?

The recommendation is, to say the least, unimpressive. The problem exists because the U.S. government does what it does and gentle requests to reconsider are unlikely to be worth the paper they are written on.

What do you think

1. (a) Explain in your own words what is meant by "extraterritoriality." Explain how extraterritoriality can affect either the Canadian economy or Canadian political policy.
   (b) Can the U.S. use the principle of extraterritoriality to stop

U.S.-owned firms in Canada from selling products to countries like Cuba?

2. Does the principle of extraterritoriality mean that the Canadian flag does not cover all goods made in Canada? What, then, is the definition of a Canadian product?

3. There are two views in this article on whether or not extraterritoriality is the most serious issue facing the United States and Canada. Which view do you agree with? Why?

4. How do some of the activities of multinational corporations resemble the activities of governments? Can a host country effectively exert sovereignty over a multinational corporation short of nationalization? If so, how?

3. THE "TIME" AND "CITIBANK" AFFAIRS

Kari Levitt described in her influential book, Silent Surrender *(Toronto: Macmillan, 1970) two events in Canada-U.S. relations which revealed American efforts to influence Canadian public policy.*

Canada's ability to withstand economic and diplomatic pressure from her southern neighbour is determined by the strength of Canadian vested interest—whether private or public—in relation to the American corporations and lobbies. Sectors where ownership is Canadian, and markets are not subject to special arrangements or concessions from the United States, have significantly more freedom. Thus, in the case of wheat sales to communist countries, American wheat producers could do little more than express displeasure and envy. Furthermore, the gains from the special wheat deals to the prairie farmers, to the transportation industry and to the politicians who were instrumental in negotiating them, have been substantial.

An instructive example of unsuccessful American penetration against strongly organized Canadian interests was provided by the Mercantile Bank affair. In this instance, a sharply-worded diplomatic protest was delivered to Ottawa informing the Canadian government that its banking legislation was "unacceptable" to the government of the United States. Neither this intervention nor the threat by American commercial banks to withdraw clearing facilities from Canadian banks was successful in securing entry for the First National City Bank into the Canadian banking system. Citibank had purchased a controlling interest in the Mercantile Bank of Canada, after being warned that Canadian banking legislation would not permit the acquired bank to be expanded into a larger corporation. Both the warning and the Canadian legislation were ignored on the miscalculation that sufficient pressure could be mounted to break the monopoly of the

Canadian banking system. But eventually Citibank had to retreat and finally was forced to bargain for the opportunity to sell their holdings in the Mercantile Bank on terms which would minimize their loss.

Although a good case could be made for more competition in the Canadian banking system, the American bank was effectively excluded because Canadian banking is tightly monopolized by a small number of very large Canadian-owned banks. This structure has been well secured by federal legislation. Canadian predominance in banking, transportation and communication is a historical legacy dating from the days of mercantile economy. Canada is one of the few countries who have not permitted American banks to enter—a striking contrast to the permissive attitude she has adopted towards American branch-plant industry.

In contrast, American intervention successfully protected the privileged position of *Time* magazine. The Canadian edition sold 356,000 copies in 1967. It has the most "select" readership of its size in Canada; the average income of *Time* subscribers was reported to be $13,000. The man who assembles the four Canadian pages of *Time* was once described by a federal cabinet minister as "just about the most influential newspaperman in Canada." With an editorial product already paid for in the United States, *Time* raked in $6.5 million of advertising revenue in Canada in 1966. The magazine split its press runs in five regional and even local editions, apart from the Canadian edition. Together with *Reader's Digest,* it absorbed close to 60 percent of Canadian advertising revenue. The result was that Canadian mass circulation monthlies such as *Maclean's* magazine or *Chatelaine* were no longer financially viable without subsidy.

In a House of Commons debate, spokesmen from the New Democratic Party called *Time* "disreputable," "deplorable" and "intrinsically vicious." In the same debate, then opposition leader John Diefenbaker said that the magazine "has devoted itself to interpreting the news and rewriting it so as to direct Canadian thinking. It is not a Canadian magazine. It has three or four pages of Canadian news in each issue, which makes it a counterfeit magazine when it pretends to be Canadian. It uses these four pages to give its viewpoint, which is not a Canadian viewpoint, to Canadians week after week. To what purpose? Is it to tell Canadians what they should do?" Walter Gordon's comment: "Influential? Yes, perhaps too darn much so, as a Canadian power directed from New York."

In 1960 a Royal Commission investigated what should be done to save Canadian magazine publishing from extinction by unfair competition from *Time* and *Reader's Digest*. The chairman was one of Canada's distinguished newspaper editors, Senator Grattan O'Leary. The O'Leary Commission recommended that expenditures on advertising placed in Canadian editions of foreign magazines should no longer be tax-deductible. Implementation of the recommendations of the O'Leary Commission would have driven *Time* out of the competition for the Canadian advertising dollar. The original U.S. edition would of course have continued to enter Canada, like any other American magazine. "It may be claimed," wrote the Commissioner, "that the communications of a nation are as vital to its life as its defences and should receive at least as great a measure of protection."

No less a person than President Kennedy interceded to inform the prime minister of Canada that he wished *Time* to be exempt from any legislation based on the O'Leary Report. Washington put pressure on the Pearson administration by making exemption a pre-condition for agreement to the pending treaty on partial free trade in automobiles and parts. As Walter Gordon wrote in his book, *A Choice For Canada:* "Approval of the automobile agreements might have been jeopardized if a serious dispute had arisen with Washington over *Time.*" *Time* and *Reader's Digest* were both exempted from the bill, passed in 1965, which denied tax deductability for advertising in any foreign-owned publication aimed at the Canadian market. The effect was to leave these two "branch-plant" magazines stronger than ever, protected against future competition from the United States. Senator O'Leary was outraged. He termed it "the probable death sentence on Canada's periodical press with all that can entail for our future voyage through history."

There were no vested interests in Canada strong enough to counter the pressure mounted by Mr. Henry Luce. Furthermore, in the automobile negotiations the Canadian government was in the position of begging favours not only from U.S. Congress but from the Big Three. In such delicate bargaining even Walter Gordon added that "in the circumstances, the decision to grant the exemptions was realistic." The unfortunate Mr. Gordon added that "explaining the reasons to the Liberal Party caucus was one of the most unpalatable jobs I had to do during my period in government." The lesson was not lost on Mr. Gordon. Sovereignty is not compatible with branch-plant status: the greater the degree of foreign ownership and control of Canadian industry, the narrower the freedom of choice in economic as well as political matters.

What do you think?

1. *What tactical moves were made by Washington to protect* Time *and* Reader's Digest?
2. *How were the American reactions to the "bank" and "magazine" affairs similar? Why was Canada able to "win" the bank struggle but "lose" the magazine dispute?*
3. *Why would the U.S. president intervene in a matter concerning the publication of magazines in Canada?*
   (a) *Is such an intervention an example of how economics can influence national culture? Why?*

(b) Is this example more important for showing how economics can influence political decisions? Why?

(c) Do you consider the backing of American firms in Canada by a U.S. president to be an aspect of American foreign policy? Why?

4. Should Mr. Walter Gordon have taken a stronger line on the *Time* case? Why? Would a finance minister today act in a similar way? Why?

4.   PARLIAMENT IS THE GUARDIAN

Professor Ian MacLeod, in an article entitled "Foreign Ownership: Villain or Scapegoat" (Peter Russell, ed.: Nationalism in Canada (McGraw-Hill-Ryerson, 1966), contends that Canada's political sovereignty is indeed protected by Parliament.

Sovereignty means final governmental control (shared in this country between the federal and provincial governments) over the territories of the nation, along with complete freedom to alter the nation's laws and policies. In the political sphere, interference with national sovereignty and the institutions of government would present serious and fundamental difficulties, even if such behaviour were consistent with Canadian economic interests. The economic portion of sovereignty applies to the fundamental decision-making processes in areas and activities affecting the economic life of the nation, and such economic sovereignty is ultimately controlled by the laws of the land. As long as non-residents are behaving as good corporate citizens, there is no danger; if they are not, our political sovereignty still leaves us entirely free to control them. American capital has not come into this country as part of an imperialist plot, and Parliament remains sovereign as the appropriate guardian of the public interest should foreign-owned firms behave in a manner that threatens Canadian independence or sovereignty.

What do you think?

1. Professor MacLeod defines two areas of sovereignty. What are they? According to Professor MacLeod which one is in control of the other and how? Do you agree? Why or why not?

2. If political sovereignty resides in Parliament, the guardian of public interest, and the public elects Parliament, under what circumstances could Canada's political sovereignty be endangered? Could this ever happen? Why?

Foreign Affairs

In world affairs, can Canada pursue policies quite different from those of the U.S.? What geographic, economic and military factors determine the relationships between Canada's foreign policy and that of the U.S.? Do these factors make an "independent" foreign policy impossible or impractical? Is an "independent" foreign policy necessarily a "good" thing? Can Canada better serve the world by being closely allied with the U.S.?

This section does not attempt to examine in detail every aspect of every situation in this complex issue. Rather, the authors have attempted to present you with the general outline of the debate. In the field of defence policy you will probe the pros and cons of Canada's military alliance with the U.S., NATO and NORAD. In the area of foreign affairs you will be encouraged to discuss the opposing schools of Canadian diplomacy: the "quiet" and the "independent."

In each case you are urged to judge for yourself what is the best course for Canada to take, not merely in terms of the country's relationship with the U.S., but also with the rest of the world.

1. NATO AND NORAD

In their book, Canadian Foreign Policy: Options and Perspectives *(Toronto: McGraw-Hill-Ryerson, 1971), Dale C. Thompson and Roger F. Swanson assess these two military alliances.*

From Canada's viewpoint, a disengagement of the two national security systems would not necessarily protect her from the consequences of a nuclear holocaust: the intercepted missiles would still be likely to explode over Canadian heads. And whether they liked it or not, Canadians would remain under the American military umbrella. In the circumstances, the choice facing the Government is not between military integration with the United States and military independence, but between degrees of both. The challenge is to devise a military policy between these two extreme positions that will assure national security against a threat from outside North America, and maximize national sovereignty within it.

*   *   *   *   *

Among the factors that must be taken into account in the re-assessment of the Canadian-United States defence relationship are the defence production sharing arrangements, which, since their conception in 1941, have been of considerable benefit to the Canadian economy. On the other hand, they have proved an embarrassment, for instance, when war matériel produced in Canada has turned up in Vietnam. Another relevant consideration is the fact that the Canadian armed forces have aligned themselves on American standards, and use a large proportion of American equipment; to abandon them would pose almost insoluble problems. Such an attempt can be discounted. The White Paper on defence that was released as expected in the summer of 1971, indicated that Canada will continue a moderate supportive role in assuring continental security, but will concentrate her efforts on the less spectacular functions of assuming a military presence in the Arctic, and internal security farther south. The Bomarc sites will soon be dismantled. On the whole, the Canadian-U.S. defence relationship will continue to be highly asymmetrical, and even somewhat detached, but not necessarily incongruent.

Militarily, Canada passed during the period of World War II from the British to the United States security system. This transition was heralded by President Roosevelt when he declared at Kingston, Ontario, as early as 1936, that "the people of the United States will not stand idly by if the domination of Canadian soil is threatened by any other empire." Canadian-United States military cooperation was given specific form with the creation of a Permanent Joint Board on Defence in August, 1940, and the negotiation of an agreement to coordinate war production in August, 1941.

The Cold War changed this relationship from one of coordination to one of at least partial integration. When NATO was created, Canadian forces, together with those of other Allies, were placed under the orders of an American general in Europe. In North America, through the NORAD agreement of 1958, the air defences of the two countries are under a fully integrated joint command. According to the agreement, the Commander of this North American Air Defence Command is an American, the Deputy Commander a Canadian, and each is in full control of the entire system when the other is absent. In a war situation, the last word rests with the heads of the two governments. The costs of this joint enterprise are shared by the two countries roughly in proportion of their respective economic strength; that is, in a ratio of about ten to one. While this arrangement undoubtedly gives Canada a significant voice in relation to North American defence, it ties her to the United States militarily, and exposes her to the charge of being a mere military satellite.

What is meant by?

"security system"
"military satellite"
"military umbrella"

What do you think?

1. (a) What is NATO? When was it formed? Who belongs to it? Who plays the dominant role in NATO? What is meant by the "cold war"? How did the conditions of the "cold war" create the need for NATO?
   (b) Is the international scene the same today as when NATO and NORAD came into being? If not, how has it changed?
   (c) If the international scene has changed, what are the implications for Canada's role in NATO, if any?
2. Explain why NORAD can be viewed as a threat to national sovereignty.
3. Why can Canada not choose between military independence and military integration?
4. Explain how NATO and NORAD alliances have laid Canada open to the charge of being a "mere military satellite of the U.S." Do you agree with this charge? Why?

2.   TRUDEAU DEFINES CANADA'S NATO ROLE

In 1969-70 Prime Minister Trudeau and his Liberal government conducted a review of Canada's foreign policy, including Canada's role in NATO. This speech was delivered by the prime minister to the House of Commons, April 23, 1969.

I might emphasize as well that, apart from the United States, Canada is at present the only member of NATO which is carrying out an extensive NATO military role on two continents. In summary, we feel that Europe, twenty years after NATO, can defend itself better and we hope that NATO's European member countries, with the support of the United States and Canada, can reach some agreement with the Warsaw Pact countries to de-escalate the present tension. For our part we are not now advocating a reduction of NATO's total military strength, although we hope that this may become possible, but a readjustment of commitments among NATO members.

It follows, and our defence review has made it clear, that a Canadian military presence in Europe is not important so much on the grounds that we fulfil a military role as we do a political role. We contribute in some measure to the "resolve" of the organization, to the will of the Alliance to respond to any aggression. This being the case, the Canadian military function in NATO may be seen to be a manifestation of our political policy.

This is consistent with one of the important roles of NATO, which is political—the accommodation with the Warsaw Pact countries of the outstanding differences between the two alliances and agreement on arms control and arms limitation.

It is this search for détente which is one of the compelling reasons for remaining a member of NATO. Quite apart from any military role, there is, we believe, an important political role for NATO and for Canada within NATO in this attempt to remove or reduce the underlying political causes of potential conflict through steps toward political reconciliation and settlement.

The efforts expended in search of a secure Canada and a peaceful world in the last 25 years are in some ways inappropriate for the next 25 years . . . Following the same careful type of study and with the same resolve that launched Canada in 1945 into a then new and effective role in the world, we believe Canada is now on the threshold of another new role. This does not mean, however, that our present posture or our present attitude must necessarily be totally changed.

JANUARY 29, 1969.

It is obvious from the foregoing that the government has rejected, for example, any suggestion that Canada assume a non-aligned or neutral role in the world. To do so would have meant the withdrawal by Canada from its present alliances and the termination of all co-operative military arrangements with other countries. That would be wrong; it is necessary and wise to continue to participate in an appropriate way in collective security arrangements with other states in the interests of Canada's national security and in defence of the values we share with our friends.

The precise military role which we shall endeavour to assume in these collective arrangements will be a matter for discussion and consultation with our allies and will depend in part on the role assigned to Canadian forces in the defence of North America in cooperation with the United States. They will be consistent as well with our belief that, as a responsible member of the international community, we must continue to make forces available for peace-keeping roles.

The world, Mr. Speaker, is embarked upon a revolutionary period which dwarfs by comparison the changes of the past centuries. Our era combines a technological revolution with a revolution of rising expectations of billions of people who for the first time in history are projecting themselves to the forefront of our consciences as they seek their proper place in the international community. This is the excitement, this is the challenge, recognized by so many of our youth.

We as Canadians would not be fulfilling our potential for good if we remained aloof from these events. This government intends to re-organize our resources and our energies to play a role in the world as it is, not to dream of things as they were. Those in this House and elsewhere who say that our defence policy represents a turn toward isolationism are pro-claiming only that, in their fixation on old wars and on old problems, they are isolated—isolated from the world of now and the world of the future.

Canada has the opportunity to play a role in the world of today, Mr. Speaker, a role which, hopefully, will act as an incentive to other like-minded states, a role which will emphasize the need to devote energies to the reduction of tension and the reversal of the arms race—a role which will acknowledge that humanity is increasingly subject to perils from sources in addition to an east-west conflict centred in Europe, and which will permit us to make the intellectual and resource investments necessary to do our part to meet those perils. This is why we are insisting that our defence policy be directed by our foreign policy, and not vice versa. This is why we are placing emphasis on imaginative concepts of assistance to developing countries. This is why we are insisting that our defence policy be rational and not a rationalization.

The government, Mr. Speaker, recognizes that the challenge of future world social and political events will not be met by a stagnant cautious attitude. We must anticipate, not react; we must think, not conform; we must have courage to discard conventional wisdom in our quest for a secure and peaceful world. If this requires change, so be it.

What is meant by?

"Warsaw Pact"
"de-escalate"
"détente"
"non-aligned"
"neutral"
"collective security"

What do you think?

1. In the 1968 federal election campaign Mr. Trudeau was quoted as saying: "We had no defence policy so to speak of except that of NATO. And our defence policy had determined all of our foreign policy."
    (a) Explain in your own words what Mr. Trudeau meant by this remark. What does his analysis imply about U.S. influence on Canadian foreign policy? Why?
    (b) How does this statement help account for the policy given in the speech you have read above, if at all?
    (c) What had determined Canada's foreign policy?
2. "Canada is on the threshold of another new role."
    (a) According to Mr. Trudeau, what changing world conditions prompted a review of Canada's foreign and defence policies?
    (b) What general directions was Mr. Trudeau suggesting Canadian foreign policy should take in April, 1969? Do you think these new directives are reinforced by his NATO position? Why?
3. (a) Were these new Liberal policy directives, in part, a reaction against U.S. influence on Canada and Canadian foreign affairs? Explain.
    (b) What new relationship with the U.S. did the new policies imply? Why?

3. CANADA IS AMERICA "WRIT LARGE"

Professor Michael Brecher is an authority on the politics of under-developed nations. In his testimony before the House of Commons Standing Committee on External Affairs and National Defence given on February 13, 1969, Professor Brecher discussed some of the disadvantages of military alliances for Canada.

My observation is based on a combination of personal experience at other levels and also from considerable reading over a period of 15 years how people in the third world look upon Canada. Whether or not it is correct to state, as I do, that this image is not so much a tarred image as a non-existent one, or whether Mr. Macquarrie is correct or not in saying that there is a distinctive identity, I still submit that there is a pronounced perception of Canada as a kind of natural geographic and cultural extension of its southern neighbour. Canada is America "writ large," if you wish. It is true that in some ways Canadian foreign aid is more acceptable and more effective, though of a much smaller dimension, precisely because it is known that relatively speaking Canada is a small power that does not constitute in any sense a threat to the existence of any one of these states as an independent entity, and in a sense—to the extent that an image of Canada exists—it is positive rather than negative. I accept this.

However, to go to your more basic point, I can only reiterate an observation which was made this morning. It seems to me that Sweden by its posture of conscious and, if you wish, committed non-alignment—despite its refusal to sacrifice its basic values, its culture, its democratic political system, its pattern of life which has grown out of its own historic experience and regardless of the pressures that may be placed upon it—has managed through its posture of non-alignment to exert far greater influence of a positive character in links with the third world in her role through the United Nations in peace-keeping enterprises, and I am suggesting that Canada by virtue of its presence in NATO, whether or not it exerts any influence therein, is automatically blurred in the minds of many who look upon NATO as simply one of two bloc military organizations engaged in a long-term conflict, if you wish, for the soul of Europe.

The only answer I can give you, Mr. Macquarrie, is that the classic defence of the continued Canadian membership in NATO is predicted on what I would call the series of essentially outmoded assumptions about the role of NATO, the importance of Canada's participation therein, the kinds of problems that will confront Canadian foreign policy in the next decade or more, and they are focussed upon the role of Canada simply as part of a North Atlantic triangle or a West European-North American geographic region. That may be important but it is not the total frame of reference in which a country like Canada must operate. I would go further and say that with the increasing stabilization of the East-West conflict in Europe, the challenge to Canada's foreign policy does not lie in Europe but rather in what is emerging as the traumatic conflict of a continental racial level of development character between the West-North, if you wish, and the South and East with all of the racial overtones and the internal instability that characterize these societies and which highly exaggerate perceptions of mistrust. So that you may well be correct in saying that Canada has managed to maintain a distinctive image. Though I disagree with you on this I yield to your superior experience in this but I would argue nonetheless that what is disturbing about the great debate over Canadian foreign policy is that it continues to take place essentially within a mold that fits the world of the 1940s and 1950s, not the world of the 1970s, and it is precisely those assumptions that I challenge.

What is meant by?

> *"third world"*
> *"non-alignment"*
> *"East-West conflict"*

What do you think?

1. *Explain why Professor Brecher's arguments against Canada's involvement in NATO stem from his belief that "Canadian foreign policy . . . continues to take place essentially within a mold that fits the world of the 1940s and 50s, not the world of the 1970s."*
   (a) *According to Professor Brecher how has the world changed? Does Mr. Trudeau agree? Do you? Why or why not?*
   (b) *What role do you think Professor Brecher sees Canada playing in the world of the 1970s? According to Professor Brecher how would Canada's role in NATO circumscribe this role? Do you agree? Why?*
   (c) *Taking into account Canada's special relationship with the U.S. do you feel Professor Brecher's suggestion is feasible? Why or why not?*

4. WITHDRAWAL THE WORST MISTAKE

Bruce Hutchison is a senior editor with the Vancouver Sun. *In this article, printed in the* Globe and Mail, *February 20, 1969, he defends Canada's place in NATO.*

During the present year of fateful decisions throughout the world Prime Minister Pierre Trudeau might commit, or avoid, the worst mistake in Canadian history. If the reader considers this an exaggerated statement he has not seen Washington, as I have seen it lately, or realized what Canada's withdrawal from the North Atlantic Treaty Organization would mean not only to the ancient friendship of North America but to the affairs of the international community.

Should Mr. Trudeau choose a neutral foreign policy he will, first, shatter the alliance which alone defends the safety of Canada and largely nourishes its economy; second, he will destroy Canada's influence in world affairs; third, as the leader of a small people, he will approach the U.S. giant without friends in naked impotence; and, fourth, as I have good reason to believe, he will split his cabinet, his party and his nation at the very moment when he is striving, in visible agony, to unite them.

*   *   *   *   *

The issue is not whether the structure of NATO should be remodeled, since it will be remodeled, and drastically, in any case: The issue is not whether Canada should maintain more or fewer troops in Europe since Canada's presence there has no serious military significance, though it has a psychological and political significance of the highest importance. The issue is not whether Canada should spend more or less on defense when actually it is spending less, in proportion to its means, than any NATO ally except Iceland.

No, the issue, as stark and simple as any issue of private morality, and as practical as any sum in arithmetic, is whether Canada should contract out of the Western world, knife its friends in the back, insure disastrous consequences, moral and commercial, end its self-respect and make Canada a lonely pariah on the cold northern slope of the planet.

I know, of course, that Mr. Trudeau will not see the issue in this light. He, and an inner brains trust more powerful than the cabinet, can argue, quite honestly, that by abandoning NATO, establishing an independent foreign policy and perhaps using defense money to help the underdeveloped countries, Canada can create a new identity, a new world-wide influence and a noble example to mankind. But having argued that proposition, as presumably they are doing now, they will find that it leads to precisely the opposite results.

The first result could be the most devastating quarrel between Canada and the United States.

*   *   *   *   *

A man who may well be the next president of the United States said to me: "If Canada actually thinks of getting out of NATO it's an insult to my country. No, much worse than an insult. It would be a betrayal. Our people would never forgive it. And believe me they would express their hurt by means that would hurt Canada far worse than you can imagine."

That is the precise description of the feelings I found in the Senate. The men who belatedly have read Mr. Trudeau's confused and contradictory statements are not so much angry as hurt, because no man can be really hurt except by his friends.

I am not trying to argue that Canada should remain in NATO and NORAD (North American Air Defense) for fear of angering the United States. My argument (as shared by many members of the Trudeau Government) is much simpler and purely Canadian—that by repudiating Canada's 20-year contract, Canada would betray its own paramount national interests and, if such an old-fashioned word is still in the dictionary, its national honour.

In the first place, if Mr. Trudeau's emerging foreign policy means anything it means that he seeks to expand Canada's influence in the world, and especially in Western Europe, the ancestral home of Canada's two founding races. As he has written, his whole philosophy of politics is based on the use of "counterweights" and in Europe he hopes to find a counterweight to U.S. influence on Canada. This strategy, it seems to me, is entirely sound and constructive.

But it must collapse and become nonsense if he abandons the alliance that defends Europe and quarrels with the United States, which defends the non-Communist world in general and Canada in particular. For once it is out of the alliance, Canada will have no more influence on the allies, no part in their military planning or, even more important, in their present determined attempt to come to terms with the Soviet Union.

In these great affairs, now changing the whole structure of world power, Canada will have no voice. And in its own special relations with the United States on many fronts it will not approach Washington, the capital of the world's giant, as a member of a team with influence but alone, powerless, distrusted and discredited.

In short, if Mr. Trudeau had deliberately set out to diminish Canada as a factor in the human equation he could not have done better than to threaten Canada's withdrawal from its company of friends, the only reliable friends it has anywhere.

What do you think?

1. Why is Mr. Hutchison opposed to Canada's withdrawing from NATO? How effective is his case?
2. According to Mr. Hutchison how would a Canadian withdrawal from NATO affect Canadian-American relations? Do you agree with him? Why?
3. Explain why Mr. Hutchison regards NATO as a "counterweight" to the U.S.? Would Mr. Trudeau agree? Would Professor Brecher agree? Do you? Why?
4. Do you favour a Canadian withdrawal from NATO and/or NORAD? Explain your reasons.

5.   QUIET DIPLOMACY v AN INDEPENDENT APPROACH

Professor Stephen Clarkson in the concluding essay to his anthology An Independent Foreign Policy for Canada? *(Toronto: McClelland and Stewart, 1968) points up the differences between these two schools of diplomatic thought and opts for an independent approach.*

THE TWO ALTERNATIVES

Once we recognize this, we can see that the key to the often confusing debate on what Canadian foreign policy should be can be found in the underlying clash between two opposing foreign policy theories. Each theory contains a complete, if implicit, explanation of the world situation and of Canada's role in it, including a view of the American relationship and a statement of objectives for Canadian diplomacy. Let's follow current fashion and call the contending theories "quiet" and "independent." By the "quiet" foreign policy approach I mean the official policy as expressed in statements, the government's practice as seen over the last five years and the image projected by our diplomats in their execution of this policy. Although what has been referred to throughout this book as an "independent" foreign policy has not been systematically articulated as a coherent doctrine, I shall present briefly what appear to me to be the major positions of each theory in order to crystallize their differences and so make possible a choice between these opposing approaches to Canada's foreign policy.

THE INTERNATIONAL SITUATION

Quiet Approach	Independent Approach
As in the late 1940's and 1950's, the world is still polarized along ideological lines between the forces of Communism and the West. Despite the splits in the Marxist-Leninist bloc, the defence of the free world is still the major priority. Revolution is a continuing threat to world stability, especially in the under-developed continents of Asia, Africa, and Latin America. This makes it all the more important to contain Communism in Vietnam and Cuba lest the whole "third world" fall to the Reds like a row of dominoes. The United States is the only power	The stabilization of Soviet and European communism has reduced the former Communist military threat to the West, turning the Cold War into a cold peace. The major world problem is no longer the East-West ideological confrontation but the North-South economic division of the world into rich and poor. Revolution is less a Red menace than an aspect of achieving the urgently needed socio-economic transformations in the under-developed world; in any case it is no direct threat to our society. Naïve American impulses to save the world from Com-

THE INTERNATIONAL SITUATION

Quiet Approach	*Independent Approach*
able to pursue a containment policy on a world-wide basis. Its allies must support this effort.	munism are misguided, out of date, and a menace to world peace. The breakdown of the monolithic unity of both the Communist and Western blocks give middle powers like Canada greater margins for independent manoeuvre.

CANADA'S NATIONAL INTERESTS

Quiet Approach	*Independent Approach*
As a Western, democratic and industrial country, Canada's national interests are essentially similar to those of our continental neighbour and friend, the USA, which is still the arsenal and defender of the free world. Worrying about national unity is of far less importance than pulling our weight in the Atlantic Alliance. Collective security is the only defence against new Hitlers or Stalins; we must not forget the lessons of 1939 and 1948.	A less ideologically but more socially concerned view of the world shows that Canada's national interests coincide more with general progress than with the maintenance of the USA's super-power status. Our external economic and political interest in trade with Communist countries diverges from American restrictions against "trading with the enemy." Canada's internal political divisions and our national identity crisis create another urgent national task for our policy: reinforce Canada's sense of bicultural personality.

INTERNATIONAL OBJECTIVES

Quiet Approach	*Independent Approach*
In the light of this analysis of the international situation and our national interests, we should strive to defend the status quo, nurturing our influence in Washington and helping maintain the solidarity of the Western alliance as the expression of our commitment to internationalism and the defence of democracy. Our order of priorities should be the American relationship first, then the Atlantic Alliance, finally the developing countries. All our	Given the more relaxed international environment and our internal need for a more distinctive foreign activity, Canadian objectives should outgrow our anti-communism to embrace the aims of international equility and socio-economic modernization. This may entail more economic sacrifice and more tolerance of revolutionary change, but an enlightened nationalism requires re-evaluating our aims in terms of the most pressing needs of the

INTERNATIONAL OBJECTIVES

Quiet Approach	*Independent Approach*
actions should keep in mind the central importance of collective action as the appropriate activity of a middle power.	whole world and will refuse to hide behind any alliance apron strings. Accordingly the "third world" should now come first in our priorities as the affairs of the Atlantic community can more easily take care of themselves. Our American relationship should not prejudice these international priorities.

OVER-ALL FOREIGN POLICY STRATEGY

Quiet Approach	*Independent Approach*
Our general strategy should be affiliation, or close alignment and cooperation with our super-power neighbour to achieve maximum diplomatic power by our influence on the Western bloc leader. We can only enjoy this influence by accepting the American foreign policy framework and restraining our urge to criticize the Americans. This then gives us access to the inner corridors of US power.	Canada is too unimportant in Washington's world view for us to have significant direct influence on American foreign policy. Our strategy should be to act directly in a given situation after making an independent evaluation of the problem. Except for continental matters of direct Canadian-American concern, influence on Washington would normally be a secondary objective. Even then our power to affect Washington's policy will depend on our international effectiveness, not our allegedly "special" relationship.

INDEPENDENCE

Quiet Approach	*Independent Approach*
Foreign policy independence is an illusion in the present-day world unless it is defined as head-in-the-sand isolation. We might just as well try to cut Canada off from North America and float out into the Atlantic. Independence must also mean a narrow and harmful anti-Americanism.	Far from being illusory, independence—being able to control one's own socio-economic environment—is an essential condition for the healthy development of the nation-state. Independence means neither isolation nor anti-Americanism, unless making up our own minds on the merits of individual foreign policies is considered un-American.

THE AMERICAN RELATIONSHIP

Quiet Approach	*Independent Approach*
As it is this relationship which gives Canada special influence through our geographical, political, and psychological proximity, nurturing the American relationship should have highest priority. We should not question the ultimate goals of the United States that has, after all, world-wide responsibilities for the defence of the free world. In addition we must realize that Canada cannot survive economically without the goodwill of the Americans upon whom we depend for our high standard of living. It would be "counter-productive" to try to influence American policies by publicly opposing them. This would only reinforce the extremist elements advocating the policies we opposed.	Our relations with the USA are "special" because of the disparity of our power and the degree to which we depend on American trade and capital inflows. We should for this reason devote careful attention to our relations, especially if we are planning international moves of which they do not approve. The huge military and political power of the USA should make us particularly critical of American policies however well-intentioned the Average American may be. Our well-being is not a product of bounteous concessions made by the US but of economic development considered to be to both countries' advantage. Our relationship should be governed by the awareness of mutual benefit. There is no evidence that independent actions strengthen extremism in the USA. If we really wish to influence American public opinion, we have to make it clear what policy we advocate. There is no better way than actually pursuing it.

RETALIATION

Quiet Approach	*Independent Approach*
We are so dependent on the American economy that we cannot afford to do anything that might annoy them such as taking some foreign policy intiative that displeases Congress or the Administration. The price of independence would be a 25 per cent drop in our standard of living, according to Mr. Pearson. We are, after all, the little pig that must be eternally vigilant lest the big pig roll over, in Mr. Plumptre's phrase. We cannot increase this risk	The possibility of retaliation is present in all international relationships. It is true that we are more vulnerable to American than the US is to Canadian retaliation, but we must not forget that retaliation is a reaction of last resort showing that all milder negotiation has failed. By being willing to use the whole armory of diplomatic weapons—bilateral and multilateral, informal and public—we could reduce the dangers of retaliation conjured up by

RETALIATION

Quiet Approach	*Independent Approach*

by provoking it to roll deliberately. In such areas as the Defence Production Sharing Agreements we gain enormously from being able to bid on American defence contracts. The share of the US market we have won pays for our own purchases of American war material at prices cheaper than we could produce it ourselves. We cannot afford the luxury of independence, whatever our conscience might say, since independent actions might jeopardize these arrangements.

the all-or-nothing approach of Quiet Diplomacy. We must realize that as the little power, we have important advantages. We can concentrate our whole attention on defending our interests in the continental relationship which, from the American point of view is but one of dozens of issues of greater importance. We have important hostages in Canada, the very subsidiaries that are the instruments of US political and economic pressure. We can also use the threat of mobilizing public opinion to strengthen our hand against possible intimidation and economic blackmail. Our goodwill and our favourable image in the US as a long-standing friend is a further asset we should not ignore.

INDEPENDENCE YES, QUIET DIPLOMACY NO

However accepted this doctrine may be, I would submit that it is no longer suitable for Canadian foreign policy in the late 'sixties. It is inappropriate first of all for the reasons stated in the "independent" replies to the "quiet" positions summarized above: its view of the world is ten years out of date; its understanding of Canada's international needs and capabilities is hopelessly circumscribed.

*   *   *   *   *

To make independence the standard for our foreign policy is not to opt out of the many undramatic areas of collective diplomacy in which Canada makes a continuing major contribution at a supranational level. Nor does independence imply anti-Americanism, however much the bogey of "making a row" is raised. Deciding policies on their own merits may well lead to disagreement with American policy. . . . Still there is no reason to inflate such policy disagreements to disastrous proportions unless the defendants of quiet diplomacy really believe the Americans to be the most vindictive politicians on earth. According to Stairs' study we have followed a line directly counter to American policy on a problem of the highest sensitivity, Cuba, and still not suffered retaliation. The point is that if we diverge it is not for the sake of a quarrel but to practise what we feel to be the correct policy, after due consideration of the Americans' reasons. It is hard to believe that a more assertive Canadian foreign policy would be countered in Washington by a concerted anti-Canadian policy. The more truculent General de Gaulle has become, the gentler has been the Americans' treatment of France. With so much direct investment in Canada, it is unlikely that the Americans, in Baldwin's phrase, would want to get rid of a blemish on the finger by amputating the arm.

Independence also requires realism in our conception of the American relationship. Our interactions with the USA are so intense and multitudinous at all levels of political, economic, cultural and personal contact that we should make a fundamental distinction between our foreign policies on one hand and our American policies on the other. While pursuing what we consider to be the best policy abroad, it is in our interest to place the strongest emphasis on the maintenance of good neighbourly relations with the USA. In all matters of mutual concern, whether financial investment, tariff policy, resource development or cultural interchange, the policies of both countries toward each other must continue to be formulated in close consultation. We clearly have an essential unity of self-interests with the Americans in our continental partnership. But partnership requires equality, and equality implies independence.

That the obsession with the Americans should not stifle our foreign activity is the first message of the independent approach; that our fascination with American power should not blind us to the extent of our own influence on American policy is the second. Canada has a comparatively strong bargaining position it can use *if it wants to* in dealing with the United States. The continentalists point out the many relations of dependence exposing Canada to American pressure and retaliation. But it is elementary political science to recognize that dependence is a two-way street. Every aspect of our relationship—our resources (our highly coveted supplies of fresh water very much included), the American branch plants, our debts, our trade deficit, our goodwill as a reliable ally—can be used by a determined leadership *if necessary* to achieve its objectives. "If necessary," for most bargaining weapons are more effective as a threat than in use—as the continentalists' terror of US retaliation shows.

What do you think?

1. (a) *Describe what Mr. Clarkson means by "quiet diplomacy." Do you think Canada's foreign policy has been determined by this approach? Why?*

   (b) *What do you think Mr. Clarkson means by an "independent approach" to foreign policy? What sort of policies do you think this approach entails?*

    (c) Would you describe the approaches of Mr. Trudeau, Professor Brecher, and Mr. Hutchison as being "quiet" or "independent"? Why?

2. Which Canadian diplomatic approach would you favour and why?

3. "We should make a fundamental distinction between our foreign policy on the one hand and our American policy on the other." Is this possible? Why?

"IT'S SUNG TO THE TUNE OF SECONDHAND ROSE"

6. QUIET DIPLOMACY REVISITED

Peyton Lyon is Professor and Chairman of the Department of Political Science at Carleton University. Professor Lyon's views on the advantages of quiet diplomacy appeared in his essay "Quiet Diplomacy Revisited", written for Stephen Clarkson's An Independent Foreign Policy for Canada? *(Toronto: McClelland and Stewart, 1971).*

We would be more influential in world affairs, as . . . many . . . Canadians contend, if only we had the courage to display our independence more boldly. Alas, the contrary is closer to the truth. If our stress is on independence in an increasingly interdependent world, this can only be at the expense of Canada's ability to exercise a moderating influence upon the decisions of other governments.

* * * * *

I shall skip lightly over the direct benefits to Canada, mostly economic, of smooth relations between Ottawa and Washington. In so doing, I do not wish to imply that there is anything improper about taking into account the impact upon Canadian living standards of different foreign policy options. Some of my academic colleagues seem to believe that our activity in world affairs should be all "knight errantry"; they refuse to face up to the possibility that the foreign policy that does the most for the material well-being of Canadians might also be the policy that enables Canada to make its best contribution to world peace. If a policy doesn't hurt, they seem to feel, it must be reprehensible. If we accept democracy, however, we cannot simply disregard the evident wish of the majority of Canadians, high-minded academics included, not to be left too far behind their opulent neighbours.

My main argument for a policy of close alliance with the United States is not that it is good for Canadian living standards or national independence. Rather it is based on the following propositions.

The United States, the wealthiest and most powerful country on earth, is a significant factor in almost every situation, whether it chooses to act or not to act.

Geographic and cultural factors give Canada the opportunity to exercise more influence in Washington than is exercised by any other country of comparable power.

This influence, in favour of diplomatic flexibility and military caution, has generally been on the side of sanity.

Canada, by exploiting its close relations with Washington, exerts greater influence in world affairs than it could through its relations with any other country or group of countries.

The belief that Canada has a special standing in Washington, access to American intelligence and insight into American thinking is a source of strength in Canada's dealings with other countries, including the neutrals and Communists; it is scarcely ever a handicap.

The fact that Canada has its own views and determines its own policies can be demonstrated without prejudicing good relations with Washington by the public airing of every difference.

A policy of seeking to influence world affairs through close alliance with Washington and quiet diplomacy is easy to support if one believes, as I do, that post-war American foreign policy has been basically responsible; that, despite errors in judgment in Washington and occasional excesses, the world is a better place than it would have been had the Americans reverted in 1945 to their traditional isolationism. It does not follow, however, that the policy of close alliance should be rejected if one believes that the Americans are generally misguided. Quite the contrary. It is for the very reason that the Americans are capable of making mistakes, with tragic consequences not only for themselves but for Canadians and the rest of the world, that we should seek to maximize our influence in Washington. The more one worries about the propensity of American policymakers to make mistakes, and the greater one's confidence in the superiority of Canadian motives and wisdom, the more one should favour policies designed to increase the effectiveness of the Canadian voice in Washington.

*   *   *   *   *

The conviction of almost all Canadians who have represented Canada in Washington is that our influence is significant, even though it varies greatly from issue to issue. They also believe that the elementary rules governing the relations between friends do apply. Our official views, for example, are more likely to be received sympathetically if we do not appear to question the ultimate goals or sincerity of the Americans, or give the impression that we are playing up our differences merely to demonstrate our independence. There are occasions when it is desirable to air our differences or offer advice in public, but such occasions should be kept to a minimum, and the reasons for breaching the normal rules should be obvious.

*   *   *   *   *

Scepticism, moreover, works both ways. Whenever I become discouraged about the difficulties in the way of demonstrating the achievements of quiet diplomacy, I console myself with the thought of how much more difficult would be my task if I had to show how a policy of non-alignment and tub-thumping diplomacy would augment Canada's influence in world affairs. What unaligned country exerts significant influence upon the policies of the super-powers? Collectively, the unaligned nations are now enjoying a field-day in the United Nations; even if one takes seriously votes in the General Assembly, however, it is hard to believe that the addition of one further member to the ranks of the unaligned would make much difference. Undoubtedly the departure of Canada from the U.S.-led alliance system would create a momentary sensation. It might be applauded in the press of some nations. Within a brief period, however, the influence of Canada, even with the neutral and Communist countries, would almost certainly decline. The assumption that Canada is more influential in Washington than most other countries is one of our strongest diplomatic assets; we would not recoup the loss of this asset by seeking comparable influence in any other capital, or group of capitals.

Although few Canadians appear to favour neutralism, many demand a much more independent line within the Atlantic Alliance. It is difficult to conceive a less rewarding policy in terms of influence; we would not escape the stigma (if such it is) of members, we would lose the ability to influence their policies that alliance membership generally brings.

*   *   *   *   *

Canadian unity would certainly be strengthened if Canadians could be convinced that their country is something more than a pale carbon copy of its more powerful neighbour. The demand for policies that demonstrate both Canada's independence, and its uniqueness, is difficult to satisfy, however, without abandoning quiet diplomacy—something responsible Canadian politicians and diplomats are reluctant to do because they appreciate the probable costs in influence as well as economic well-being. Satisfying the demand might even require them to subscribe publicly to opinions about American policies that they do not in fact hold. Too often it is assumed that if Ottawa takes a stand similar to Washington's, this can only be the result of dictation, or at least of an attempt to curry favour. In fact, Canadian and American experts see many situations in much the same light because they have access to much the same information and, as North Americans, they are much the same kind of people. In many respects, moreover, the interests of the two countries are virtually identical.

*   *   *   *   *

Satisfying the demand for a posture of greater independence in Canada's foreign policy would thus almost certainly mean a reduction in Canada's influence in world affairs. The price might well be worth paying, I have suggested, if it were to make a significant contribution to the preservation of Canadian unity. This, however, is at best uncertain. Indeed, for most countries, most of the time, foreign relations bring more frustration than gratification, and we would be unwise to count on spectacular success in world diplomacy to bolster domestic unity.

We would be even more foolish to abandon a foreign policy that has been generally helpful, and admired by foreign experts, for a new policy that might well prove to be counter-productive, even in helping Canadian intellectuals to overcome their inferiority complex. The case for quiet diplomacy may not be as compelling as it was during the cold war. I don't believe that it is. On the other hand, the case for a tub-thumping, moralistic approach—one that puts more emphasis on the appearance of rectitude and independence than the reality of quiet influence—has not as yet been established. I doubt if it can be unless we adopt the escapist premise that the over-riding purpose of foreign policy is to be ostentatiously on the side of virtue, regardless of practical consequences. Is the world sufficiently secure for such luxuries?

What do you think?

1. What main argument does Professor Lyon use to defend the "quiet" approach? How would Mr. Clarkson answer him? Whom do you agree with and why?
2. Cite instances where you think Canadian influence has affected U.S. policy.
3. Why does Professor Lyon accuse the proponents of an independent approach as being tub-thumping moralizers, ostentatiously on the side of virtue? Does he have a point? Why?
4. What other factors can you think of which in your view make it difficult, impossible or impractical for Canada to take an independent foreign policy approach?

4

The Historical Background

Canada's proximity to the United States, one of the world's most powerful and vigorous nations, has influenced all aspects of Canadian development.

Canadians have debated for two centuries the pros and cons of political and economic union with the United States. Many of the arguments have only been re-stated during the sixties and the seventies.

Whether one searches the Canadian character, institutions or policies, the result of the U.S. presence will always be found. It is a *fact* that we have lived with from the outset. But somehow we have survived as a distinct national entity on this continent.

How has the presence of the United States influenced the development of Canadian society and institutions? How has Canada been able to retain her independence so far? How has the historical struggle between influence and independence contributed to the contemporary issue? What lessons, if any, are contained in the history of Canada-U.S. relations for guiding Canadian action in the future?

The 1940s and 1950s

For the most part the 1940s and 1950s marked an era of good feelings between Canada and the U.S. During the Second World War, Canada drew closer to the United States after the Allied military defeats in the early summer of 1940 showed the Canadian government that Canada was strategically dependent on the U.S. Moreover, post-war prosperity relied heavily on a huge infusion of U.S. capital into Canada. As a result, during the 1940s and pre-Diefenbaker years of the 1950s, most Canadians appeared to be satisfied with their country's favourable response to the United States.

The cordial relations between the two nations during this time made it extremely difficult for those who were apprehensive about Canada's growing dependence on the U.S. to find a hearing in Canada. However, a few did warn about the possible dangers.

In this section you will examine some of the debate surrounding Canada's military, economic and cultural relations with the United States during the 1940s and 1950s. To what extent did the events and attitudes of this period represent a departure from the historical mainstream of Canadian-American relations? How has this period influenced the attitudes of today?

1. THE MILITARY REALITIES OF THE RELATIONSHIP

President Roosevelt and Liberal Prime Minister Mackenzie King met on August 18, 1940, at Ogdensburg in northern New York State. They issued the following press release.

The Prime Minister and the President have discussed the mutual problems of defence in relation to the safety to Canada and the United States.

It has been agreed that a Permanent Joint Board on Defence shall be set up at once by the two countries.

This Permanent Joint Board on Defence shall commence immediate studies relating to sea, land, and air problems including personnel and material.

It will consider in the broad sense the defence of the north half of the Western Hemisphere.

The Permanent Joint Board on Defence will consist of four or five members from each country, most of them from the services. It will meet shortly.

[*A short time later Mr. Roosevelt and Mr. King met again and drafted the Hyde Park Declaration.*]

Declaration by the Prime Minister of Canada and the President of the United States of America regarding co-operation for war production, made on April 20, 1941.

Among other important matters, the President and the Prime Minister discussed measures by which the most prompt and effective utilization might be made of the productive facilities of North America for the purposes both of local and hemisphere defence and of the assistance which in addition to their own programs both Canada and the United States are rendering to Great Britain and the other democracies.

It was agreed as a general principle that in mobilizing the resources of this continent each country should provide the other with the defence articles which it is best able to produce, and, above all, produce quickly, and that production programs should be co-ordinated to this end.

While Canada has expanded its productive capacity manifold since the beginning of the war, there are still numerous defence articles which it must obtain in the United States, and purchases of this character by Canada will be even greater in the coming year than in the past. On the other hand, there is existing and potential capacity in Canada for the speedy production of certain kinds of munitions, strategic materials, aluminum, and ships, which are urgently required by the United States for its own purposes.

While exact estimates cannot yet be made, it is hoped that during the next twelve months Canada can supply the United States with between $200,000,000 and $300,000,000 worth of such defence articles. This sum is a small fraction of the total defence program of the United States, but many of the articles to be provided are of vital importance. In addition, it is of great importance to the economic and financial relations between the two countries that payment by the United States for these supplies will materially assist Canada in meeting part of the cost of Canadian defence purchases in the United States.

In so far as Canada's defence purchases in the United States consist of component parts to be used in equipment and munitions which Canada is producing for Great Britain, it was also agreed that Great Britain will obtain these parts under the Lease-Lend Act and forward them to Canada for inclusion in the finished articles.

The technical and financial details will be worked out as soon as possible in accordance with the general principles which have been agreed upon between the President and the Prime Minister.

What do you think?

1. What did the Permanent Joint Board on Defence mean in terms of Canadian defence policy? Why?
2. What did the Hyde Parke Declaration state concerning Canada's military relationship with the United States?
3. "In 1940 and 1941 Canada became a part of the American Empire." Do you agree? Why?

4. *When did the United States declare war? Was the Hyde Park Declaration the kind of policy one would expect from a nation not at war? Why do you think the Declaration was made?*
5. *What military and defence policies does Canada now have which reflect the principles of the 1940 and 1941 agreements? Do you think Canadian attitudes to these principles have changed? If so, why?*

2. CANADIAN FOREIGN POLICY RESTRICTED

Almost twenty years after the World War Two agreements, Mr. Harold Winch, the C.C.F. (Co-operative Commonwealth Federation) member for Vancouver East, deplored in a speech on July 2, 1959, the fact that Canada's hard-won independence had been so "short-lived."

It will be recalled that when World War Two ended Canada had at long last achieved the status of an independent though a small power. I am certain all hon. members will agree that there was no longer any doubt whatever that at that time we had at long last outgrown what might be referred to as our colonial childhood. Canada became a free nation, calling no one master, and bound to no other country by any ties stronger than those of sentiment. I am sure that this feeling of independence was pleasing to all Canadians if even though it was somewhat short-lived.

Scarcely had the war ended when the continuing communist drive for world domination became abundantly clear to all who wanted to see. By 1947 the United States was seeking the right to establish air bases throughout the Canadian north. Before very long three courses seemingly were open to us in Canada. The first was neutrality or some variant thereof. The second was an alliance with the United States. The third was an alliance with the U.S.S.R. The latter, of course, was admittedly and obviously rejected by all thinking Canadians as being morally abhorrent. Canada chose a closer alliance with our southern neighbour, perhaps principally for reasons other than defence requirements alone, and soon our defence policy evolved as if by preordination to one closely dependent upon that of the United States. Officers were exchanged between national defence headquarters in Ottawa and the Pentagon in Washington. Canadians were sent in increasing numbers on courses and attachments to United States establishments. The continued United States occupation of three bases in Newfoundland, obtained from England in its direst hour, was accepted by Canadians on Newfoundland's accession, as if permanent occupation of the nation's soil by foreign troops in time of peace was the most natural thing in the world.

This evolving dependence on our stronger neighbour under a Liberal administration has been speeded up considerably under the Conservatives. Today R. C. A. F. officers command the D . E . W. line sites but it is a United States company which operates the D. E. W. line and, as we know, all information recorded is sent directly to the United States. The D. E. W. line remains essentially a defence installation of another nation on Canadian soil in time of peace. Our jurisdiction is limited to contributing in one way or another to its maintenance.

Shortly after announcing the cancellation of the Arrow CF-105 contract the Conservative government in March of this year stated our new air defence arrangements with the United States. We will operate and maintain the radar lines and air bases, while the U.S.A.F. will man the aircraft required for the air defence of the United States and Canada. As *Le Devoir* put it, the United States will fly the planes and we will sweep the landing strips. This idea of defence sharing is merely an extension of the arrangements that existed at Fort Churchill which I visited along with others only a few years ago. There was a Canadian command there responsible for housekeeping arrangements only.

At this point I think it is well that I should stress that the United States has shown remarkable restraint with regard to the power vacuum to their north. That country has without a doubt achieved a major degree of military control over Canada which is not inconsistent, I suppose, with its vast control over our economy. We have not yet, however, and I hope we never will, surrender our political position or our political control. The net result has been for United States military demands to be based on what the United States government considers necessary for the defence of that country which, of course, for the United States is exactly as it should be, though I maintain that for Canada it may well mean our becoming a satellite of the United States. If this transpires I have no hesitation in saying that we will have no one to blame except ourselves.

*   *   *   *   *

Our interests in Canada, Mr. Chairman, are not, nor should they be, identical with those of the United States. Our desire to trade with China against United States objection is merely a small example of what I have in mind. But even if our own Canadian objectives, if our own Canadian interests were identical with those of the United States, we strongly feel that it would be wrong for us to accept such complete United States domination of and responsibility for our foreign and our defence policies.

What do you think?

1. *Explain DEW line; NATO; NORAD and "the cancellation of the Arrow CF-105."*

2. What policy was Mr. Winch advocating? How realistic was it?
3. Compare Mr. Winch's views with those of Prime Minister Trudeau (page 124) and Professor Brecker (page 127). Have the criticisms of Canadian foreign and defence policies changed since Mr. Winch's time? Why?

3.   OUR FIGHT FOR CANADA

Tim Buck, long-time leader of the Canadian Communist Party, attacked in his book, Our Fight for Canada *(Progress Books, 1951), the pro-American policies of Canadian governments.*

The St. Laurent Government is operating systematically to make Canada an economic, military and political satellite of the United States. Members of the St. Laurent government describe their aim as that of "integrating" Canadian economy and political aims with those of the United States. What they describe as "integration" is in fact the aim of the complete subordination of Canada—on terms laid down by the United States monopolists. Their aims were outlined rather frankly by the financial editor of the *Wall Street Journal* some time ago, in an article that was given wide publicity all over the United States by the slick magazine *Look.*

The financial editor of the *Wall Street Journal* emphasized Canada's abundant resources of almost priceless industrial raw materials and the great advantages that would accrue to the U.S. if U.S. monopolies would secure control of those resources and thus head off any grandiose development of industry to process them in Canada. He admitted that to accomplish that fully would involve far-reaching changes in Canada's economic perspective. He pointed out that, carried out fully, it would involve "completely free trade between the two countries, plus a co-ordinated tariff on imports from other countries. . . ." He acknowledged that such an arrangement would de-industrialize Canada, but argued that it is necessary to change the present setup in which "textiles are made in Canada at a far higher cost than in the Carolinas; and copper is mined in some western states at a far higher cost than in Canada."

He admits that it will create difficulties, including (although he doesn't say so outright) widespread bankruptcies and mass unemployment in Canada; he brushes that aside as a transitory difficulty, however. Illustrating the U.S. monopolists' disdain for existing Canadian legislation he suggests that "Labor exchanges would probably have to be established to facilitate the process of readjustment, and substantial compensation would have to be provided for workers displaced temporarily." He does not propose as an immediate solution of the problem of those workers' free emigration to the United States. He explains that such a proposal "might have to be approached slowly."

Now, the perspective outlined so bluntly for Americans by the financial editor of the *Wall Street Journal* is no more and no less than an indication of the concrete objectives that are implicit in the very guarded basic policy statements of Prime Minister St. Laurent, exemplified by his address at Toronto University (Convocation Hall, January 10, 1947), on the foundations of his foreign policy and in his statement to the Canadian Society of New York in February 1950, in favor of continuing in peacetime the co-ordination of U.S.-Canadian production provided for in the wartime Hyde Park agreement.

How clearly the members of the St. Laurent government recognize and agree with the perspectives described by the financial editor of the *Wall Street Journal,* was demonstrated by Mr. Douglas Abbott, Minister of Finance, when he described what the government really aims at in the field of economic policy in the following words:

> If we cut down the consumption of refrigerators and other articles which contain metal, we can sell the metal in its original form for dollars in the United States or anywhere else. That is one way whereby we can get United States exchange. Instead of using labor in Canada to convert the metal into things our own people consume, we shall sell the raw materials. (*House of Commons Debates,* March 18, 1948.)

A semi-official spokesman for the U.S. government, described by *Toronto Daily Star* as "A U.S. foreign policy expert . . . an authority on Canadian-U.S. relations"—who refused to permit his name to be mentioned —explained how the U.S. State Department "justifies" all those encroachments upon Canadian sovereignty. The substance of his lecture was as follows:

> . . . U.S. foreign policy cannot be conducted with an eye to Canadian approval or disapproval. Upholding United States' criticism of what he called "Canada's slowness to act" when President Truman called for imperialist intervention in Korea, and rejecting criticism of the independent U.S. behind-the-barn negotiations with Franco, he declared that "Canada is not as important to the U.S. as the U.S. is to Canada" and that, having chosen to "throw in its lot . . . under the leadership of the U.S., Canadians should accept the idea that 'he who pays the piper should be allowed to call the tune'." (*Toronto Daily Star,* August 17, 1951.)

Mr. St. Laurent may believe that the supreme need now is to save the capitalist system and re-establish its imperialist exploitation of other parts of the world. But the fact that Mr. St. Laurent, or any other person or the capitalists as a class, may hold that opinion, doesn't make it Canadian—still less does it make it right. It is not Canadian to sacrifice the national future of Canada in a reckless predatory attempt to "turn the clock back"! It is not Canadian to alienate to the U.S. in perpetuity the priceless resources that should belong to and be developed by the Canadian people as the sacred heritage of their children. It is not Canadian to subordinate our country and the lives and future of its people to the insatiable greed and ambitions of the profit-drunk, power-crazed would-be rulers of the world in Wall Street and Washington. A person who chooses such policies can't be very much concerned about maintaining the sovereign independence of Canada.

What do you think?

1. *Do you think a U.S. spokesman would make similar statements today? Why?*
2. *What government policies do you think Mr. Buck was referring to when he argued that the government was pursuing a policy of "integration"? Has government policy changed?*
3. *(a) Compare Buck's views with those of today's economic nationalists. Account for any similarities or differences.*
   (b) Do you think that Buck's analysis was valid? Why?

4.   THE MASSEY REPORT, 1951

In 1949 the Royal Commission on National Development in the Arts, Letters and Sciences was established by the Liberal Government. The Commission was under the chairmanship of the future Governor General of Canada, Vincent Massey. Its main concern was to recommend how a viable Canadian culture could exist in the midst of Americanization. The following are excerpts from the Massey Report.

Of American institutions we make the freest use, and we are encouraged to do so by the similarities in our ways of life and by the close and friendly personal relations between scholars as individuals and in groups. Not only American universities and graduate schools but specialized schools of all sorts (library schools, schools of art, of music and dramatics); great national institutions (libraries, museums, archives, centres of science and learning)—all are freely placed at our disposal. We use various American information services as if they were our own, and there are few Canadian scholars who do not belong to one or more American learned societies. Finally, we benefit from vast importations of what might be familiarly called the American cultural output. We can import newspapers, periodicals, books, maps and endless educational equipment. We also import artistic talent, either personally in the travelling artist or company, or on the screen, in recordings and over the air. Every Sunday, tens of thousands tacitly acknowledge their cultural indebtedness as they turn off the radio at the close of the Sunday symphony from New York and settle down to the latest American Book of the Month.

Granted that most of these American donations are good in themselves, it does not follow that they have always been good for Canadians.

*   *   *   *   *

Every intelligent Canadian acknowledges his debt to the United States for excellent films, radio programs and periodicals. But the prices may be excessive. Of films and radio we shall speak in more detail later, but it may be noted in passing that our national radio which carries the Sunday symphony from New York also carries the soap-opera. In the periodical press we receive indeed many admirable American journals but also a flood of others much less admirable which, as we have been clearly told, is threatening to submerge completely our national product.

*   *   *   *   *

Although during the last generation our periodicals have maintained and greatly strengthened their position, the competition they face has been almost overwhelming. Canadian magazines with much difficulty have achieved a circulation of nearly forty-two millions a year as against an American circulation in Canada of over eighty-six millions. "Canada . . . is the only country of any size in the world," one of their members has observed, "whose people read more foreign periodicals than they do periodicals published in their own land, local newspapers excluded." The Canadian periodical cannot in its turn invade the American market; for Americans, it seems, simply do not know enough about Canada to appreciate Canadian material. Our periodicals cannot hold their own except in their limited and unprotected market, nine million English-speaking readers. These must be set against the one hundred and sixty millions served by their competitors in the whole North American continent.

The American invasion by film, radio and periodical is formidable. Much of what comes to us is good and of this we shall be speaking presently. It has, however, been represented to us that many of the radio programmes have in fact no particular application to Canada or to Canadian conditions and that some of them, including certain children's programmes of the "crime" and "horror" type, are positively harmful. News commentaries too, and even live broadcasts from American sources, are designed for American ears and are almost certain to have an American slant and emphasis by reason of what they include or omit, as well as because of the opinions expressed. We think it permissible to record these comments on American radio since we observe that in the United States many radio programmes and American broadcasting in general have recently been severely criticized. It will, we think, be readily agreed that we in Canada should take measures to avoid in our radio, and in our television, at least those aspects of American broadcasting which have provoked in the United States the most out-spoken and the sharpest opposition.

American influences on Canadian life to say the least are impressive. There should be no thought of interfering with the liberty of all Canadians to enjoy them. Cultural exchanges are excellent in themselves. They widen the choice of the consumer and provide stimulating competition for the producer. It cannot be denied, however, that a vast and disproportionate amount of material coming from a single alien source may stifle rather than stimulate our own creative effort; and, passively accepted without any standard of comparison, this may weaken critical faculties. We are now spending millions to maintain a national independence which would be nothing but an empty shell without a vigorous and distinctive cultural life. We have seen that we have its elements in our traditions and in our history; we have made important progress, often aided by American generosity. We must not be blind, however, to the very present danger of permanent dependence.

What do you think?

1. What advantages did the authors of the Massey Report see in American cultural influence? What disadvantages? Do you agree with their arguments? Why or why not?
2. "Granted that most of these American donations are good in themselves, it does not follow that they have always been good for Canadians." Explain and evaluate this statement.
3. Does the Canadian cultural scene face the same problems today as it did in 1951? Why?

5.   NOTES ON THE MASSEY REPORT

Professor Frank Underhill, the distinguished Canadian historian, commented on the Massey Report in the Canadian Forum, *August, 1951.*

. . . There is one theme in the report about which some searching questions should be asked. The commissioners seek a national Canadian culture which shall be independent of American influences. Several times they speak of these influences as "alien." This use of the word "alien" seems to me to reveal a fallacy that runs through much of Canadian nationalistic discussion. For we cannot escape the fact that we live on the same continent as the Americans, and that the longer we live here the more we are going to be affected by the same continental influences which affect them. It is too late now for a Canadian cultural nationalism to develop in the kind of medieval isolation in which English or French nationalism was nurtured. The so-called "alien" American influences are not alien at all; they are just the natural forces that operate on a continental scale in the conditions of our twentieth-century civilization.

The fact is that, if we produced Canadian movies for our own mass consumption, they would be as sentimental and vulgar and escapist as are the Hollywood variety; and they would be sentimental, vulgar and escapist in the American way, not in the English or French or Italian way. Our newspapers, which are an independent local product, do not differ essentially from the American ones. The kind of news which the Canadian Press circulates on its own origination is exactly like that originated by A.P. or U.P. Like the American ones, our papers become progressively worse as the size of the city increases, up to a certain point. Somewhere between the size of Chicago and the size of New York another force comes into operation, producing a different kind of newspaper. We haven't any daily as bad as the *Chicago Tribune,* because we haven't any city as big as Chicago; but also we haven't anything as good as the *New York Times.* . . . It is mass-consumption and the North American continental environment which produce the undesirable aspects of "mass-communication," not some sinister influences in the United States.

If we could get off by ourselves on a continental island, far away from the wicked Americans, all we should achieve would be to become a people like the Australians. (And even then the American goblin would get us in the end, as he is getting the Australians). Let us be thankful, then, that we live next door to the Americans. But if we allow ourselves to be obsessed by the danger of American cultural annexation, so that the thought preys on us day and night, we shall only become a slightly bigger Ulster. The idea that by taking thought, and with the help of some government subventions, we can become another England—which, one suspects, is Mr. Massey's ultimate idea—is purely fantastic. No sane Canadian wants us to become a nation of Australians or Ulsterites. So, if we will only be natural, and stop going about in this eternal defensive fear of being ourselves, we shall discover that we are very like the Americans, both in our good qualities and in our bad qualities. Young Canadians who are really alive make this discovery now without going through any great spiritual crisis.

The root cultural problem in our modern mass-democracies is this relationship between the mass culture, which is in danger of being further debased with every new invention in mass-communications, and the culture of the few. The United States is facing this problem at a rather more advanced stage than we have yet reached; and the more intimately we study American experience the more we shall profit. What we need, we, the minority of Canadians who care for the culture of the few, is closer contact with the *finest* expressions of the American mind. The fear that what will result from such contact will be our own absorption is pure defeatism. We need closer touch with the best American universities (*not* Teachers' College) and research institutions, closer touch with American experimental music and poetry and theatre and painting, closer personal touch with the men who are leaders in these activities. The Americans are now mature enough to have come through this adolescent phase of believing that the best way to become mature is to cut yourself off from older people who are more mature than you are. It is about time that we grew out of it also. I think the Massey commissioners should use their leisure now to study the Americans much more closely than they seem to have done hitherto.

What do you think?

1. *Do you agree with Mr. Underhill that the "so-called 'alien' American influences are not alien at all?" Why?*
2. *Do you agree that the "more intimately we study American experience the more we shall profit"?*
3. *What is mass culture? To what extent are the Canadian "mass" culture and the American "mass" culture alike or different? Is there much popular support for the agitation against the American cultural invasion? Why?*
4. *"Young Canadians who are really alive make this discovery now without going through any great spiritual crisis." Do you feel this was true in 1951? Is it true today? Why?*

The 1930s: Canada's "New Deal"

During the Great Depression, many Canadians looked to the United States for their economic salvation. Franklin D. Roosevelt, the liberal Democrat who had won the presidential election of 1932, not only became the hero of Canadian socialists and liberals but he also provided the radical economic policies which the Conservative Prime Minister, R. B. Bennett, attempted to introduce into Canada in 1934 and 1935.

Why did Mr. Bennett attempt to copy the American New Deal? How did his attempt to implement a Canadian New Deal influence Canadian attitudes towards the U.S.? Do Canadians still look to the U.S. for solutions to problems? What are your feelings about adopting U.S. solutions to solve Canadian problems?

1. AMERICA FINDS A LEADER

In the early 1930s the Canadian Forum *was a socialist periodical written by and for Canadian intellectuals and academics. In an editorial of May 1933, the* Forum *praised the accomplishments of Roosevelt.*

The remarkable achievements of President Roosevelt during his first month in office are all the more spectacular because of the initial difficulties placed in his way by the American system of government. The constitution, based on the separation of powers, deliberately made any control and direction by the President almost impossible; and this has been strengthened by a jealous tradition of independence on the part of both Houses of Congress. To break down these barriers, even temporarily, and to get the direction of affairs into his own hands, was itself a major achievement on the part of the President. It called for both vigour and confidence, and for a willingness to stake his whole political future on his ability to use his exceptional powers in a way which would justify to the whole nation this extraordinary departure from established usage. To judge from the record of the first month, his confidence was extremely well founded. The envy with which other nations have watched this display of leadership must be especially acute among those who, like Canada, are blessed with what is quaintly called responsible government. Those extensive powers which are so exceptional in the American president are the normal powers of a prime minister. He does not have to fight for his opportunity against all existing tradition—it is presented to him by a complacent parliamentary majority. But where is the leadership which can take advantage of that situation? It is certainly not apparent at Ottawa at the present time.

2. WOODSWORTH PRAISES THE NEW DEAL

Mr. J. S. Woodsworth, the first leader of the C.C.F., praised many aspects of Roosevelt's New Deal. This selection is an excerpt from a speech given by Woodsworth in the House of Commons on February 19, 1937.

We have poor housing conditions. We have enormous debts that are crushing the lives out of a great many of our western farmers and making impossible recovery in many sections of this country. We can do nothing for these classes; yet no expenditure is too great and nothing is too good for those who wish to prepare for war.

A few days ago I received a very interesting copy of the *Halifax Herald* of January 28, in which there is a front page editorial dealing with the program of President Roosevelt. This is a quotation from the address of the president:

> I see millions of families trying to live on incomes so meagre that the pall of family disaster hangs over them day by day.
> I see millions whose daily lives in city and on farm continue under conditions labelled indecent by a so-called polite society half a century ago.
> I see millions denied education, recreation and the opportunity to better their lot and the lot of their children.
> I see millions lacking the means to buy products of farm and factory and by their poverty denying work and productiveness to many other millions.
> I see one-third of a nation ill-housed, ill-clad, ill-nourished.

And he added:

> It is not in despair that I paint you that picture. I paint it for you in hope—because the nation, seeing and understanding the injustice of it, proposes to paint it out.

The editorial comments:

> What the president of the United States has said about his country applies with equal force to this country. Canada, with its population of around eleven million people, is in no better case proportionately than the neighbouring republic.
> And what the president of the United States has demanded in social justice and social security for the people of his own country, is what is being demanded for the Canadian people.
> I wish that this government, calling itself by the name of Liberal, would follow a lead of that kind instead of falling back on age-old methods which have in the past proved so futile.

What do you think?

1. *Why did the* Forum *and Mr. Woodsworth praise President Roosevelt?*
2. *Why did socialist favourable comment in the 1930s turn into*

socialist attacks and criticism of the United States in the 1960s and 1970s?

3. THE LIBERAL CENTRE

At a Liberal party conference at Port Hope, Ontario, in September 1933, T. W. L. MacDermot, a university teacher, suggested that Roosevelt's New Deal provided the Liberal Party with the key to electoral victory.

The New Deal is of profound significance to Canada for two reasons. First, it is a polite name for the first real revolution that has struck Anglo-Saxon America and is taking place at our very doors, indeed, over our very threshold; second, its main principles are quite easily applicable to this country. For Canada is at about the same political, economic and intellectual stage in its development as the United States. As we investigate the New Deal, therefore, it is useful to remember that we are North Americans and observers of an experiment that was born in much the same political and commercial air as that which we normally breathe. . . .
. . . For the New Deal has a peculiar relevance to Canada. National experiments are now commonplace and Canadians have sought vigorously amongst them for precept and warning. To the hearty radicals, to whom nothing is obscure, Russia quickly became the great storehouse of revolutionary lore; and we have been deluged with selections from it. But interesting as Russia is, and much as we can learn from it, it is a country as different in history, people, temperament, from Canada as a country very well could be.

     *   *   *   *   *

America is different. We are familiar with the business outlook and all its organized forms. We have effusively embraced the Service Club, the movie hero, and the dollar standard. So that the analogy between American effort and our own is not difficult to establish, and is therefore highly illuminating.

If we are to study the New Deal, we must above all form a clear idea of the *whole thing*. It has two general aspects, which I shall separate for the sake of analysis, but which are at bottom inseparable. They are the economic and socio-political aspects. The first, the economics of raising prices and wages, fixing prices, dealing with debt charges, monetary stabilization and so on, has had the greater share of attention, as its immense importance deserves. For that reason, and because I am no economist, I shall be discreet, and add but one word. It is that the New Deal is based on a consistent and thought-out theory of economics, and is quite able to defend itself in debate: it fits into and belongs to the complete ground plan of the New Deal. There is, of course, another and diametrically opposed, theory of economics, and the horns of the economists are locked over the two. But those whom God hath joined together let no man put asunder.

Supplementing the economic action of the plan is the confidence, the national exhilaration of which its launching has given rise, and I gather from the economists that this unpredictable force may be a potent instrument in making or marring the whole scheme. For it is not the legislation itself, but the fact that it was passed that has affected the mind of the people.

As a social and political phenomenon the New Deal might be described as an historical climax: a man, a body of legislation, and a set of ideas. The swift chapter of events of last spring came at a time when many old ideas were being dropped in the United States, when the phrase "rugged individualism" and all that it stood for was passing into contempt and derision; when the Democratic Party was summarily and boldly changing its course, and when the financial and industrial world of the United States seemed ready to crash about their ears. The Man, of course, is Mr. Roosevelt, endowed with great public gifts, an education, and a winning smile, and now personifying the new national spirit of the country. His name is used to push on codes, to settle strikes, to calm industrialists; and in the tactical prosecution of a new policy, the personal factor represented by him cannot, and should not, be overlooked for a minute.

*   *   *   *   *

The general principles I have enumerated are, I believe, completely applicable to Canada. They appeal to the emotional demands of the day, and to the canons of common sense. They harmonize with the note in Canadian thought, the claim and desire of all Canadians to join democratically in the economic and political salvaging of their country. They touch, too, the springs of hope and are capable of releasing a tremendous political force. They are based on a belief in humanity, and are founded on the facts of our lives, and their objectives answer to the deeper satisfactions of the common man. Abroad, the sharpest resentment is felt against the shocking disorder of all our affairs; and a plan founded on a conception of the nation as a real unity, as a free unity, and as a unity working towards order and stability in its daily life, irresistibly appeals.

I believe the Revolution of Control could take place in Canada without the danger of Fascism accompanying it, though I doubt if it will. Certainly we should have difficulty in view of the present set-up of political affairs to fill in all the parts of the formula. We need a Man who can lead and with the courage and wit to act; a body of thinkers cooperating on a definite set of ideas; and a prepared legislative plan which will give scope to the leadership, and at one blow consolidate the nation into some kind of unanimity on national policy. But the powers of the closed mind are great; and it is easy to be pessimistic about the probabilities of this country's realizing to the point of action the significance of the New Deal to Canada.

What do you think?

1. *According to Mr. MacDermot, what was at the heart of the "New Deal"?*
2. *Why did the author feel that Canada could accept and implement the principles of the New Deal very easily? In general, do you feel that American solutions can be applied to problems in Canada? Why?*
3. *Compare the New Deal and the New Left. How similar were their respective impacts on Canada? How dissimilar?*
4. *Do you think that the inclination of Canada to imitate policies conceived by the U.S. has increased or decreased since the 1930s? Why?*

4. A CONSERVATIVE POSITION

Mr. W. D. Herridge, Prime Minister R. B. Bennett's brother-in-law, was the Canadian envoy in Washington. While in the American capital Herridge was converted to the principles of the New Deal. He sent the following message to Mr. Bennett on April 12, 1934.

There is little abatement in the popular support of the President. The people still look upon him as the man who gave them the New Deal and as a leader who, in some way not wholly revealed, will lead them out of the wilderness of depression. This New Deal is a sort of Pandora's box, from which, at suitable intervals, the President has pulled the N.R.A. and the A.A.A. and a lot of other mysterious things. Most of the people never understood the N.R.A. or the A.A.A. any more than they understood the Signs of the Zodiac, but that did not matter very much: they were all part of the New Deal, and the New Deal meant recovery, because the President had so promised. . . .

We need a Pandora's box. We need some means by which the people can be persuaded that they also have a New Deal, and that the New Deal will do everything for them *in fact* which the New Deal here has done *in fancy*.

Moreover, we must fully develop the plan which may rightfully be called a New Deal and which when tested in practical ways, will contain the elements which are the seeds of a new order of prosperity. . . .

One may profitably attempt a comparison between the way things are done in Washington and in Ottawa. Here, the New Deal was struck out with a single blow, and so presented to the people. The different parts of the New Deal were then hastily devised. . . . At Ottawa, there is in preparation a New Deal, but there is no acknowledgment of that fact. . . . What we are doing has not been regarded as a whole. . . . Failure of complete integration and the balancing of each element in terms of the whole invites a very real danger. This danger is that we may find, proceeding as we do along unrelated and parallel lines, that our finished projects are in some respects mutually repugnant and tend to cancel one another out. . . .

. . . It has been said that on March 4th, 1933, President Roosevelt was given a national instrument of extreme sensitivity upon which to play. It has been argued that we cannot reasonably conceive of a parallel situation in Canada, and that, at any rate, none such exists. I do not know how much truth there is in this, but I believe that there is in Canada today a situation which can be almost amazingly influenced by the right treatment. I believe that . . . the national heart is at this time highly responsive and will incline with profound fervour to the right sort of lead.

That you alone can give. That you have the power to give. With your decision to do so, there can without difficulty be worked out the necessary supporting plan. . . .

What do you think?

1. Why, according to Mr. Herridge, did Canada need a New Deal?
2. How important were Roosevelt's qualities as a leader in creating a favorable impression of the New Deal? Did Canadians have the same attitudes as Americans about strong leaders during the 1930s? Are Canadian attitudes on this question more or less like U.S. attitudes today? Why?

5. R. B. BENNETT'S NEW DEAL

On January 2, 1935, Prime Minister Bennett made his New Deal views public on a nation-wide radio network. Like Roosevelt, Bennett was attempting to use the radio to build up his following.

In the last five years, great changes have taken place in the world. The old order is gone. It will not return. We are living amidst conditions which are new and strange to us. Your prosperity demands corrections in the old system, so that, in these new conditions, that old system may adequately serve you. The right time to bring about these changes has come. Further progress without them is improbable. To understand what changes and corrections should be made, you must first understand the facts of the present situation. To do that, you should have clearly in mind what has taken place in the past five years; the ways in which we have made progress, the ways in which we have not. To do that—to decide wisely—you must be in a position to judge those acts of Government which have palliated your hardships, which have preserved intact our industrial and financial structure, and which have prepared the way for the reforms which must now take place.

  * * * * *

 . . . if you believe that things should be left as they are, you and I hold contrary and irreconcilable views. I am for reform.

 And, in my mind, reform means Government intervention. It means Government control and regulation. It means the end of *laissez faire*. Reform heralds certain recovery. There can be no permanent recovery without reform. Reform or no reform! I raise that issue squarely. I nail the flag of progress to the masthead. I summon the power of the State to its support.

 Who will oppose our plan of progress? It will be interesting and instructive to see. It seems to me that the party which supports *laissez faire,* which demands that Government do not interfere with business, which says that the State has no such part to play in these critical times—it seems to me that that party may have a change of heart when it sees how the rest of us feel about the matter, and may decide to come along with you and me. Well, if it will denounce its hereditary chieftain, which is reaction, abandon its creed of inaction, and pledge its allegiance to action, to progress, to reform—it will be welcome if it is really sincere. *For I am working, and working grimly, to one end only; to get results.*

  * * * * *

 I am willing to go on, if you make it possible for me still to serve you. But if there is anyone better able to do so, I shall gladly make way for him. And it is your duty to yourselves to support him, and not me. Your country's future is at stake. *This is no time to indulge your personal prejudices or fancies.* Carefully and calmly, look well into the situation. Then pick the man and the policy best fitted to deal with it. And resolutely back that man and that policy. The nation should range itself behind them. *In war you fought as one. Fight now again as one.* For the task ahead demands your war-time resolution and your war-time unity.

  * * * * *

. . . if you believe in progress, if you believe in reform, if you believe that the present situation cries aloud for betterment, if you believe that it is the duty of government, by all right and fair means, to strive to secure betterment, if you believe that in Big Business, that in capitalism, there are abuses which work hardship upon the people of this country, if you believe that the faults of capitalism have brought about injustices in our social state, if you believe that these injustices manifest themselves in lower wages and too high costs of living and unemployment—then support my Party . . .

. . . For my Party has already undertaken and will pursue to the end, a programme of reform which will rid the system of these disabilities. It stands for the freedom of the individual and private initiative and sound business, but it stands with equal certainty for permanent and better relationship between the people and those instruments of commerce and finance which are set up to serve them. It stands not for traditions which are outworn or practices which belong to another age or for economic faiths which if pursued now, mean economic hardships. My Party stands simply for the greatest good of the greatest number of the people. And it shapes and will continue to shape its policy of reform, to make that sure.

I have just one more thing to say. This policy of reform will force, inevitably, a political re-alignment. Because this policy of reform comprises the great issue before the people. And never since Confederation, has that issue been raised in this way. Do you want reform, or do you not want reform? If you do not want it, back the Liberal Party. If you do want it, back my Party.

You know that my whole programme is by no means complete. The first stage has been well begun. The second stage we will immediately initiate. And so on and on, until the job is done. If there is a more workable plan than mine, I will be very glad to hear of it.

As I say, in details we may differ; but all earnest men and women who put their country first will, on the broad principle and practice of reform as I have stated it, unite with me. For you agree that our success depends upon our unity. And so, all together, we will drive forward, confident that the might of the Canadian people will reclaim this land from trouble and sorrow, and bring back happiness and security.

What do you think?

1. What was "laissez-faire"? Why did Mr. Bennett want to get rid of it?
2. How deeply do you think the prime minister had been influenced by the New Deal?
3. What do you think the attitude of the average Canadian in 1935 would have been towards Mr. Bennett's adoption of these reform

policies? Would the fact that they originated in the United States affect this attitude? Why?

4. *How would the Conservatives in the 1970s react to adopting an American programme? Why?*

The 1920s

During the 1920s Canada's economy and culture came increasingly under American influence. Some Canadians, a very small minority, began to express a certain anxiety about what they considered to be the growing Americanization of Canadian life. But the majority of Canadians wanted their country to share in U.S. economic prosperity. Even those who attacked the U.S. cultural invasion often looked favourably at the commercial success of the United States and at the infusion of American capital into Canada. How has the Canadian response to U.S. influences changed since the 1920s? In what ways has it remained the same?

1.   CANADA IS A U.S. COLONY

In 1920 the distinguished Nova Scotian scholar, Professor Archibald MacMechan, argued that Canada had virtually become a colony of the United States.

The threats of American politicians, editors, and Fourth of July orators, the organized effort for "commercial union" in 1891 . . . the possibility of a quarrel between Canada and the United States ending in an appeal to arms, may be lightly dismissed. The danger is far more subtle and far more deeply to be dreaded. It lies in gradual assimilation, in peaceful penetration, in a spiritual bondage—the subjection of the Canadian nation's mind and soul to the mind and soul of the United States. No long argument is needed to prove the imminent and deadly menace of this danger, and nothing should touch the pride of a young, strong, and ambitious people like accepting tamely a position of inferiority to a powerful neighbour. Without any outward fetter it is the situation of a spiritual slave. Enforced political subjection is the lesser evil; it would be easier to bear, for the spirit could still be free. . . .

It is inevitable that the United States should exert a tremendous influence upon Canada. Our domains march together for three thousand miles. The same speech, the same laws, the same religions prevail on both sides of the border, as Goldwin Smith was never weary of preaching. Intercourse between the countries is easy. A standard gauge and common courtesy have made the continent one country for purposes of railway transportation. C.P.R. cars may be seen in Texas, and Omaha and Santa Fe in Cape Breton. Traffic between Canada and the United States is far easier than between the separate colonies of the Australian Commonwealth. Then, our neighbours are many and rich; we are few in the land, and until lately we were very poor. Hundreds of thousands of Canadians have been drawn across the border, because of the better opportunities for making a living, and for making money, under the Stars and Stripes. All these things were inevitable, and tend to make of Canada nine more states not yet brought formally under the control of Washington.

But our spiritual subjection goes deeper. Canada has definitely, if tacitly, declared her position as between American and English ideals. To begin with the individual. The most popular set of caricatures ever designed in this country were Racey's portrayal of the green "young Englishman" and his mistakes, much as the "new chum" is represented in Australia. The Englishman's accent, voice, manner, clothes are considered odd, departing from the norm. The American's are not, because they do not strike us as different from our own.

Take the most potent influence at work to-day upon the popular mind, our journalism. Hundreds of thousands of Canadians read nothing but the daily newspaper. Not only is the Canadian newspaper built on American lines, but it is crammed with American "boiler-plate" of all kinds, American illustrations, American comic supplements. American magazines, some of them distinctly anti-British in tone and tendency, flood our shops and book-stalls. Every new Canadian magazine is on an American model, some of them borrowing an American title and changing only the national adjective. . . .

Another potent influence for bringing Canada into spiritual subjection to the United States is the moving-picture show. The films are made for American audiences, naturally, to suit their taste. Then, they come to Canada. We originate none, practically. I dropped into a "movie" theatre in a small Nova Scotian town. It was filled with noisy, excited children. The point of the plot was the continual thwarting of a villain through the agency of several small boys and girls. They occurred and recurred in a sort of procession, the leader carrying the Stars and Stripes; and whenever they appeared the little Bluenoses cheered like mad.

American influence is seen even more plainly in our universities. The curriculum, text-books, methods of teaching, over-sight of students, "credits", are borrowed from the United States. Organization and administration are on the American model. Among the students, American ideas prevail. Such matters as Greek letter societies, class organizations, with president, prophet, critic, and "exercises," down to the big initial on the football sweater and the curious war-cries known as class and college yells, are borrowed directly from American colleges. Our students did not originate these ideas; they borrowed them. The Dalhousie "yell," for example, was introduced by an American teacher of music.

Canadian sport has become more and more American. Our one native game, lacrosse, is dead. Cricket, which flourishes in Australia, is here a sickly exotic. But baseball is everywhere. Our newspapers are filled with reports of the various "leagues."

In minor matters, the popularity of such toys as the Teddybear, that curious tribute to the worth of an American president, the spread (by seductive advertising) of the chewing gum habit, the establishment of the automatic chewing gum machine, that monument of progressive civilization, are all to be reckoned with. Our fashions in clothes are decreed for us in New York, whither our tailors resort yearly to ascertain "what will be worn"; and our youths develop knobbly shoulders, semi-detached trousers with permanent cuffs or hour-glass waists, according to the whim of certain multiples of nine in the commercial metropolis of America. All these are straws showing how the wind blows.

The list of such straws might be extended indefinitely. No Canadian ever invents a new slang term. All our slang is brought in and distributed by the American "shows," of one kind or another.

*   *   *   *   *

We invent nothing. The various fraternal orders invade us from the United States. The Rotary Club is another instance. It is, no doubt, an admirable organization, though intrigued by the title I was personally disappointed to find that the Rotarians did not rotate on their own axles like the Whirling Dervishes. But why did not a Canadian invent it? Why must we be always borrowing ideas from our big neighbour?

Reviewing all these facts, the pessimist may well shake his head and sigh; "Perhaps, after all, it is not worth while struggling on, trying to make Canada a distinct nation. Best give up the struggle. Work along the line of least resistance. Perhaps the utmost we can ever hope to become is a poor pale imitation of the United States."

What do you think?

1. What did Professor MacMechan mean when he referred to Canada's "spiritual subjugation"?
2. According to Professor MacMechan, what factors were responsible for the Americanization of Canada?
3. Compare Mr. MacMechan's views with those of the Massey Report

(page 150), and the statements made by various commentators in the 1960s and 1970s. What similarities do you notice? What differences? Account for any you find.
4. Are Canadians today more or less likely to be influenced by U.S. values transmitted by media than they were in the 1920s? Why?

2. A NEW KIND OF RELATIONSHIP

Professor Frank Underhill became one of the founding members of the CCF, the forerunner of the New Democratic Party. In spite of his inclination towards socialism, Underhill unlike MacMechan was quite sympathetic to the United States. This selection is an excerpt from an article he wrote for the July 1929 issue of the Canadian Forum.

On the subject of Americanism the ordinary Canadian behaves like a fundamentalist discussing modernism. No one in his senses can deny that the social and economic bonds between the two North American peoples are becoming every day more intimate and more complex. The process is as inevitable as the movements of the tides, and even in Eastern Canada our political Mrs. Partingtons with their tariff brooms are coming to be recognized as slightly ridiculous. King Street and St. James Street are more and more dominated by Wall Street, and business men pass to and fro between New York and Toronto or Montreal as unconscious of the national boundary lines as they are of the state boundary lines when they pass between New York and Chicago or Philadelphia. There is not a man in Canada under fifty years of age who would not pack up and move to the States tomorrow if he got a good business offer. Most of those patriots who talk so loudly about their determination to remain in Canada have managed to preserve their virtue simply because it has never been exposed to temptation. We are reaching a condition on this continent in which men change their citizenship as easily as they change their wives.

*   *   *   *   *

The truth is that we are working out on this continent a new kind of relationship between two peoples such as the world has never seen before. We fail to understand it ourselves because our minds are still dominated by political ideas about nationality which were imported from Europe. But the interpenetration of the lives of the two peoples has already become so far-reaching and so complex that it is absurd to talk to us as if we were like Frenchmen and Germans in Europe. We need a new set of political categories. North America is destined to give the political pluralists of our day a great deal of new ammunition for their guns. Exactly what form the political relationship of the next generation will take no one can predict. The one thing that is certain is that annexation talk on both sides of the border will die away. When the non-political ties have multiplied, as they are bound to do, far beyond what they are already, everyone will come to realize that to abolish Ottawa would be as meaningless a gesture as to abolish the royal veto in England. We on the north side of the boundary line shall have to learn how to reconcile our allegiance to Canada with our acceptance of these other non-political facts. Indeed we are learning already. No one would worry about the matter if our professional patriots would let us alone.

*   *   *   *   *

The real problem on this continent is not the political relationship between two supposedly mutually exclusive and independent entities called Canada and the United States, but the economic relationship between the classes who make up the North American community. What is this Americanism about which we hear so much? It is government of the people by big business and for big business. It is the doctrine that a millionaire is the noblest work of God. It is the new economic feudalism which is every day making our political democracy more meaningless. But all these things we have in Canada already. The Canada of our business men is completely Americanized now. But it does so happen that we have developed some other elements in our life which may act as a corrective to this overwhelming capitalism. The Wheat Pools on the prairies, the Canadian National Railways, the Ontario Hydro, are examples of another way of doing things, in which the common man exists for some other purpose than that of being exploited by his betters. The question whether Canada is to become wholly American depends on which elements in her economic life will ultimately prevail. Our big business men are our chief American influences, and the tendency of their activities is not one whit altered by the vigour with which some of them wave the old flag. If they prevail indefinitely Canada will become only a geographical expression.

What do you think?

1. *According to Professor Underhill, what was the unique "new relationship" being worked out between Canada and the United States? Is that relationship still being worked out? Give reasons.*
2. *How does Professor Underhill deal with the various points raised by Professor MacMechan? Whose case is stronger? Why?*
3. *What does Professor Underhill mean when he argues that: "The real problem on this continent is not the political relationship . . . but the economic relationship between the classes who make up the North American community"?*
4. *Which nineteenth century Canadians expressed views similar to those of Professor MacMechan and Professor Underhill?*

5. Compare Professor Underhill's views here with his views in 1951 (page 152). Do you see a change? If so, account for it.
6. Judging from the views of Professor MacMechan and Professor Underhill, have Canadian attitudes changed since the 1920s? Why or why not?

3. THE GANGSTER ERA

The following three articles were published in the periodical Saturday Night, *in August and November, 1925. The articles, on gangsterism, were among hundreds published in Canada in the 1920s.*

WHERE LAWLESSNESS IS TOP DOG

The records of the courts, together with the crime sheets of the City of Chicago, show that a murderer has better than a hundred to one chance of not having his neck stretched. So it is that the premier city of Illinois is the prize murder centre of the world, barring perhaps a certain section of Asia at the moment. Just the other day five hold-up men staged a robbery at the fashionable Drake Hotel in that City. The net result was two robbers and one hotel clerk killed, two women injured, two robbers captured, while one escaped with some ten thousand dollars' worth of booty. Of course this is only one little incident of the many that have taken place in Chicago within the past year or two.

There are laws against murder in Illinois as in other parts of the world. In fact there is, as is common over the international boundary, a multiplicity of laws. So many indeed that a goodly proportion of citizens forget where one begins and the other leaves off. The trouble in Chicago seems to be that law is one thing and law enforcement quite another.

Perhaps it would be quite in order to invite the 125 U.S. evangelists who are now visiting Great Britain where there are less murders than in one American city with the idea of telling the British people how to live to visit their own country and straighten out this business of lax law enforcement.

(*Saturday Night*, August 8, 1925)

CHICAGO HABITS IN CANADA

Chicago people who visit Canada should leave their Chicago habits at home. Here is a case in point. A resident of the Windy City by the name of Phillips was arrested the other day in Montreal. He was drunk, armed with a revolver and in charge of an automobile. It took some shooting on the part of the police to bring the inebriated gentleman to a standstill. He was incidentally condemned to pay a fine of $100 or spend a month in jail.

Chicago people visiting Canada should play safety first and leave their firearms behind.

(*Saturday Night*, August 22, 1925)

THE ILLINOIS CRIME CALENDAR

Periodically we obtain new tips on the administration of justice from the state of Illinois. A recent issue of the *Chicago Tribune* contains some piquant revelations as to the kindly spirit in which youthful robbers are treated there. "Pick your own penitentiary" is the latest judicial motto. At Waukegan, Illinois, a lively youth named Jack Durand was recently convicted of robbing the summer home of the president of the Armour corporation and remanded on bail for sentence. In the interim he motored with a party of friends to visit the reformatory at Joliet and decided that its appointments and surroundings were not to his taste. When he came up for sentence he objected to being sent to Pontiac but expressed a willingness to give Joliet penitentiary a trial. It was announced that he would motor out there next day and inspect it before making up his mind on the question of appeal. Inasmuch as he is likely to spend not less than three years and not more than twenty years there his interest was natural.

Young Durand's conviction does not seem to have diminished his popularity with the younger set. The *Tribune* states that he starred on the gridiron on Sunday, November 1. He is captain of the Lake Bluff eleven and made some brilliant plays against the Highwood team. It was announced that he would make his farewell appearance on the football field before leaving for the penitentiary on Sunday, November 8. No doubt he was given a good send-off, and his fellow townsmen expressed their sorrow at his hard luck in getting caught after yielding to the temptation to rob a millionaire.

Further stimulating news as to criminal justice in Illinois was forthcoming at the trial at Chicago of the Genna gang, an influential coterie of bootleggers. They were not arraigned for breaches of the liquor law, but for murder. Not long ago they were guilty of a faux pas. They slew two policemen in a running automobile fight. Their explanation is that they mistook the policemen for bandits. Thus an ill-adjudged attempt to assist the course of law and order landed them in jail, and they feel aggrieved, because, according to their story, their relations with the police were friendly. They claim that they have been paying 300 Chicago policemen for protection in connection with their liquor business and that their payroll for this purpose was $8,000 per month. Evidently the police were not greedy. These figures mean only about $25 per month per cop. But possibly there were many other bootleggers similarly open-handed, so that the police were not asked to starve on a mere pittance. Unfortunately a few indiscreet officers went and spoiled it all by starting a gun-fight. A Chicago policeman when he meets a bootlegger should show his badge and ask for money.

Then there would be no chance of a well-intentioned and kindly bootlegger mistaking him for a bandit.

(*Saturday Night,* November 14, 1925.)

What do you think?

1. (a) How would stories like these influence Canadian attitudes to the U.S.?
   (b) Does Canadian popular writing about the U.S. today exhibit tendencies similar to those seen in the three articles above?
2. Why were some Canadians in the 1920s so concerned about "American injustice"?
3. To what extent can a "superiority complex" account for Canadian attitudes toward the U.S.? Has this tendency increased or decreased since the 1920s? Why?

4. CANADA: BRITISH NOT "POLYGLOT"

Mr. R. B. Bennett, the leader of the Conservative Party in 1928, had another reason for being concerned about Americanization. In a speech delivered in the House of Commons on June 7, 1928, the future prime minister of Canada urged Canada to retain the characteristics of "British civilization".

Read the history of the United States, read what is written in every magazine in that country by thoughtful men, and you will find that the principle of the melting pot has failed; and they are quite apprehensive. Every thoughtful man in the United States, every keen observer, every man who travels, every author, everyone who shapes and moulds public opinion in the universities and in the great foundations—all these are bewailing the fact that uncontrolled immigration has been permitted into that country, to such an extent that there is now in the United States a polyglot population, without any distinctive civilization, and one about which many of them are in great despair. That is the answer to my hon. friend. And, sir, it is because we desire to profit by the very lessons we learned there that we are endeavouring to maintain our civilization at that high standard which had made the British civilization the test by which all other civilized nations in modern times are measured. . . .

We have Germans and Ukrainians; we have people from other countries, Norwegians, Swedes, Danes, Finns, Germans, some Swiss, some Dutch, some Belgians, a few old country French, some Austrians; I recall a very considerable settlement of people from that country. We have people from Poland, a few from Roumania; I have never seen any from Lithuania, but that was part of another country before the war, and the same might be said with respect to Esthonia and Latvia. I have seen some few settlers from Czechoslovakia and Jugoslavia, which countries were parts of Serbia before the war. These people have made excellent settlers; they have kept the law; they have prospered and they are proud of Canada, but it cannot be that we must draw upon them to shape our civilization. We must still maintain that measure of British civilization which will enable us to assimilate these people to British institutions, rather than assimilate our civilization to theirs. That is the point; that is all that may be said with respect to it, and it is the point I desire to make at this time. We earnestly and sincerely believe that the civilization which we call the British civilization is the standard by which we must measure our own civilization; we desire to assimilate those whom we bring to this country to that civilization, that standard of living, that regard for morality and law and the institutions of the country and to the ordered and regulated development of this country. That is what we desire, rather than by the introduction of vast and overwhelming numbers of people from other countries to assimilate the British immigrants and the few Canadians who are left to some other civilization. That is what we are endeavouring to do, and that is the reason so much stress is laid upon the British settler . . .

What do you think?

1. (a) What did R. B. Bennett mean when he talked about: "The American melting pot"? "a polyglot population"?
   (b) Is U.S. society a "melting pot"? Is Canadian society a "mosaic"? Give reasons.
2. (a) According to Mr. Bennett, what role was "British civilization" playing in Canada with respect to immigration?
   (b) How successful do you think a conscious adherence to the "British way" would have been in keeping Canadian culture distinct from the U.S.? Why?
3. (a) From your reading so far in this section dealing with the 1920s, describe what you think was the "atmosphere" of Canadian society at that time.
   (b) How has that atmosphere changed? Is Canadian society today more or less like U.S. society than in the 1920s? Give evidence to support your answers.
   (c) Have changes in the nature of Canadian society affected Canadian attitudes to the U.S.? Justify your answer.

5. GOOD FRIENDS

On January 30, 1923, the Kingston Daily British Whig *published the following article applauding the "undefended border."*

Not long ago an arch was erected on the Canadian-American boundary line at Blaine, Washington, to commemorate more than a century of peace between Canada and the United States. During that time more than the ordinary number of occasions have arisen which might have led to war. "This fact," says Dr. Nicholas Murray Butler, "is of itself an eloquent testimony to the temper and self-restraint of English-speaking peoples."

There are additional reasons for the friendly relations between these two great countries. Canada as a nation holds sacred traditions and ideals which are similar to those of the United States. The two countries have common parentage in Great Britain, and of late years have grown more nearly alike in the matter of government. No two nations in the world are like these with such a far-reaching common boundary line, and in maintaining so little in the way of defensive fortifications.

That this dominion has advanced to the extent of assuming in a measure her own diplomatic relations with the United States is another cause for congratulation. Our increasing responsibility will make for more rapid development of leaders who will plan ahead for the expansion of our industries and the extension of our trade and commerce.

Canada and the United States share so much in common that they may expect the centuries of friendship and mutual good will to continue into the future of time.

What do you think?

1. How accurately did this statement reflect Canadian attitudes towards the U.S. in 1923? How accurate is it for today?
2. "Canada and the United States share so much in common that they may expect the centuries of friendship and mutual good will to continue into the future of time." Discuss.

6.   THE ECONOMIC DEBATE: CONCERN

A prophetic article by J. Marjorie van der Hoek appeared in August, 1926, in the Canadian Forum. *She suggested that the "branch plant" problem was quite serious.*

At the beginning of the twentieth century, foreign investors suddenly realized that Canada was an attractive field for the investment of capital. Until then only a few British bankers had taken up the Canadian government bonds and the railroad securities. By 1900, however, the Canadian Pacific Railway, a pioneer line, had opened up the Canadian West and made this rich region of undeveloped resources accessible. The British bankers then began to invest more heavily in Canada, but, since they were moved chiefly by the desire to obtain a safe interest, most of their capital went into railroads and government bonds and only very little into industrial enterprises.

Just at this period when Canada was opening as a field for investment, the United States experienced an important change in internal development. With the passing of the frontier lands, the United States changed from an agricultural country to one predominantly industrial. The new status necessarily altered her economic policy from the development of internal resources to the search for new markets and raw materials. The country was prosperous and the American business man, looking for likely opportunities to invest his profits, found them in the undeveloped resources of the prairie provinces. Unlike the British, the American investments, made with the idea of seeking profits and developing resources and industries, were largely speculative and industrial.

. . . The outbreak of the World War had its effect on Canadian finance insofar as England, in need of every available shilling for war purposes, was soon unable to invest money abroad. During the war the increased demand for Canadian goods necessitated more capital for enlarging the factories, and the municipal and provincial governments also were putting out large quantities of bonds. Since England could not furnish the capital, the Canadians turned to the United States. During the war, and for a period after it, the permanent loans from the United Kingdom were practically stationary, increasing slightly in 1915-1916 but decreasing almost the same amount in 1920-1921. The flow of British capital to Canada was retarded even after the war by the fact that the pound was at a discount. Thus in 1920 the British had practically the same amount invested in Canada as in 1914, while the United States had one billion four hundred and fifty million dollars, or almost twice as much as in 1914, and 52 percent as much as the British.

*   *   *   *   *

Perhaps the most striking feature of the penetration of American capital is the establishment of branch plants of American industries. During the war the assembling and distributing houses were converted into full-fledged factories, and by 1922 there were over seven hundred American branch factories in Canada.

. . . The problem to-day is what effect the penetration of American capital will have on Canada. Opinions differ widely on this subject—from that of a member of the Canadian Parliament who recently expressed his belief that American imperialism was greatly to be feared, to those who see nothing more than the rapid development of the country. The financial organs take an optimistic view of the movement. The Banker's Trust Company of New York asserts that the capital will develop Canada into a powerful nation which, since it will enlarge the market for the United States, is beneficial, while the *Financial Post* declares that the flow of capital has added but another common interest between the two countries:

> Eventually American capital must have attained the ascendancy in Canada, for geographically, ethically, and economically, there could have been no resisting the movement of American wealth northwards to find new fields for productive use. The war, of course, which shut off the supply of the British capital greatly increased American wealth, brought the movement to a head much sooner than it could possibly have developed in the ordinary course of events. . . . There is no reason why Englishmen should regret the situation. Canada, politically, is firmly attached to the British Empire, no matter where her economic affiliations are the strongest. American capital is making Canada a stronger and richer nation; if that makes her a stronger asset of the British Commonwealth of Nations, then the other British nations have no cause to regret the advent of American capital. And when the problem of exchange has been settled, Britain will have equal opportunities with the United States to invest in Canada.

But Scott Nearing believes that a conflict inevitably arises whenever the economic and political controls are in different hands. He asserts that economic activities are followed by political complications—the capital migrating to foreign countries makes demands upon the governments of these countries under the authority of concessions, and when satisfactory treatment is not accorded, the American investors appeal to the United States for support. Nearing is convinced that Canada is only at the first stage of this process, and, although as yet there has been no change in politics, the time will come when Canada will become part of the United States either by force, by peaceful annexation due to the propaganda fostered by American investors, or by organization of an American producers' federation.

What do you think?

1. *Why did Americans invest in Canada?*
2. *What are "branch plants"? Why might this article be considered "prophetic"?*
3. *What is the basic argument put forward by Scott Nearing? Who in Canada today is putting forward the same argument?*
4. *What benefits did American capital bring to the Canadian economy at this time? Do these benefits still exist? Why?*

Reciprocity, 1911

In the 1911 federal election campaign the Conservatives and Liberals continued their late nineteenth-century political battle over the advantages and disadvantages of closer economic relations with the United States. The Liberals were led by Prime Minister Wilfrid Laurier, and the Conservatives by Robert Borden. In many respects the election was very much similar to the one of 1891, but it was to be the last Canadian federal election campaign dominated by the central issue of Canadian-American relations. Why do you think this was the case?

1. THE CONSERVATIVE CRITIQUE

On February 9, 1911, George Foster, the Conservative Party's chief financial critic, savagely attacked the Liberal Government's reciprocity proposal.

But I not only take President Taft then, I take President Taft since. He is now stumping the United States in favour of reciprocity, and as he goes he grows a little more and a little more decided. At Columbus, Ohio, he declared:

> The greatest reason for adopting this agreement is the fact that it is going to unite two countries with kindred people and lying together across a wide continent, in a commercial and social union to the great advantage of both.

What says Mr. Hill, the railway magnate?

> I want to say to you that we cannot afford to let this opportunity pass. It is said that "opportunity calls once at every man's door," but that if you leave the door open it will come again. Let me say to you that the conditions in the British Empire are such that if we let it pass it will never come again. If we neglect the opportunity that is now manifesting itself, if that is refused, it is almost a certainty that imperial federation will follow, and if it does, where is your independence, where is your market?

What says Senator Beveridge? What says Governor Foss? What say the newspapers from one end of the country to the other? What is the allusion, what is the call to the United States for viewing this question, not simply from the low business standpoint, but from far-sighted reasons of statesmanship and National Policy? What does it mean? It means that the old objective is there, it means that the methods have changed, they propose to have the Trojan horse with its big gifts introduced into the fortress. Sir, "I fear the Greeks when they are bearing gifts."

I could go on quoting from one and another; these are but samples of what I could quote, and therefore are indicative of the general trend in the United States. All their methods of the past we have withstood and met, and we are on terms of absolute good friendship with the United States. I want to repeat what I said before, that to-day they have more respect for us in Canada, and more admiration for our enterprise and our work, than at any other period in the history of these two countries; and we on this side have just as high an appreciation of them as they on their side have of us. There is absolutely to-day no cause of dissatisfaction or ill will between us and the United States. But it does not follow that, because you are friendly with your neighbour and are doing each other good turns, you should give him half or three-quarters of your house and install him in it. Neither does it follow that because we want to be on good terms with the United States we are to hand over the rich possessions we have hewn out and made for ourselves, and go into a dangerous partnership with them. Nor does it agree with our policy, our instincts and our ideals. It was the conquest of Canada aimed at in 1775; it was the conquest of Canada aimed at in the years around 1812, and since; it was the conquest of Canada and its incorporation with the United States aimed at by the methods I have spoken of in respect to our trade and fisheries; and the dominant spirit in the United States that is pushing reciprocity through to a successfully enactment today is not economic, it is political. It is still the conquest of Canada. But it is conquest of Canada by peaceful means and large gifts, to bring about the time when, from the frozen north to the Mexican gulf, there shall be but one power predominant, and that the United States of America, and when British and European influence shall be banished forever from this North American continent. . . .

. . . This land of ours, we have made it, we and our fathers—please God we will keep it for our children and our children's children, to the remotest generation. We have not wrought so in order to bestow a great gift upon a rich nation, we have wrought to build ourselves a national home with a fireside and altars for ourselves and for those who come after us in this great far-flung country that God has given to us for our own.

This proposal cuts square across that national ideal, challenges it at every point, will endanger it undoubtedly, may destroy it entirely. Should we not think before we enter into it? Ninety-three millions to the south of us mean it in the way of absorption and hegemony and mean it in no other way, hence these gifts. This proposal cuts our country into sections and at every section bleeds the life blood from it. The well-filled arteries of interprovincial trade will be drained until the whole system grows anemic and flabby. Do not treat it lightly. The sustained pressure of ninety-three millions to eight millions, the far-reaching effect of business affiliation, the close proximity and constant efflux and influx, the seductions of commercialism, the constant intercourse of business, social and official life, will inevitably weaken the ties of empire and wean the thoughts of our newer generations, if not of ourselves, towards the predominant power, and create new attachments, until like Samson we would arise and would shake ourselves and find that our strength is gone.

I utter the most solemn words I have ever uttered in my life, and I believe them to the very bottom of my heart, that there is danger, and deep danger ahead. This path entered upon leads us away from home to a strange country. I pray, Sir, that the full meaning of this first step may sink into the hearts of members of parliament and into the hearts of the people of this country until there shall burst forth a protest of such strength that the steps contemplated will be recalled to the old paths, leading east and west, in and out amongst our own people, converging on the great metropolis of the mother land, and which we may follow without uncertainty and without menace to our national existence.

What do you think?

1. (a) Describe Mr. Foster's views of the U.S.
   (b) What relationship do you think he wanted to see between Canada and the U.S.?
   (c) Why did he fear reciprocity? What arguments did he use against reciprocity? What do you think of his arguments and why?
2. (a) What importance did Britain have in forming Foster's views? What part did Britain play in Canada's "national ideal"?
   (b) Could Canada have a national ideal without an external friend or foe? Why?

2.   SOME LIBERALS BOLT

A few very influential members of the Liberal Party split with Laurier over the reciprocity issue. Among them was Clifford Sifton, a powerful Liberal from the West. Sifton attacked reciprocity in the House of Commons, February 9, 1911.

What will be our future relations with the United States? I read the argument presented by the hon. member for North Toronto (Mr. Foster) upon that aspect of the case. I see no possible answer to it. It seems to be perfectly clear to me that every day in which we adapt ourselves to the markets of the United States, that every day in which we cater to those markets, that every day in which we adapt all our arrangements to catering to those markets strengthens the grip of the United States upon Canada. And while everybody, of course, repudiates as absurd the idea of any conscious interference either with our political independence, or with our commercial independence, I do not believe that if this treaty goes into effect there will ever again, so long as it goes on, unless a rupture takes place, be a revision of our tariff in which United States interests, United States lobbyists, and United States pressure will not be brought to bear on this parliament. What is the only possible effect? The only possible effect is domination of the smaller by the larger, and if you say you do not think there is any danger of any domination I say that I think the domination has come now, that we have it in the discussion of this treaty. How did it get here, what brought it about? For 30 years the United States had nothing to say to us, and then, when we have finally, definitely won our commercial independence and put ourselves into such a position that we were perfectly independent, what happened? They shook a club over our heads, they threatened a surtax. It was threatened a year ago. Then our friends of the government were asked to make concessions in order that this surtax might be avoided. The government made some concessions. I think they were very trifling in character: I do not think they were of much importance, but I do think it would have been as well if the government had stood its ground at the start. Nevertheless, we all know that in international matters it is necessary to leave a great deal to the government. You cannot know everything that passes, and you must leave a great deal to the discretion of the government in international matters. But I am prepared to say now that I think we all made a mistake. I think the time to have stood our ground was the first time the club was flourished. What has been the history of our relations with the United States? For the last 30 or 40 years we have been ignored and buffeted by them, and during all that time we have taken our way secure, firm, serene under the strong arm of the British Empire. Now we come to the point when we are of some use; we are just beginning to be of some use. Up to nearly the present time we have been more or less of a nuisance to the Empire; now we are beginning to get to the point when we add something to the prestige of the British Empire, to the point when, if necessary, we can send some men, or some ships, or some money; we can be of some use to the Empire that has given us our liberties and all the traditions of our citizenship. When we get to that point what happens? The United States beckons from Washington and we are asked, the first time anybody beckons, to turn from the path that leads to the capital of the empire, and to turn towards the path that leads to Washington. I say, so far as I am concerned: Not for me.

What do you think?

1. Why did Sifton split with the Liberal Party over reciprocity?

2. What does Sifton mean by "shaking the clubs"? Is Canada vulnerable today to such actions? Why?

3. LAURIER REPLIES TO CRITICISM

In the House of Commons, February 9, 1911, Laurier defended his reciprocity policy against harsh criticism.

One other thing cannot be denied, that at this moment, amongst the thoughtful men of the American union, the feeling is growing up that the policy which they have pursued towards us for the last fifty years has been wrong, that it has been injurious to themselves as well as to us, that it is selfish and narrow; and they are prepared to retrace their steps and to enter with us into a mutually profitable commercial intercourse. Now, when we reach that stage, it is inconceivable that we in Canada should be told that this retrograde policy, long followed by the United States and which they are now on the eve of abandoning, should become the Canadian policy and that we should follow a policy of non-commercial intercourse with them. It is incredible, and yet we have heard that idea proclaimed again and again in this House. We are told that unless this retrograde policy is maintained Canada is exposed to danger, and we are threatened that unless this policy of non-intercourse is maintained we are doomed to annexation. Annexation! Annexation! Once upon a time there was a very strong annexationist movement in this country, and it received its first check when Lord Elgin brought back from Washington the reciprocity treaty of 1856. From that day to this the desire for annexation has dwindled and dwindled, until there is not a vestige of it left in any part of this country.

Once upon a time—this is also a matter of history—the conviction of every American citizen was that the Canadian confederation should become a part of the American union. Recent events have shown that there are still men in the United States who harbour that hope. But there are also men who are beginning to perceive that the republic, though its career has been glorious, has yet many questions to solve and many dangers to face; and many of them are beginning to recognize that the solution of their difficult problems would be seriously complicated, perhaps fatally impaired, if, in the territory of the republic, was to be included another territory as large as their own, with a people not yet as numerous, but destined to be as numerous as their own, with problems of their own also to solve, and whose union with the United States would only add to the complications which the American people have to meet. If my poor voice could be heard throughout the length and breadth of this country, and if, without any presumption, it could be heard also beyond the frontier, I would say to our American neighbours: flattering as may be to your pride, the idea that the territory of the republic should extend over the whole continent from the waters of the Gulf of Mexico to the waters of the Arctic ocean, remember that we Canadians were born under the flag of your ancestors, a flag under which perhaps you may have suffered some oppression, but which to us has been, and is more than ever, the emblem of freedom. Remember that if you have founded a nation upon separation from the motherland, we Canadians have set our hearts upon building up a nation without separation; remember that in this task we are already far advanced, that with our institutions, with our national entity as a people, and with everything that constitutes our national home we are just as devoted as you are to yours. Remember that the blood which flows in our veins is just as good as your own, and that if you are a proud people, though we have not your numbers, we are just as proud as you are, and that, rather than part with our national existence, we would part with our lives. If my voice could be heard that far, I would presume to say to our American friends: There may be a spectacle perhaps nobler yet than the spectacle of a united continent, a spectacle which would astound the world by its novelty and grandeur, the spectacle of two peoples living side by side along a frontier nearly 4,000 miles long, with not a cannon, with not a gun frowning across it, with not a fortress on either side, with no armament one against the other, but living in harmony, in mutual confidence, and with no other rivalry than a generous emulation in commerce and the arts of peace. To the Canadian people I would say that it is possible for us to obtain such relations between this young and growing nation, and the powerful American republic, Canada will have rendered to old England, the mother of nations, nay, to the whole British Empire, a service unequalled in its present effects, and still more in its far-reaching consequences.

What do you think?

1. Why do you think reciprocity had fallen into disfavour in Canada by 1911?
2. How did Laurier meet the "annexation threat" argument of those opposed to reciprocity?.How effective do you think he was? Could this argument be used today? Why?
3. Examine Laurier's rhetorical devices. How effective are they and why? Would Laurier have used the same devices in an essay? Why?

4.   THE CAMPAIGN: THE CONSERVATIVE CASE

The reciprocity issue was argued vociferously in the press. The first document seen here is an appeal to industrial workers taken from *the September 20, 1911 issue of the* Kingston Daily Standard. *The second is the editorial position of the* Montreal Daily Star, *published September 16, 1911.*

(a) THE KINGSTON DAILY STANDARD

WORKINGMEN, YOUR JOBS ARE IN DANGER.

THAT IS WHAT RECIPROCITY MEANS TO YOU!

THE PRO-RECIPROCITY PEOPLE ARE TELLING THE FARMERS THAT IT MEANS HIGHER PRICES TO THEM ON WHAT THEY SELL.

THEY ARE NOT DARING TO TELL YOU THAT IT MEANS HIGHER PRICES FOR THE ONE THING YOU SELL—YOUR LABOUR.

IF WHAT THEY TELL THE FARMER IS TRUE, THEN RECIPROCITY MUST MEAN HIGHER PRICES ON WHAT YOU BUY—FOOD PRODUCTS.

IF RECIPROCITY WILL INCREASE THE COST OF FARM PRODUCTS, IT IS OBVIOUS THAT IT WILL INCREASE THE COST OF LIVING.

YOU WILL PAY MORE TO LIVE: AND—BY WAY OF REWARD—YOU WILL GET LESS IN YOUR PAY ENVELOPE.

THIS LAST IS THE POINT YOU SHOULD CONSIDER MOST CAREFULLY.

NOW HOW CAN RECIPROCITY GET YOU HIGHER WAGES?

NO ONE IS FOOLISH ENOUGH TO TRY TO TELL YOU IT WILL!

IT CERTAINLY WILL NOT SEND WAGES UP.

ON THE OTHER HAND, IT WILL AT ONCE ROB OUR EAST-AND-WEST RAILWAYS OF MUCH OF THEIR BUSINESS. THE LOCAL INDUSTRIES WILL BE HIT. THE PORT OF KINGSTON WILL BE BADLY CRIPPLED. THIS MEANS THAT RAILWAY HANDS AND DOCK HANDS WILL BE DISCHARGED, AND WILL COMPETE IN OUR LABOUR MARKET. WE WILL HAVE NO MORE WORK TO SHARE: BUT MANY MORE WORKERS TO SHARE IT. COMPETITION WILL BEAT WAGES DOWN.

THEN OUR DOCK LABOURERS WILL BE OUT OF WORK; FOR OUR SHIPPING WILL GO TO AMERICAN PORTS. AGAIN, MORE LABOUR ON THE MARKET WILL CUT WAGES.

CERTAIN LOCAL INDUSTRIES WILL BE CRIPPLED OR SMASHED. AMERICAN FIRMS WILL STOP BUILDING BRANCHES IN CANADA. LESS WORK, AGAIN; AND MORE WORKERS. OUR FACTORIES WILL RUN ON SHORT TIME, AND WAGES WILL FALL.

THEN TAFT AND THE GRAIN GROWERS SAY THAT RECIPROCITY WILL LEAD TO "FREE TRADE IN EVERYTHING." THAT MEANS THE CLOSING OF ALL PROTECTED INDUSTRIES. IT PROBABLY MEANS THE CLOSING OF YOUR INDUSTRY.

AWAY GOES YOUR OWN JOB.

VOTE AGAINST RECIPROCITY, KEEP THE PRICE OF LABOUR UP AND THE "COST OF LIVING" DOWN. VOTE RIGHT EVEN IF YOU PUT POLITICIANS OUT OF EASY BERTHS.

(b) THE MONTREAL DAILY STAR

No one now doubts the possible future of Canada. We have made it sure. We are not a boastful people; but we may be forgiven if we boast a bit of our determination, our faith in the face of discouragement, our unyielding loyalty to our native land. We have believed in Canada; and she has justified our belief. She is the richest, most promising, most prosperous country in the modern world.

We have believed, furthermore, in our people. We have been confident that they would "make good." And they have. They are the possessors of El Dorado of the twentieth century; and they have proven their capacity to guide its development and carry it forward to its high destiny.

The capacity we have. Have we the courage? That is the issue today. Just at the climax of our success, we are asked by the shrewd nation which scorned us when we were weak and scouted us when we sought her favors, to give it all up—to abandon the ideal for which our fathers faced the bleak north—to share with her the rich harvest which we sowed in bitter hardship and cherished through long years of suffering and lonely sacrifice.

Shall we do it?

Shall we surrender just when the battle is won?

Shall we let the men, who deserted us in the dark days, now come in as full-fledged "American citizens" and take over the country they did not think worth living in?

Shall we give it to them to say that they have judged better than we have all along—that they cleverly escaped the digging and the planting, the dull days of rain and deadly days of drought, but that now they get a Prodigal's share of the feast? They will have reversed the parable. They went abroad and found—not a diet of husks—but the richest living, leaving the "lean commons," to us; and, now they come to us as citizens of a foreign country, expecting that the "fatted calf" will be served to them.

Shall we give up, too, the glorious future which beckons us—the chance that we will become the chief state in the British Empire and the most powerful nation in the world?

Shall we bring the sacrifices of the Fathers to naught?

Shall we re-tread the path, with apology on our lips and our price in our hands, that the United Empire Loyalists trod with stern lips and a priceless loyalty in their hearts?

Shall we admit to the refuge they found, and made sacred, the very flag whose intolerance they fled?

The answer to these questions will all be given on polling day. This is not a party election. It is a national crisis. We are, in truth, "at the parting of the ways." We will either continue to march on the highway toward national greatness with the flag of Canada floating in our clear northern air over our heads; or, we will turn aside toward absorption in the "great and glorious Republic," to the south of us, surrendering to a calculating smile what we have long defended from hostility in every form— armed invasion, tariff persecutions, bullying over boundaries, even insolent disregard of treaty obligations.

What do you think?

1. *To whom was the Daily Standard appealing and why? How convincing were its arguments and why?*
2. *What techniques did the Daily Standard use to get its argument across to the reader? What do you think of this type of appeal and why? Can you think of some modern examples of this type of appeal?*
3. *What is the function of an editorial? How does an editorial differ from a news report? What techniques did the writer of the Montreal Star use to appeal to his audience? Compare them to the techniques used by modern-day editorial writers. (See pages 12, 20 and 104.) Account for any differences that you notice.*
4. *What did the Montreal Star mean when it asked: "Shall we admit to the refuge they [the Loyalists] found and made sacred, the very flag whose intolerance they fled"?*

5. THE LIBERAL CASE

Leading Liberals pleaded the case of reciprocity during speaking tours across the country. This selection is an excerpt from a speech by W. S. Fielding, Laurier's chief Maritime lieutenant and the minister responsible for the reciprocity negotiations. The speech was delivered in Halifax on August 19, 1911.

Never was a policy submitted to the Canadian people which gave more widespread promise of advantage. The agreement offers the prospect of increased trade in every province of the Dominion. While, for reasons already stated, an agreement for a general free exchange of manufactured goods would not be fair to our workers in those lines, there are few Canadians who do not believe that in most of our great industries—farming, fruit-growing, fishing and lumbering—Canada need fear no competitors at home or abroad. Enlarged markets for our products have been diligently sought by our Government. With this object in view we have subsidized steamers and sent commercial agents to distant parts of the earth. Would it not be strange if we failed to avail ourselves of the opportunity to share in the markets of ninety-two millions of the richest consumers in the world?

To no part of the Dominion does this agreement bring greater hope than to the Maritime provinces. While conditions have, we are glad to know, somewhat improved in these provinces in recent years, it must be acknowledged that our growth and progress fall far short of what we ought to expect. The western country has been developing rapidly. We in the lower provinces recognized the conditions which have brought this about, and we have cheerfully borne our share of the large outlays which have been necessary to open up that country. We view with every satisfaction the progress and prosperity of our western land and will cordially co-operate in every movement for its further advancement. But we cannot be expected to be indifferent to the conditions that are nearer to us. Freer trade relations with the United States have been the dream of every leading Canadian statesmen for nearly half a century. In the lower provinces particularly the importance of such better trade relations has been universally recognized. The Conservative policy of higher tariff was only accepted by its own friends because it was declared by Sir John Macdonald himself and by other statesmen of his party to be the best possible road towards obtaining reciprocity with the United States. The increase of our interprovincial trade and our trade with Great Britain is gratifying and we must see that every reasonable effort is made for their further expansion. But if, in addition to these, we can give our people that access to the United States markets for many of our natural products which they have been seeking for so many years, we shall undoubtedly bring new life and new hope and new strength to this eastern part of the Dominion.

The great industries of Nova Scotia, New Brunswick and Prince Edward Island are farming, fruit growing, fishing, lumbering and mining. Every one of these industries has been well considered and cared for in the reciprocity agreement.

Nothing more clearly shows the weakness of the case against reciprocity than the fact that our opponents have to resort to the device of waving the British flag and accusing the advocates of reciprocity of disloyalty. It is an old and well worn trick which will not deceive intelligent people. The glorious flag of the Empire was never intended to be used for so mean a purpose. Never were the people of British North America more loyal or more contented with British institutions than during the period of the old reciprocity treaty. It was in the very midst of that period that His late Majesty King Edward, then Prince of Wales, visited British North America and received everywhere such splendid evidence of the loyalty and devotion of our people. Sir John Macdonald, Sir Charles Tupper, Sir John Thompson, Mr. Foster and other public men of the Conservative party were not deemed disloyal when they laboured without success to obtain a reciprocal trade arrangement with the United States. It will be difficult to persuade anybody that the Canadian Ministers of to-day are disloyal when they have carried on reciprocity negotiations which have been crowned with the success that was denied to their predecessors. No Canadian who is trading today with citizens of the United States, in money or in merchandize, feels that he thereby in any way compromises himself as a loyal citizen of Canada and a loyal subject of the King, nor will any feeling of that kind be experienced by other citizens of Canada who will avail themselves of the larger opportunities of trade which we believe will be opened up to them by the reciprocity agreement. The pretence that the Canadian farmer, fisherman or lumberman who sells his products in the United States impairs his loyalty to His Majesty is an insult to loyal Canadians and will, I feel sure, be resented by them.

Even if we desired to do so, we could not be indifferent to our commercial relations with the people of the neighbouring republic. Touching each other as the two countries do along a border line of thousands of miles, the people of both should always desire the best relations in commercial and all other affairs. Irresponsible speakers and writers of either nation may feel free to indulge in foolish and, too often, offensive utterances concerning the other. But responsible ministers in London, in Ottawa and in Washington, with the support of the best people in each country, will realize the importance of cultivating between Canada and the United States those friendly commercial relations which will make for both continental and imperial peace. It is in that spirit that our Government have welcomed the approaches of the authorities of the United States and have joined them in this effort to establish better trade relations between the two counries.

What do you think?

1. Compare Fielding's views with those of Mr. Stephen Weyman page 36). What do you notice? How can you account for this?
2. If you had been able to vote in 1911 which party would you have supported? Why?
3. Why do you think the Liberals were more sympathetic than the Conservatives to the United States?
4. If the Liberals had won the 1911 election and if reciprocity had been introduced, would Canada still be independent today? How do you justify your answer?
5. Many of the Conservative anti-reciprocity arguments in 1911 and 1891, and earlier, stressed that it was best for Canada to remain closely associated with Great Britain.
   (a) Was this sound reasoning? Why?
   (b) Is it sound reasoning today? Why?
   (c) How do you think Canadian-American relations in the pre-1911 period affected Canada's relationship with Great Britain?

The Alaska Boundary Dispute

The Alaska Boundary Dispute is important not only in the area of Canadian-American relations, but also in regard to Anglo-Canadian relations. The dispute arose over the location of the boundary between southern Alaska and Canada. In October 1903, when the controversial Alaska Boundary Award was announced, Canadians realized that the British authorities had sacrificed Canadian interests to ensure better Anglo-American relations.

In theory, the dispute was submitted to an arbitration tribunal consisting of "six impartial jurists of repute." In fact, the three Americans appointed by President Theodore Roosevelt were committed to Roosevelt's bellicose anti-Canadian point of view. There were two Canadians on the tribunal and a British Lord Justice, Lord Alverstone.

What was the Canadian reaction to the tribunal's decision? How can this reaction be accounted for? How did the decision affect Canada's attitude towards Britain and the United States?

1. AMERICAN IMPARTIALITY?

Senator Henry Cabot Lodge, one of the three Americans on the tribunal, described his experiences.

Several Senators came to see me, especially Senators from the northwest, and said that they must be assured as to the men whom the President would appoint as members of the tribunal, because they could not agree to having anybody on that tribunal who would yield on the American claim, which they rightly believed to be wholly sound. I told the President of the situation and asked if he would allow me to tell Senators in confidence whom he intended to appoint. He gave me permission to do so and I told Senator Teller—who was the leader perhaps of those from the West who felt very strongly about the question—that it was the President's intention to appoint Mr. Root (then Secretary of War), Senator George Turner of Washington and me. When these selections of the President were made known in confidence to Senators there was no further objection to the treaty and it was ratified by the Senate, unanimously as I remember, on the 11th of February, 1903. It was ratified by Great Britain and by the President and ratifications were exchanged on the 3rd of March, 1903.

What do you think?

1. *Explain the term "wholly sound."*
2. *Why were the Americans so eager to ensure that a pro-American decision would be given by the tribunal?*

2.   A BRITISH RESPONSE

In November, 1903, the Governor General of Canada, Lord Minto, cogently summed up his response to the decision.

. . . It is impossible to exaggerate the bitter feeling caused by the Alaska Award towards Alverstone's supposed actions, whilst it has also set all the rooted dislike to "the States" in a blaze. The American flag was hissed recently both at Ottawa and Montreal during a performance at the theatre.

As regards the history of the Alaska Tribunal I suspect that a want of appreciation of the intense sensitiveness of the Canadian Commissioners accounts for a good deal of the soreness which exists . . . one of the complaints made to me is that Alverstone ignored the great abilities of his colleagues, treated them as juniors, and assumed for himself the position of an umpire. . . .

*   *   *   *   *

The whole position is full of meaning which it is impossible to deal with in a short letter . . . there is undoubtedly a genuine wish throughout Canada for 'closer relations' with Great Britain and I do not think the Alaska friction has at all injured Mr. Chamberlain's objects . . . on the other hand there is this feeling of Canadian nationality, which I confess it is sometimes difficult to reconcile strictly with loyalty . . . and there is the not quite satisfactory attitude of the people at the head of affairs who might have been more genuinely hearty in their wish to allay the storm. I do not like entertaining suspicions but I doubt if the recent criticism of the Motherland was as absolutely unwelcome to everyone as one could wish it to have been.

As far as I can judge from the information I have, Alverstone seems to have changed his mind as to the Portland Channel during the course of the discussions. I see no reason why he should not do so if there were sufficient reasons to influence him . . . but I do not know whether or not he sufficiently consulted his colleagues as to such a change—personally I believe his to have been the only judicial mind on our side.

The future is full of problems. I believe in an Imperial sense we are much nearer the parting of the ways than I had thought. If Mr. Chamberlain's preferential proposals are not accepted, the result here will be an impression that the Canadian advances have been received with cold water by the Old Country, and influences will at once assert themselves here which Canadians at present will not acknowledge the existence of . . . viz. the influence of the U.S. markets, and the ultra-national feeling tending to separations and independence—the chief argument against the latter being that Canada is not strong enough at present to stand alone. . . . Still if the idea gains ground that the Old Country is not in complete sympathy with the Dominion, the struggle here will ultimately be between independence and annexation to 'the States'. The position is an anxious one and it is very necessary it should be well understood at home.

What do you think?

1. *What did Lord Minto mean when he wrote "There is this feeling of Canadian nationality, which I confess it is sometimes difficult to reconcile strictly with loyalty"?*
2. *Why did Minto feel that "in an Imperial sense we are much nearer the parting of the ways than I had thought"?*
3. *Who was "Mr. Chamberlain"? What were his views concerning the Empire?*
4. *. . . "The struggle here will ultimately be between independence and annexation to 'the States'."*
   (a) Explain what you think Lord Minto's views were concerning Canada's relations with Britain and the U.S.
   (b) What do you think he meant by "independence"?
   (c) Was Lord Minto's prediction correct?

3.   SOME CANADIAN REACTIONS

The following selections form a survey of Canadian reaction to the Alaska boundary decision.

THE HOUSE OF COMMONS, OCTOBER 23, 1903

Mr. Seymour E. Gourlay (MP, Colchester, N.S.): Thank God it will create a bitter feeling towards the United States . . . from this moment no Canadian will cherish anything but the most fearful dislike to the people who have wronged us out of our territory . . . there will grow up in the hearts of the people of Canada a determination to have nothing to do with these people who have wronged us out of territory that justly belonged to this country and therefore I see in this award the destruction . . .

of a reciprocity treaty. I hope that now we will build up a tariff wall against these people and let them know we are Canadians.

Prime Minister Wilfrid Laurier: . . . I have often regretted, Mr. Speaker, and never more than on the present occasion, that we are living beside a great neighbour who, I believe I can say without being deemed unfriendly to them, are very grasping in their national acts, and who are determined upon every occasion to get the best in any agreement which they make. I have often regretted also that while they are a great and powerful nation, we are only a small colony, a growing colony, but still a colony. I have often regretted also that we have not in our own hands the treaty-making power, which would enable us to dispose of our own affairs. But in this matter we were dealing with a position that was forced upon us—we have not the treaty-making power. I am sorry to say that the whole correspondence which we have had upon this question since 1899 has not yet been placed before Parliament; I am sorry not only that we have not the treaty-making power, but that we are not in such an independent position that it is in my power to place before Parliament the whole of the correspondence as it passed between the Canadian government and the British government. But we shall have that correspondence, and it will be placed before Parliament at the next session—the whole of it, no matter what protest may come from abroad, we shall have the whole of it, and then this country may know exactly what has taken place, and what share of responsibility must rest upon each of the parties concerned in this matter. But we have no such power, our hands are tied to a large extent owing to the fact of our connection—which has its benefits, but which has also its disadvantages—the fact of our connection with the Mother-country making us not free agents, and obliging us to deal with questions affecting ourselves through the instrumentality of the British ambassador. . . .

The difficulty, as I conceive it to be, is that so long as Canada remains a dependency of the British Crown, the present powers that we have are not sufficient for the maintenance of our rights. It is important that we should ask the British Parliament for more extensive power, so that if ever we have to deal with matters of a similar nature again we shall deal with them in our own way, in our own fashion, according to the best light that we have.

SOME CANADIAN NEWSPAPERS RESPOND

Ottawa Citizen, October 23, 1903.
The whole incident as outlined in the dry phrases of red tapedom is eloquent of the unprincipled character of "one great branch of the Anglo-Saxon race" on the one side; the well-bred, unsuspecting credulity of the other party to the case, and Canada in the pathetic role of the perfectly sophisticated unwilling but dutiful sacrifice.

Victoria Colonist, October 23, 1903.

The feeling of indignation in Vancouver over the Alaskan award is so intense that prominent citizens openly give voice to sentiments hostile to England. . . . One of the ways in which this sentiment has found expression is in pledges being made by the more hot-headed citizens that they will not sing "God Save the King" again until England has justified herself in the eyes of Canada. . . . Taking advantage of the general expression of opinion around the city that an Independence Club should be formed, Mr. George Perry, a well-known newspaperman, has invited, through the press, all those who wish to join such a club to hand in their names. . . .

Toronto Globe, October 21, 1903.

One of the Canadian commissioners afterwards said to a representative of Associated Press: "This award affects much more the relations between the Dominion and the Mother Country than most people here seem to realize, and almost marks the parting of the ways, at least so far as leaving any such question for Britain to decide for us."

A Canadian who has been most intimately and prominently associated with the Alaska case said: "It is the hardest blow the Imperial idea has ever received. . . . [Canada] must now face the fact that when Imperial interest or friendships require it her territory will be handed over without the slightest hesitation. . . ."

Toronto Mail and Empire, October 27, 1903.

However much we may all regret the judgment in the Alaskan boundary case, we must deplore still more the circumstance that it has been followed by a suggestion of separation from the Empire. . . .

Why are people asked to regard Great Britain as an enemy and to yearn for the severance of the tie? There is a movement for closer British union on foot. Is it possible that this Alaskan incident is being used illogically, and as it appears untruthfully, with mischievous ends in view?

OTHER RESPONSES

[*F. H. Turnock, a Canadian journalist, discussed the anti-British feeling unleashed by the dispute, in* The Outlook, *November 7, 1903.*]

The callousness, the selfishness, and the bad faith with which Canadians consider Britain has treated Canada in this matter will long rankle in the breasts of Canadians. It is bound to affect Canada's destiny. What the ultimate outcome may be, it is perhaps too early yet to predict. But it will sensibly loosen the tie which binds Canada to Great Britain. It will quench the spirit of Imperialism which has for some time been growing in Canada in spite of much discouragement from Great Britain.

Canadians now realize how little their services in the cause of the Empire have been appreciated.

*   *   *   *   *

With the decadence of Imperialism will come the serious discussion of Canada's national future. If there is to be no federated empire, independence or annexation to the United States are the only other courses open. Naturally, the idea of annexation will not be popular at the present time—though many a Canadian has said in his wrath in discussing the boundary award, "We may as well go in for annexation, body and breeches, if Great Britain is going to allow us to be annexed piecemeal." Independence will be the idea to which Canadians will naturally first turn. The outcome much depends on the future attitude of the United States.

[*For Goldwin Smith the Alaska Boundary Dispute provided further proof that Canada had no future as an appendage of Great Britain. He wrote the following in* The Canadian Magazine *early in 1904.*]

The British Government, in consequence of this Alaska decision, is once more upbraided with careless sacrifice of Canadian interests. This complaint, in which the voice of even the late Sir John Bourinot is heard, derives some colour of probability on the present occasion from the assiduity with which Great Britain is now just deeming it politic to cultimate American friendship. Nevertheless it is baseless. The British Government has always done for us the best that diplomacy could do. In the Oregon dispute it went to the very verge of war. Beyond the verge it could not possibly have gone. It has pleaded our case to the utmost of its ability, and through the best advocates that it could command. But it has had no *ratio ultima*. Would its people have allowed it, for a belt of territory on the other side of the Atlantic which they could not point out in the map and pictured to themselves only as a snowy waste, to engage in mortal conflict with a powerful nation of their own race, defeat in which would have been not only loss and dishonour, but almost ruin? . . .

What do you think?

1. *What lessons did Mr. Gourlay, Prime Minister Laurier and Goldwin Smith learn from the Alaska Boundary Dispute? Who was right? Why?*
2. *Had Canada been an "unwilling but dutiful sacrifice"? Support your answer with some major arguments from the material in this section.*
3. *Account for and describe the anti-British feeling triggered by the dispute. How important was pro-British sentiment in explaining nineteenth-century Canadian views of the U.S.?*
4. *How important is pro-British feeling in Canada today? Why?*

The Great Debate Continues

During the 1870s but more particularly in the 1880s and the early 1890s, a furious and often bitter controversy raged between Canadians who favoured closer economic ties with the United States and those who were vigorously opposed. How are the views of the men of this period like or unlike today's views on this question? What has caused any change you notice in the debate? Why are some aspects still the same?

1. MACDONALD WARNS OF MANIFEST DESTINY

On November 26, 1875 the Montreal Gazette *carried the following speech made by John A. Macdonald.*

. . . suppose that annexation had taken place then in 1849, what would have been the consequences? Gentlemen your sons would have been slain in the civil war, and many homes and many families would have bowed over the graves of slaughtered children; and you would now have been suffering under the ruinous amount of taxation, which clogs, impedes and obstructs the prosperity of that great country the United States. We run no such dangers as we would run, if annexation should take place, when we are living under the aegis of Great Britain, and in the enjoyment of peace, liberty, happiness, intellectual, moral material and physical— secured by remaining as we are British subjects. . . . We are now in greater danger than we were before the civil war, the whole of the southern states being slave holding were opposed to the addition of other free states, but now slavery being abolished, the southern Americans entertain exactly the same feeling that pervades the most of the United States—that the inevitable destiny of that country was to govern the whole of this continent, and to absorb the whole of this continent—a doctrine instilled into the children of the less educated classes from their first fourth of July celebrations until they are twenty-one. It is said that the great and good and the wise men there, the educated classes would not permit this; but the educated classes do not rule there—the many govern, the many-headed monster governs that country. . . . With such a long frontier how many causes of quarrel would arise? While now, while backed by the power of England, we are now free from all that. Standing alone, it might be gentlemen, that the lion and the lamb would be down together, but, as had been said, the lamb would be inside the lion.

What do you think?

1. *What did Macdonald mean by the "many-headed monster"? How different were American and Canadian attitudes towards democracy during this period? To what extent to the two countries display different attitudes towards democracy and authority today? Why?*
2. *How much of Macdonald's fear about American Manifest Destiny was justified? Give evidence to support your answer.*

2. THE NATIONAL POLICY

Macdonald was determined to ensure that an economically viable Canada would exist north of the United States. To accomplish this he introduced his National Policy. There was to be a protective tariff to safeguard Canadian industry from American competition. The CPR would have to be finished to make certain that the Canadian West would not join the United States.

On March 14, 1879, Sir Leonard Tilley, Macdonald's finance minister, made the following speech to the House of Commons introducing the new tariff.

. . . But if we undertake, as the present Government have undertaken, to readjust and reorganize, and, I may say, make an entirely new tariff, having for its object not only the realisation of $2,000,000 more revenue than will be collected this year, but, in addition, to providing for that deficiency, to adjust that policy, or that tariff with a view of making what has been, and is to-day, declared the policy of the majority of this House—I mean the protection of the industries of the country—the magnitude of the undertaking will be better appreciated. . . . We have invited gentlemen from all parts of the Dominion, and representing all interests in the Dominion, to assist us in the readjustment of the tariff. . . . We did not feel that we were prepared without the advice and assistance from men of experience with reference to these matters, to readjust and make a judicious tariff. We, therefore, invited those who were interested in the general interests of the country, or interested in any special interests. . . . I have this to say to our American friends: In 1865 they abrogated the Reciprocity Treaty, and from that day to the present a large portion of the imports from that country into the Dominion have been admitted free. We have hoped, but hoped in vain, that by the adoption of that policy we would lead our American friends to trust us in a more liberal spirit with regard to the same articles. Well, after having waited twelve years for the consideration of this subject, the Government requiring more revenue, have determined to ask this House to impose upon the products of the United States that have been free, such a duty as may seem consistent with our position. But the Government coupled with the proposal, in order to show that we approach this question with no unfriendly spirit, a resolution . . . containing a proposition to this effect. That, as to articles named, which are the natural products of the country, including lumber, if the United States take off the duties in part or in whole, we are prepared to meet with equal concessions. The Government believes in a reciprocity tariff, yet may discuss free-trade or protection, but the question of to-day is—shall we have a reciprocity tariff, or a one-sided tariff? The Government propose to do more. We had not been long the advisers of His Excellency before we decided that it was of the utmost importance to extend our trade with the British and foreign West India Islands, and, if possible, with South America. . . . The time has arrived, I think, when it will become our duty to decide whether the thousands of men throughout the length and breadth of this country who are employed, shall seek employment in another country, or shall find it in this Dominion; the time has arrived when we are to decide whether we will be simply agriculturists raising wheat, and lumbermen producing more lumber than we can use, or Great Britain and the United States will take from us at remunerative prices; whether we will confine our attention to the fisheries and certain other small industries, and cease to be what we have been, and not rise to be what I believe we are destined to be under wise and judicious legislation, or whether we will inaugurate a policy that will, by its provisions, say to the industries of the country, we will give you sufficient protection; we will give you a market for what you can produce; we will say that while our neighbours build up a Chinese wall, we will impose a reasonable duty on their products coming into this country; at all events, we will maintain for our agricultural and other productions, largely, the market of our own Dominion. The time has certainly arrived when we must consider whether we will allow matters to remain as they are, with the result of being an unimportant and uninteresting portion of Her Majesty's Dominions, or will rise to the position, which I believe Providence has destined us to occupy, by means which I believe, though they may be over sanguine, which the country believes are calculated to bring prosperity and happiness to the people, to give employment to the thousands who are unoccupied, and to make this a great and prosperous country, as we all desire and hope it will be.

What do you think?

1. (a) What reasons did Tilley give for the new tariff? Which, in your opinion, was the most important to the Macdonald Government? Why?

(b) Which reasons given by Tilley are still relevant today, if any? Explain why.

2. What did Tilley say that the tariff would mean for Canada's future? Was he correct? Give reasons.

3. Has the tariff contributed to Canada's so-called "branch plant" economy? If so, how?

3. CANADA'S POLITICAL DESTINY

Goldwin Smith was an outstanding scholar and writer. After teaching at Oxford and at Cornell University, he moved to Toronto in 1871. In June 1871, in The Canadian Monthly, *he cogently expressed his continentalist point of view.*

Canadian nationality being a lost cause, the ultimate union of Canada with the United States appears now to be morally certain; so that nothing is left for Canadian patriotism but to provide that it shall be a union indeed, and not an annexation; an equal and honorable alliance like that of Scotland and England, not a submission of the weaker to the stronger; and at the same time that the political change shall involve no change of any other kind in the relations of Canada with the mother-country. The filaments of union are spreading daily, though they may be more visible to the eye of one who sees Canada at intervals than to that of a constant resident. Intercourse is being increased by the extension of railways; the ownership and management of the railways themselves are forming an American interest in Canada; New York is becoming the pleasure, and, to some extent, even the business, capital of Canadians; American watering-places are becoming their summer resort; the periodical literature of the States, which is conducted with extraordinary spirit and ability, is extending its circulation on the northern side of the line; and the Canadians who settle in the States are multiplying the links of family connection between the two countries. . . .

To Canada the economical advantages of continental union will be immense; to the United States its general advantages will be not less so. To England it will be no menace, but the reverse: it will be the introduction in the councils of the United States, on all questions, commercial as well as diplomatic, of an element friendly to England, the influence of which will be worth far more to her than the faint and invidious chance of building up Canada as a rival to the United States. In case of war, her greatest danger will be removed. She will lose neither wealth nor strength; probably she will gain a good deal of both. . . .

What do you think?

1. *If Goldwin Smith were alive today, how might he account for the fact that "Canadian nationality" has, to this point at least, not been a "lost cause"?*
2. *Which present-day writers on Canadian-American relations have views quite similar to those of Smith? Why?*
3. *What were the major arguments put forward by Smith to justify his conclusion? What do you think of these arguments? To what extent are they relevant today?*
4. *"Reunion . . . not annexation." What did Smith mean? Was Smith's proposal viable in the 1880s and 1890s? Why? Is it viable today? Why?*

4. AN AMERICAN COMMENT

On March 1, 1889, the American House of Representatives debated a resolution concerning commercial union with Canada.

The House having under consideration the joint resolution to promote commercial union with Canada, Mr. Butterworth said:

I regret that the limited time we may devote to the consideration of the pending resolution will prevent that full discussion of the points involved which the importance of the subject obviously demands. The resolution reported from the Committee on Foreign Affairs by my honorable friend is a move in the right direction. It looks to extending the area of the trade and commerce of our country and extending it in a direction which promises the best possible results.

I cordially indorse what my friend has said touching the great advantage which would result to the people of the United States and to the people of Canada from removing the barriers which now intercept the sweep of our commerce towards the north. The resolution suggests commercial union. I believe that business relation would be of advantage to both countries. I have advocated full and unrestricted reciprocal trade. That relation being promptly rejected by Sir John Macdonald's Government, political union is proposed as an alternative for imperial federation and as presenting advantages which are greater and more permanent than would result from any other possible arrangement.

I have never doubted, and do not doubt now, that unrestricted reciprocal trade is desirable; that commercial union is desirable; and that political union is still more desirable.

I have advocated removing every barrier and hindrance to full and free trade between Canada and the United States. I have believed, and do now, that such unhampered trade relations would lead to political union. I have deemed political union indispensable to the peace, prosperity, and happiness of our race in North America. I have believed, and do now, that we can no more avert it than we can change the course of the seasons.

The attitude of some of our Canadian friends toward political union is amusing and in some cases ridiculous.

Occasionally some patriot breaks voice and becomes violent at the thought of what he in patriotic frenzy denounces to be a scheme to induce Canadians to sell their country, etc. As if the proposed union had in it any element of humiliation for our kinsman across the border. How absurd to suggest that a proposition to admit a Canadian province, or the Canadian provinces, each to an equal share with the empire States of New York, Pennsylvania, Ohio, and Illinois in the control and management of the American Republic could work the humiliation of such province or provinces. If there is in it anything that smacks of humiliation it is not on the side of Canada. The proposition looks to the exaltation of Canada, not to her abasement. It looks to enlarging the opportunities of her people, not to restricting them.

*   *   *   *   *

The reason this [political union] should be consummated speedily is that the result may be attained in a manner worthy of the civilization of the age; worthy of the members of one great family, who are, whatever their affected differences may be, bound together by indissoluble ties, which can not be severed without destroying one or both and leaving scars which a century of peace could not heal. But I repeat again, this is the people's question. It is not wise to let it rest until the consummation of this great event will be made to serve the ambition of a few or to lay the foundations of vast fortunes for a few more. It is the people's highway of commerce that we ask to open. It is for the opportunity for the people to become enriched that we plead. It is for the broader and fuller privilege of the people on both sides of the line that we seek this consummation. A man's first loyalty is to his God. Next, to his country and his home. That loyalty which is constant to God and the home circle is sure to be in consonance with the well-being of the country to which loyalty is due. . . .

I have often referred to the material advantage that would result to my countrymen if this union of the Dominion of Canada and the United States under one government could be consummated. It enlarges the opportunities of our people an hundred-fold. It secures to us with the blessings of lasting peace upon this continent the permanent supremacy of free institutions founded upon suffrage. It establishes upon an enduring basis an enlightened civilization based upon the precepts of Christianity. It would unite on this continent in indissoluble bonds the two great branches of the

English-speaking family. The swelling tide of our commerce toward the north would cease to break upon the line which marks our northern boundary and roll back upon ourselves, but would grow with each coming month, and rushing on find new and ever-increasing markets, while sources of wealth in great variety and exhaustless in quantity would be opened up to the enterprise and industry of our people.

Our Canadian kinsmen should discuss this proposition in the light of all the factors involved in its right solution. Loyalty to country is a noble sentiment, but a sentiment that should call practical common sense to sit in judgment with it.

What do you think?

1. *According to Congressman Butterworth, what were the advantages of commercial union for Americans and Canadians?*
2. *Do you think it likely that any American politician today would seriously put forward a resolution like Butterworth's?*
3. *Why do you think Butterworth emphasized that it was the "people's question"? Would a Canadian politician of the time agree?*
4. *"Loyalty to a country is a noble sentiment, but a sentiment that should call practical common sense to sit in judgment with it."*
   (a) *Has the "common sense" factor increased or decreased in significance since Butterworth made his resolution? Why?*
   (b) *Has Canada's survival depended on abandoning "common sense"? Explain why or why not.*

5. THE ELECTION OF 1891

The Liberal Party in 1891 supported closer economic ties with the United States. The Conservatives, led by Prime Minister John A. Macdonald, did not. The Toronto Globe was the political mouthpiece of the Liberals.

(a) THE TORONTO GLOBE

January 1, 1891: Ontario manufacturers would get American iron, bituminous coal and all the other articles which they require at first cost . . . without the addition of the onerous Canadian duty . . . their customers, the farmers and artisans of Canada, would be benefited by having free access for the products of their labour to the United States, for it would be within our power to turn the natural resources of the country to good account . . . the trade of Manitoba and the other outlying provinces would be lost in part to the American manufacturers, but it would be to the advantage of the settlers there if they were able to buy nearer home, whilst the Ontario manufacturers would obtain compensation by invading the neighbouring states.

January 19, 1891: The restrictionists' appeal to loyalty has no effect. The Conservatives of the country know that they are no more loyal than their Liberal neighbours, and are naturally suspicious of a cry which they feel must be raised for an ulterior purpose. That purpose they suspect is to hold them in the bondage of the tariff mercenaries. Not a few feel, as Mr. Frank Hunt put it at Sir Richard's St. Thomas meeting, that "you can't shout for the Queen on an empty stomach."

February 13, 1891: Most Americans are too much immersed in their own affairs to bestow a thought upon the subject of political union. Those who discuss the question in academic fashion are persuaded that if we continue to heap up debt, to impoverish all classes, and to wage a commercial war against them, we shall one day be found begging for admission at their gate. . . . It rests with the Canadian people to decide on March 5th which course shall be pursued in the future—whether we are to be neighbourly as becomes neighbours, or whether the Dominion is to challenge the United States to a prolongation of the hostilities which have led to the adoption of mutually hurtful tariffs. . . . Let us cease to be the victims of an ancient feud, and clasp the hand of fellowship which our neighbours are ready to extend to us. . . .

February 17, 1891: Fifty years ago the British Empire had a commercial policy of its own. . . . But when that arrangement was abolished at the demand of the British people, the commercial policy of the Empire ceased to exist. Britain no longer troubles her head about encouraging colonial development. Her investors lend us money because we pay a high rate of interest and for no other reason, and if she buys our goods it is only when they are cheaper than those of our rivals. Equity would suggest that Canada on her part should be equally at liberty to adopt what seems to be the most advantageous course for herself.

February 20, 1891: Our history . . . from first to last shows the friends of progress fighting against contumely and justifying "the ways of God to men" amid trials many and great, whilst the enemies of progress took their stand on appeals to ignorance, hoisting the flag of Britain over misdeeds and abuses and manifold outrages on the rights of people.

(b) JOHN A. MACDONALD, FEBRUARY 1891

. . . For a century-and-a-half this country has grown and flourished under the protecting aegis of the British Crown. The gallant race who first bore to our shores the blessings of civilization passed by an easy transition from French to English rule, and now form one of the most law-abiding portions of the community. These pioneers were speadily recruited by the advent of a loyal band of British subjects, who gave up everything that men most prize, and were content to begin life anew in the wilderness rather than forego allegiance to their Sovereign. To the descendants of these men, and of the multitude of Englishmen, Irishmen, and Scotchmen who emigrated to Canada, that they might build up new homes without ceasing to be British subjects—to you Canadians I appeal, and I ask you what have you to gain by surrendering that which your fathers held most dear? Under the broad folds of the Union Jack, we enjoy the most ample liberty to govern ourselves as we please, and at the same time we participate in the advantages which flow to manage our domestic concerns, but, practically, we possess the privilege of making our own treaties with foreign countries, and, in our relations with the outside world, we enjoy the prestige inspired by a consciousness of the fact that behind us towers the majesty of England. The question which you will shortly be called upon to determine resolves itself into this; shall we endanger our possession of the great heritage bequeathed to us by our fathers, and submit ourselves to direct taxation for the privilege of having our tariff fixed at Washington, with a prospect of ultimately becoming a portion of the American union? I commend these issues to your determination, and to the judgment of the whole people of Canada, with an unclouded confidence that you will proclaim to the world your resolve to show yourselves not unworthy of the proud distinction that you enjoy, of being numbered among the most dutiful and loyal subjects of our beloved Queen.

As for myself, my course is clear. A British subject I was born—a British subject I will die. With my utmost effort, with my latest breath, will I oppose the "veiled treason" which attempts by sordid means and mercenary proffers to lure our people from their allegiance. During my long public service of nearly half a century, I have been true to my country and its best interests, and I appeal with equal confidence to the men who have trusted me in the past, and to the young hope of the country, with whom rests its destinies for the future, to give me their united and strenuous aid in this, my last effort, for the unity of the Empire and the preservation of our commercial and political freedom.

What do you think?

1. What was at the core of the Liberal pro-American stance in 1891?
2. What are the strengths and weaknesses in Macdonald's argument?
3. Compare and contrast attitudes to the U.S. of various 19th Century

Canadians with the attitudes of Canadians in the 1960s and 1970s.
(a) What changes, if any, do you see?
(b) How do you account for these changes or for the absence of change?

Confederation or Continental Union?

Fear of the United States together with the constitutional lessons learned from the American Civil War were of critical importance in bringing about Confederation. Why were so many Canadians afraid of the United States in the 1860s? How did the constitutional lessons learned from the Civil War affect the nature of Confederation?

1. JOHN A. MACDONALD AND CONFEDERATION

During the Confederation debates of 1865, John A. Macdonald, who more than any other Canadian politician helped to create a united Canada, discussed some of the ways by which the United States had influenced Confederation.

If we are not blind to our present position, we must see the hazardous situation in which all the great interests of Canada stand in respect to the United States. I am no alarmist, I do not believe in the prospect of immediate war. I believe that the common sense of the two nations will prevent a war; still we cannot trust to probabilities. The government and legislature would be wanting in their duty to the people if they ran any risk. We know that the United States at this moment are engaged in a war of enormous dimensions—that the occasion of a war with Great Britain has again and again arisen, and may at any time in the future again arise. We cannot say but that the two nations may drift into a war as other nations have done before. It would then be too late when war had commenced to think of measures for strengthening ourselves, or to begin negotiations for a union with the sister provinces. . . .

And I am strong in the belief—that we have hit upon the happy medium in those resolutions, and that we have formed a scheme of government which unites the advantages of both, giving us the strength of a legislative union and the sectional freedom of a federal union, with protection to local interests. In doing so we had the advantage of the experience of the United States. . . . We can now take advantage of the experience of the last seventy-eight years, during which that Constitution has existed, and I am strongly of the belief that we have, in a great measure, avoided in this system which we propose for the adoption of the people of Canada, the defects which time and events have shown to exist in the American Constitution. . . . Ever since the union was formed the difficulty of what is called "State Rights" has existed, and this had much to do in bringing on the present unhappy war in the United States. They commenced, in fact, at the wrong end. They declared by their Constitution that each state was a sovereignty in itself, and that all the powers incident to a sovereignty belonged to each state, except those powers which, by the Constitution, were conferred upon the General Government and Congress. Here we have adopted a different system. We have strengthened the General Government. We have given the General Legislature all the great subjects of legislation. We have conferred on them, not only specifically and in detail, all the powers which are incident to sovereignty, but we have expressly declared that all subjects of general interest not distinctly and exclusively conferred upon the local governments and local legislatures, shall be conferred upon the General Government and Legislature. We have thus avoided that great source of weakness which has been the cause of the disruption of the United States. We have avoided all conflict of jurisdiction and authority, and if this Constitution is carried out, . . . we will have in fact, as I said before, all the advantages of a legislative union under one administration, with, at the same time the guarantees for local institutions and for local laws, which are insisted upon by so many in the provinces now, I hope, to be united. . . .

What do you think?

1. (a) What are the main differences between a "legislative union" and a "federal union"?
   (b) Why did Macdonald favour a legislative union?
2. Do you think that the type of government set up by the BNA Act represented an attempt to construct a society in North America radically different from that of the United States? If so, how?

2.   D'ARCY McGEE AND THE "WARNING VOICES"

This selection is from a speech given by McGee on February 9, 1865, during Parliamentary debates on Confederation.

All, even honorable gentlemen who are opposed to this union, admit that we must do something, and that that something must not be a mere temporary expedient. We are compelled, by warning voices from within and without, to make a change, and a great change. . . . Then . . ., there came what I may call the other warning from without—the American warning. (Hear, hear.) Republican America gave us her notices in times past, through her press, and her demagogues and her statesmen,—but of late days she has given us much more intelligible notices—such as the notice to abrogate the Reciprocity Treaty, and to arm the lakes, contrary to the provisions of the addenda to the treaty of 1818. She has given us another notice in imposing a vexatious passport system; another in her avowed purpose to construct a ship canal round the Falls of Niagara, so as "to pass war vessels from Lake Ontario to Lake Erie"; and yet another, the most striking one of all, has been given to us, if we will only understand it, by the enormous expansion of the American army and navy. . . . Another motive to union, or rather a phase of the last motive spoken of, is this, that the policy of our neighbors to the south of us has always been aggressive. There has always been a desire amongst them for the acquisition of new territory. They coveted Florida, and seized it; they coveted Louisiana, and purchased it; they coveted Texas, and stole it; and then they picked a quarrel with Mexico, which ended by their getting California. (Hear, hear.) They sometimes pretend to despise these colonies as prizes beneath their ambition; but had we not the strong arm of England over us, we should not now have had a separate existence. (Cheers.) The acquisition of Canada was the first ambition of the American Confederacy, and never ceased to be so, when her troops were a handful and her navy scarce a squadron. Is it likely to be stopped now, when she counts her guns afloat by thousands and her troops by hundreds of thousands?

What do you think?

1. How important to Canadian politicians was the fear of U.S. military aggression in their acceptance of the Confederation scheme?
2. Summarize the role the U.S. played in Confederation.
3. "The survival of an independent Canada has depended to a large extent on its farsighted politicians who have seen the seriousness of the American threat, and have responded by taking the initiative, often in the face of apathetic and disinterested citizens." Discuss the above statement in relation to the following events:
   (a) Confederation,
   (b) the building of the CPR,
   (c) the CRTC regulations on broadcasting.

3. NOVA SCOTIA'S ATTITUDE

Many people in Nova Scotia were violently opposed to Confederation. Their hatred of "Upper Canada"—as they spitefully referred to

the provinces of Ontario and Quebec—was more intense than their
suspicion of the United States. And as a result, for a few years after
Confederation, there was a significant annexationist movement in
Nova Scotia. A leading annexationist newspaper, the New Glasgow
Eastern Chronicle, *explained its position on May 5, 1869.*

Annexation is one of the legitimate consequences of Confederation.
If that measure had not been forced upon the country against the well
understood wishes of the people . . . years might have elapsed ere the
question of Annexation could have been mooted in Nova Scotia. But the
evil has been done, the people saw their rights trampled upon, have been
refused investigation into their grievances, their faith in "historic delusions"
has been shaken, their loyalty has been unsettled, and as a consequence we
have vast numbers of our people looking to Washington and openly advocating annexation. . . . While confederation has done all this and a great
deal more, it has done one good thing—it has aroused Nova Scotians from
their apathy and Rip Van Winkle slumbers, and shown them that their
true interests lie, not in being connected with a country 3000 miles away,
not in being part of a straggling and poverty-stricken Dominion, but in
being incorporated with the United States—a great, free and prosperous
nation—union with which will open to us the markets of 34,000,000 of
freemen—"will place factories on all our streams, ensure capital for all
legitimate enterprises, open up a career for ourselves and our children, and
ensure adequate protection for ever by land and sea."
    . . . the interests of commerce, of peace and of humanity all
demand that the imaginary line which separates these provinces from the
United States should be wiped up—that one flag should wave, one code of
laws be established, one tariff prevail, over the North American continent.
    But we advocate annexation because we wish to see lasting peace
prevail on this continent, because we wish to see the United States and
Great Britain bound to keep the peace by more substantial arguments
than frowning fortifications bristling with cannons, iron-clads and ships
of war, and armed men trained to murder each other on the most approved
scientific principles—because we wish to see these two great nations united
in interest, in sentiment, in commerce going hand in hand in the noble
work of civilizing and Christianizing the world. This can never take place
so long as an imaginary line separates British America from the United
States.

What do you think?

1. *If you were an editor of a pro-Confederation Nova Scotian news-*
   paper in 1869, how would you answer the Eastern Chronicle's
   main arguments? Prepare a brief anti-annexationist statement.
2. *Why did the Nova Scotia annexationists fail?*

3. *Are any of the* Eastern Chronicle's *arguments relevant in the Canada of the 1970s? What is more important as far as you are concerned, economic prosperity or national integrity? Why?*

Continental Union?

From the 1840s until the Reciprocity Election of 1911 many Canadians vigorously debated the advantages and disadvantages of closer commercial relations with the United States. For many people on both sides of the debate closer economic ties would mean eventual political union. It is especially interesting that throughout this period most Americans did not care about absorbing Canada into the republic. Without question, there was far more enthusiasm in Canada than in the United States both for closer economic relations *and* for annexation. It was especially during periods of severe economic recession that Canadians looked to the United States for their economic salvation. What arguments were used against the early "continentalists"? Are they similar to the "nationalist" arguments of today? How has the debate changed since 1849 and how has it remained the same?

1. THE 1849 ANNEXATION MANIFESTO

In October, 1849 a number of leading Montreal businessmen decided that annexation to the United States provided the only answer for their commercial and political problems. They resented the growing political power of the French Canadians and the fact that they no longer were given preferential treatment in trade with Great Britain. The Montreal annexationists were also supported by merchants in New Brunswick and what is now Ontario.

Of all the remedies that have been suggested for the acknowledged and insufferable ills with which our country is afflicted, there remains but one to be considered. It propounds a sweeping and important change in our political and social condition involving considerations which demand our most serious examination. THIS REMEDY CONSISTS IN A FRIENDLY AND PEACEFUL SEPARATION FROM BRITISH CONNECTION AND A UNION UPON EQUITABLE TERMS WITH THE GREAT NORTH AMERICAN CONFEDERACY OF SOVEREIGN STATES.

We would promise that towards Great Britain we entertain none other than sentiments of kindness and respect. Without her consent we consider separation as neither practicable nor desirable. But the colonial policy of the parent state, the avowals of her leading statesmen, the public sentiments of the Empire, present unmistakable and significant indications of the appreciation of colonial connection. That it is the resolve of England to invest us with the attributes and compel us to assume the burdens of independence is no longer problematical.

The proposed union would render Canada a field for American capital, into which it would enter as freely for the prosecution of public works and private enterprise as into any of the present States. It would equalise the value of real estate upon both sides of the boundary, thereby probably doubling at once the entire present value of property in Canada, whilst, by giving stability to our institutions, and introducing prosperity, it would raise our public corporate and private credit. It would increase our commerce, both with the United States and foreign countries, and would not necessarily diminish to any great extent our intercourse with Great Britain, into which our products would for the most part enter on the same terms as at present. It would render our rivers and canals the highway for the immigration to, and exports from, the West, to the incalculable benefit of our country. It would also introduce manufacturers into Canada as rapidly as they have been introduced into the northern states; and to Lower Canada especially, where water privileges and labour are abundant and cheap, it would attract manufacturing capital, enhancing the value of property and agricultural produce, and giving remunerative employment to what is at present a comparatively non-producing population. Nor would the United States merely furnish the capital for our manufacturers. They would also supply for them the most extensive market in the world, without the intervention of a custom house officer. Railways would forthwith be constructed by American capital as feeders for all the great lines now approaching our frontiers; and railway enterprise in general would doubtless be as active and prosperous among us as among our neighbours. The value of our agricultural produce would be raised at once to a par with that of the United States, whilst agricultural implements and many of the necessaries of life, such as tea, coffee and sugar, would be greatly reduced in price.

The simple and economical State government, in which direct responsibility to the people is a distinguishing feature, would be substituted for a system, at once cumbrous and expensive.

In place of war and the alarms of war with a neighbour, there would be peace and amity between this country and the United States. Disagreements between the United States and her chief if not only rival among nations would not make the soil of Canada the sanguinary arena for their disputes, as under our existing relations must necessarily be the case. That such is the unenviable condition of our state of dependence upon Great Britain is known to the whole world, and how far it may conduce to keep prudent capitalists from making investments in the country, or wealthy settlers from selecting a fore-doomed battle-field for the home of themselves and their children, it needs no reasoning on our part to elucidate.

But other advantages than those having a bearing on our material interests may be foretold. It would change the ground of political contest between races and parties, allay and obliterate those irritations and conflicts of rancour and recrimination which have hitherto disfigured our social fabric. Already in anticipation has its harmonious influence been felt—the harbinger may it be hoped of a lasting oblivion of dissensions among all classes, creeds and parties in the country. Changing a subordinate for an independent condition, we would take our station among the nations of the earth. We have, now, no voice in the affairs of the Empire, nor do we share in its honors or emoluments. England is our parent state, with whom we have no equality, but towards whom we stand in the simple relation of obedience. But as citizens of the United States the public services of the nation would be open to us,—a field for high and honorable distinction on which we and our posterity might enter on terms of perfect equality.

Nor would the amicable separation of Canada from Great Britain be fraught with advantages to us alone. The relief to the parent state from the large expenditure now incurred in the military occupation of the country,—the removal of the many causes of collision with the United States, which result from the contiguity of mutual territories so extensive —the benefit of the larger market which the increasing prosperity of Canada would create, are considerations which, in the minds of many of her ablest statesmen, render our incorporation with the United States a desirable consummation.

To the United States also the annexation of Canada presents many important inducements. The withdrawal from their borders, of so powerful a nation, by whom in time of war the immense and growing commerce of the lakes would be jeopardized—the ability to dispense with the costly but ineffectual revenue establishment over a frontier of many hundred miles—the large accession to their income from our customs—the unrestricted use of the St. Lawrence, the natural highway from the western states to the ocean, are objects for the attainment of which the most substantial equivalents would undoubtedly be conceded.

What do you think?

1. *Why did the annexationists want to break away from Great Britain?*
2. *Why did Great Britain abandon preferential trade with Canada? What was the effect of the action on the Canadian farmer, merchant and manufacturer?*
3. *How important are Canada's tariff arrangements with the U.K. today? Will Britain's membership of the European Common Market change Canadian attitudes towards economic relationship with the U.S.?*

4. Why were the annexationists of 1849 anxious for closer economic ties with the U.S.? Compare their reasons with those expressed by Canadians favouring such a move today. Account for any similarities or differences.

2. RESPONSE TO THE MANIFESTO

On October 30, 1849, a public meeting was held at Cobourg, Ontario, "to express disapprobation of the annexation movement at Montreal."

Resolved: That this meeting view with feelings of regret and indignation, the course pursued by those of our fellow-subjects in Montreal, who, forgetful of their allegiance to the best of Sovereigns, have deliberately, yet rashly, affixed their names to a document recommending the separation of these colonies from the British Empire, and their annexation to the neighboring republic.

2. That it is the opinion of this meeting that, from the loyal and patriotic feeling displayed by the inhabitants of this province upon former trying occasions, to preserve the integrity of the Empire, the same spirit would again be exerted if necessary for the same purpose.

3. That, although suffering (temporarily, we trust,) from a great depression in trade, in the same manner as other countries have occasionally suffered,—we believe that relief can, and will be obtained by the co-operation of the provincial with the imperial legislature, without foregoing our allegiance to the parent state.

4. That by a sound system of legislation—a calm resolve to drop old party strife—a submission to the rule of a constitutional majority—and a rigid economy in the administration of the government, this colony can better re-establish her credit, and regain her wonted prosperity, than by severing her connexion from the greatest Empire of the earth, and forming instead a dependent State of the American Union.

5. That this meeting is pleased to find that two prominent members of the Provincial administration, the Honble. Robert Baldwin and the Honble. Francis Hincks, have publicly and plainly expressed their views on the subject for which this meeting is assembled, and that such views meet with the full and unqualified approbation of this meeting.

6. That this meeting is of opinion that this country owes a great debt of gratitude to the parent state, for the large amount of her treasure which she has from time to time expended in the colony for its protection and defence, as well as in the erection of that magnificent work the Rideau Canal, which, while it is so beneficial to the province, is a continual expense to the Mother Country, and productive of scarcely any revenue.

7. That a committee . . . be appointed to prepare a protest against the annexation movement, in accordance with the foregoing resolutions, and to express our firm and unalterable adherence to British connexion, and to the British throne and constitution, and that the committee be further requested to circulate the said protest for general signature.

What do you think?

1. Why did the Cobourg meeting oppose the annexationists?
2. Who were Robert Baldwin and Francis Hincks? Why were they mentioned here?
3. How have the anti-continentalist arguments changed since 1849 and why?

3. A U.S. RESPONSE

Also in response to the Annexation Manifesto, the legislature of Vermont passed the following resolutions.

Whereas, by the original articles of the Confederation adopted by the States of this Union it was provided that "Canada, acceding to this Confederation and joining in the measures of these United States, shall be admitted into and entitled to all the advantages of this Union."

And whereas recent occurrences in the said Province of Canada indicate a strong and growing desire on the part of the people thereof to avail themselves of the advantage of the foregoing offer, and to apply for admission among the sovereign States of this Union;

Therefore, Resolved by the Senate and the House of Representatives, that believing the admission of Canada into this Union to be a measure intimately connected with the permanent prosperity and glory of both countries, the government of the State of Vermont is earnestly desirous to see such reunion affected, without a violation, on the part of the United States, of the amicable relation existing with the British Government, or of the law of voters.

Resolved; the peaceful annexation of Canada to the United States, with the consent of the British Government, and the people of Canada, and upon just and honorable terms, is an object to the highest degree desirable to the people of the United States. It would open a wide and fertile field to the enterprise and the industry of the American people; it would extend the boundaries and increase the power of our country; it would enlist a brave, industrious and intelligent people under the flag of our nation; it would spread wide the liberal principles of republican government, and promote the preponderance of free institution in this Union. We therefore trust that our national government, in the spirit of both peace and courtesy to the British Government and the people of Canada, will adopt all proper and honorable means to secure the annexation of Canada to the United States.

What do you think?

1. *According to the Vermont Resolutions, what were the major advantages of annexation?*
2. *How was the union of the two countries to be realized?*
3. *How would you account for the basic differences between the Vermont Resolutions and Hull's Proclamation of 1812 (page 215)?*

A Separate Nation

During the early months of the American Revolution, during the War of 1812, and again in 1838 and 1839, thousands of American troops invaded what would come to be known as Canada. They came for a variety of reasons, but the most important was probably their desire to liberate "Canadians" from British rule. Instead of accomplishing this goal, however, the Americans significantly strengthened the desire of most Canadians to build a separate and British nation north of the neighbouring republic.

Why were the Americans rejected by most Canadians? How did these early events affect Canadian-American relations in the post-1840 period? How did they influence what may be referred to as Canadian national feeling? How do Canadians regard these events today? Why?

Revolution Rejected

The American Revolution can be considered one of the more crucial events in Canadian history. The Revolution not only shattered the vast British North American colonial empire, but it also profoundly affected the historical evolution of Canada. For many, the Revolution represents the beginning of a distinct and unique Canadian identity. Consequently the refusal of Quebec and Nova Scotia to become a part of the Revolution in 1775 and 1776 has become a fascinating field of historical inquiry in that it might provide part of the answer to the problem of Canada's national identity.

Why did Quebec and Nova Scotia refuse to join the Thirteen Colonies? Was there in the Canadian colonies at that time a sense of distinctness from the colonies to the south? Or was the refusal based on more "practical" reasons? What light does the Canadian rejection of the Revolution shed on the riddle of our national identity, if any at all? How do you think the U.S. thrust and the Canadian reaction in 1775 has affected later relations between the two countries?

1. WASHINGTON'S PROCLAMATION

In the autumn of 1775, General George Washington, the commander in chief of the American Revolutionary forces, issued the following proclamation to the 90,000 colonists of Quebec.

Friends and Brethren: The unnatural contest between the *English* Colonies and *Great Britain* has now risen to such a height that arms alone must decide it. The Colonies, confiding in the justice of their cause and the purity of their intentions, have reluctantly appealed to that Being in whose hands are all human events. He has hitherto smiled upon their virtuous efforts. The hand of tyranny has been arrested in its ravages, and the British arms, which have shone with so much splendour in every part of the globe, are now tarnished with disgrace and disappointment. Generals of approved experience, who boasted of subduing this great continent, find themselves circumscribed within the limits of a single city and its suburbs, suffering all the shame and distress of a siege, while the freeborn sons of America, animated by the genuine principles of liberty and love of their country, with increasing union, firmness, and discipline, repel every attack, and despise every danger. Above all, we rejoice that our enemies have been deceived with regard to you; they have persuaded themselves, they have even dared to say, that the *Canadians* were not capable of distinguishing between the blessings of liberty and the wretchedness of slavery; that gratifying the vanity of a little circle of nobility would blind the eyes of the people of *Canada;* by such artifices they hoped to bend you to their views, but they have been deceived; instead of finding in you that poverty of soul and baseness of spirit, they see, with a chagrin equal to our joy, that you are enlightened, generous, and virtuous; that you will not renounce your own rights, or serve as instruments to deprive your fellow-subjects of theirs.

Come, then, my brethren, unite with us in an indissoluable union; let us run together to the same goal. We have taken up arms in defence of our liberty, our property, our wives, and our children; we are determined to preserve them or die. We look forward with pleasure to that day, not far remote, we hope, when the inhabitants of *America* shall have one senti-ment, and the full enjoyment of the blessings of a free government. Incited by these motives, and encouraged by the advice of many friends of liberty among you, the grand *American* Congress have sent an army into your province, under the command of General *Schuyler,* not to plunder, but to protect you; to animate and bring forth into action those sentiments of freedom you have disclosed, and which the tools of despotism would ex-tinguish through the whole creation. To cooperate with this design, and to frustrate those cruel and perfidious schemes which would deluge our fron-tiers with the blood of women and children, I have detached Colonel *Arnold* into your country, with a part of the army under my command. I have enjoined upon him, and I am certain that he will consider himself, and act as in the country of his patrons and best friends. Necessaries and accommodations of every kind which you may furnish he will thankfully receive, and render the full value. I invite you, therefore, as friends and brethren, to provide him with such supplies as your country affords; and I pledge myself not only for your safety and security, but for ample com-pensation. Let no man desert his habitation. Let no one flee as before an enemy. The cause of *America* and of liberty is the cause of every virtuous *American* citizen, whatever may be his religion or his descent. The United Colonies know no distinction but such as slavery, corruption, and arbitrary domination may create. Come, then, ye generous citizens, range yourselves under the standard of general liberty, against which all the force and arti-fice of tyranny will never be able to prevail.

What do you think?

1. What did General Washington mean when he referred to the British "hand of tyranny"?
2. If you had been living in Montreal in November, 1775, how would you have reacted to the proclamation? Why?
3. How did General Washington try to persuade the Quebec colon-ists to join the American Revolution?

2.   A QUEBEC RESPONSE

A letter to Mr. Richard Montgomery, Brigadier-General of the Con-tinental Army, from the residents of three Montreal suburbs follows.

Sir,
          The shadows in which we were enveloped are at last dispersed—the day has dawned, our chains are broken, and a happy freedom restores us to ourselves—a freedom which we have long desired, and which today

makes it possible for us to bear witness to our satisfaction at being united with our colonial brothers of whom you are worthy representatives.

Although the citizens of the city of Montreal have heaped scorn upon us and continue to do so every day, we declare that we abhor their conduct towards our brothers and friends. We declare that the capitulation proposed by them is a treaty between enemies, and not a pact of association and fraternal union.

These same citizens have always regarded us, and still regard us, as rebels. We are not offended by this designation since we share it with our brothers in the Colonies, but in spite of them and in accordance with our own desire, we accept the union.

3.   THE BISHOP OF QUEBEC REPLIES

The influential Roman Catholic bishop of Quebec, Jean-Olivier Briand, warned his people not to listen to the seditious propaganda of the American rebels. On May 22, 1775, Bishop Briand issued the following statement.

To all the peoples of this colony, greeting and benediction.

A troop of subjects in revolt against their lawful Sovereign, who is also yours, has invaded this province, less in the hope of being able to maintain a position there than with a view to involving you in their revolt, or at least engaging you not to oppose their pernicious design. The singular kindness and leniency with which we have been governed by His Very Gracious Majesty King George III since the arbitrament of war has made us his subjects, and the recent benefits with which he has favoured us, in restoring the use of our laws and the free practise of our religion and in allowing us to enjoy all the privileges and advantages of British subjects, these are favours great enough in themselves to inspire your gratitude and your zeal to promote the interests of the British Crown. But at this moment your hearts should be stirred by still more urgent motives. Your religion and the oaths which you have taken impose upon you an indispensable obligation to defend to the utmost your country and your King. Close your ears, therefore, dear Canadians, to the voices of sedition which seek to destroy your happiness by stifling the sense of submission to your lawful superiors graven in your hearts by your education and your religion. Be joyful in the execution of orders from a beneficent government which seeks no other goal than your interest and your happiness. There is no question of carrying the war into distant provinces; you are being asked merely to help repulse the enemy and turn back the invasion which threatens this province. Your religion and your interests unite to guarantee your zeal in the defence of our frontiers and our property.

What do you think?

1. Why do you think some Quebec colonists supported the American invaders?
2. What do you consider Bishop Briand's major argument? Why?
3. How do Canadians today use an "anti-Revolution" argument to support the continuance of a separate Canada?
4. How do you account for the failure of the "American liberation" movement?

4.   THE NOVA SCOTIA RESPONSE

In 1775 Nova Scotia had a population of about 20,000. More than half were recent immigrants from New England, so it might have been expected that the colony would have quickly joined the Revolution. Instead, most Nova Scotians would have agreed with the sentiments of the 1775 petition by the people of Yarmouth.

We do all of us profess to be true Friends and Loyal Subjects to George our King. We were almost all of us born in New England, we have Fathers, Brothers and Sisters in that Country, divided betwixt natural affection to our nearest relations, and good Faith and Friendship to our King and Country, we want to know, if we may be permitted at this time to live in a peaceable State, as we look on that to be the only situation in which we with our Wives and Children, can be in any tolerable degree safe.

What do you think?

1. Compare and contrast the responses in Quebec and Nova Scotia to the Revolution.
2. Explain the source of what has been called Nova Scotia's "neutrality".
3. Why did the Revolution not destroy the strong feelings of kinship between Americans and some British North Americans? Give other historical and recent examples of kinship surmounting divided opinion between the two countries. Why did the bonds last in these cases?

The War of 1812

The War of 1812 was unique in that it was, apparently, won by both sides. Most of the serious fighting took place in Upper Canada. There was no fighting in the Maritime colonies; and Lower Canada was largely by-passed by the events of the war. It should be remembered that in 1812 there were about 130,000 people in Upper Canada. Sixty percent of the population were recent American immigrants, twenty percent were of Loyalist origin, and twenty percent of British origin.

The war, it has been argued, was critical in shaping Canadian nationalism. It seemed to confirm the Loyalist conviction that the Americans were dangerous, aggressive imperialists, bent on destroying the neighbouring British colonies. How justified were these fears? How did they contribute to the attitudes of later generations? Are their effects still being felt?

1. HULL'S PROCLAMATION

On July 13, 1812 Hull, commander of the North Western army of the United States, issued the following proclamation at Sandwich, near what is now Windsor, Ontario.

Inhabitants of Canada! After thirty years of Peace and prosperity, the United States have been driven to Arms. The injuries and aggressions, the insults and indignities of Great Britain have *once more* left them no alternative but manly resistance or unconditional submission. The army under my Command has invaded your Country and the standard of the United States waves on the territory of Canada. To the peaceful unoffending inhabitant, It brings neither danger nor difficulty. I come to *find* enemies not to *make* them. I come to *protect,* not to *injure* you.

Separated by an immense ocean and an extensive Wilderness from Great Britain you have no participation in her counsels, no interest in her conduct. You have felt her Tyranny, you have seen her injustice; but I do not ask *you* to avenge the one or to redress the other. The United States are sufficiently powerful to afford you every security consistent with their rights & your expectations. I tender you the invaluable blessings of Civil, Political, & Religious Liberty, and their necessary result, individual and general prosperity: That liberty which gave decision to our counsels and energy to our conduct in our struggle for INDEPENDENCE, and which conducted us safely and triumphantly thro' the stormy period of the Revolution.

That Liberty which has raised us to an elevated rank among the Nations of the world and which has afforded us a greater measure of Peace & Security wealth and prosperity than ever fell to the Lot of any people.

In the name of my Country and by the authority of my Government, I promise you protection to your *persons, property, and rights.* Remain at your homes, Pursue your peaceful and customary avocations. Raise not your hands against your brethren, many of your fathers fought for the freedom & *Independence* we now enjoy. Being children therefore of the same family with us, and heirs to the same Heritage, the arrival of an army of Friends must be hailed by you with a cordial welcome. You will be emancipated from Tyranny and oppression and restored to the dignified station of freemen. Had I any doubt of eventual success I might ask your assistance, but I do not. I come prepared for every contingency. I have a force which will look down all opposition and that force is but the vanguard of a much greater. If, contrary to your own interest & the just expectation of my country, you should take part in the approaching contest, you will be considered and treated as enemies, and the horrors and calamities of war will Stalk before you.

If the barbarous and Savage policy of Great Britain be pursued, and the savages are let loose to murder our Citizens and butcher our women and children, this war will be a war of extermination.

The first stroke with the Tomahawk, the first attempt with the Scalping Knife, will be the Signal for one indiscriminate scene of desolation. *No white man found fighting by the Side of an Indian will be taken prisoner.* Instant destruction will be his Lot. If the dictates of reason, duty, justice, and humanity cannot prevent the employment of a force, which respects no rights & knows no wrong, it will be prevented by a severe and relentless system of retaliation.

I do not doubt your courage and firmness; I will not doubt your attachment to Liberty. If you tender your services voluntarily they will be accepted readily.

The United States offer you *Peace, Liberty,* and *Security*: your choice lies between these, & *War, Slavery, and destruction.* Choose then, but choose wisely; and may he who knows the justice of our cause, and who holds in his hand the fate of Nations, guide you to a result the most compatible with your rights and interests, your peace and prosperity.

What do you think?

1. *What was Hull's attitude to the Canadians? Why?*
2. *What are the similarities between Hull's Proclamation of 1812 and that of Washington in 1775?*
3. *Why was Hull so concerned about the Indians?*

2. BROCK'S ANSWER

Sir Isaac Brock was the commander of the British troops in Upper Canada and was also in charge of civil affairs in the colony. An outstanding military officer, Brock died in the famous battle of Queenston Heights.

The unprovoked declaration of War, by the United States of

America, against the United Kingdom, of Great Britain and Ireland, and its dependencies, has been followed by the actual invasion of this Province in a remote Frontier of the Western District by a detachment of the Armed Force of the United States. The Officer commanding that detachment has thought proper to invite his Majesty's Subjects not merely to a quiet and unresisting submission, but insults them with a call to seek voluntarily the protection of his Government. Without condescending to repeat the illiberal epithets bestowed in this appeal of the American Commander to the people of Upper Canada on the Administration of his Majesty, every Inhabitant of the Province is desired to seek the confutation of such indecent slander in the review of his own particular circumstances: Where is the Canadian Subject who can truly affirm to himself that he has been injured by the Government in his person, his liberty, or his property? Where is to be found in any part of the world, a growth so rapid in wealth and prosperity as this Colony exhibits,—Settled not 30 years by a band of Veterans exiled from their former possessions on account of their loyalty, not a descendant of these brave people is to be found, who under the fostering liberality of their Sovereign, has not acquired a property and means of enjoyment superior to what were possessed by their ancestors. This unequalled prosperity could not have been attained by the utmost liberality of the Government or the persevering industry of the people, had not the maritime power of the Mother Country secured to its Colonists a safe access to every market where the produce of their labor was in demand.

The unavoidable and immediate consequence of a separation from Great Britain, must be the loss of this inestimable advantage, and what is offered you in exchange? to become a territory of the United States and share with them that exclusion from the Ocean, which the policy of their present Government enforces.—you are not even flattered with a participation of their boasted independence, and it is but too obvious that once exchanged from the powerful protection of the United Kingdom you must be reannexed to the dominion of France, from which the Provinces of Canada were wrested by the Arms of Great Britain, at a vast expense of blood and treasure, from no other motive than to *relieve* her ungrateful children from the oppression of a cruel neighbor: this restitution of Canada to the Empire of France was the stipulated reward for the aid offered to the revolted Colonies, now the United States; the debt is still due, and there can be no doubt but the pledge has been renewed as a consideration for Commercial advantages, or rather for an expected relaxation in the Tyranny of France over the Commercial World.—Are you prepared Inhabitants of Upper Canada to become willing Subjects or rather Slaves, to the Despot who rules the Nations of Europe with a rod of Iron? If not, arise in a Body, exert your energies, co-operate cordially with the King's regular Forces to repel the invader, and do not give cause to your children when groaning under the oppression of a foreign Master to reproach you with the richest Inheritance on Earth.—a participation in the name, character and freedom of Britons.

The same spirit of Justice, which will make every reasonable allowance for the unsuccessful efforts of Zeal and Loyalty, will not fail to punish the defalcation of principle: every Canadian Freeholder is by deliberate choice, bound by the most solemn Oaths to defend the Monarchy as well as his own property; to shrink from that engagement is a Treason not to be forgiven; let no Man suppose that if in this unexpected struggle his Majesties Arms should be compelled to yield to an overwhelming force, that the Province will be eventually abandoned; the endeared relation of its first settlers, the intrinsic value of its Commerce and the pretensions of its powerful rival to repossess the Canadas are pledges that no peace will be established between the United States and Great Britain and Ireland, of which the restoration of these Provinces does not make the most prominent condition.

What do you think?

1. What were Brock's answers to Hull's main arguments?
2. If you had been, in 1812, a recent arrival from New York living near Windsor, how would you have reacted to the two proclamations? Why?
3. (a) Judging from Brock's proclamation, how powerful was the attachment to the British monarchy in Canada? Why?
   (b) How important is the monarchy to Canadians today? How does the monarchy contribute to the desire of Canadians to remain independent of the U.S. today? Why?

3.   SOME UPPER CANADIAN RESPONSES

Some Upper Canadians responded favorably to the Americans; others did not. For example, Brock felt compelled to report in July 1812 on the apathy of many Canadians to the war.

My situation is most critical, not from anything the enemy can do, but from the disposition of the people—the population, believe me is essentially bad—and full belief possesses them all that this Province must inevitably succumb. This prepossession is fatal to every exertion—Legislators, Magistrates, Militia officers, all, have imbibed the idea, and are so sluggish and indifferent in their respective offices that the artful and active scoundrel is allowed to parade the Country without interruption, and commit all imaginable mischief.

[*Two years later another British army officer, General Gordon Drummond, commented on Upper Canadian morale.*]

Having said so much with respect to the disaffected spirit evinced by some, it is at the same time but justice to say that the greater part of the inhabitants are well disposed, and many have on various occasions manifested their loyalty and devotion to the service by their actions in the field.

[*About the same time, in 1814, two Upper Canadian women experienced some of the horrors of war.*]

As my mother and myself, wrote Mrs. John Harris, were sitting at breakfast, the dogs kept up a very unusual barking. I went to the door to discover the cause; when I looked up, I saw the hill-side and fields, as far as the eye could reach, covered with American soldiers. . . . Two men stepped from the ranks, selected some large chips, and came into the room where we were standing, and took coals from the hearth without speaking a word. My mother knew instinctively what they were going to do. She went and asked to see the commanding officer. A gentleman rode up to her and said he was the person she asked for. She entreated him to spare her property, and said she was a widow with a young family. He answered her civilly and respectfully, and expressed his regrets that his orders were to burn, but that he would spare the house, which he did; and he said, as a sort of justification of his burning, that the buildings were used as a barrack, and the mill furnished flour for British troops. Very soon we saw columns of dark smoke arise from every building, and of which at early morn had been a prosperous homestead, at noon there remained only smouldering ruins. . . . My father had been dead less than two years. Little remained of all his labours excepting the orchard and cultivated fields.

What do you think?

1. How do you acocunt for Brock's pessimistic report?
2. Why do you think General Drummond could report in 1814 that "the greater part of the inhabitants are well disposed"?
3. (a) Do you think the American soldiers were justified in burning the farm? Why?
   (b) Since this was not an uncommon occurrence, how would such incidents affect the attitudes of most Upper Canadians?
   (c) How lasting do you consider these impressions to have been? To what extent do you think they can explain later anti-American feeling?

Rebellion and the Patriot Hunters

Pro-American feeling helped to incite the unsuccessful 1837 and 1838 rebellions led by William Lyon Mackenzie and Louis-Joseph Papineau. In 1838 Mackenzie, from his American refuge on the New York side of the Niagara River, issued his "republican" proclamation. But few Upper Canadians were sympathetic. Later that year, thousands of Americans living near the Canadian border decided to use force to accomplish what Mackenzie's proclamation had obviously failed to do. These Americans joined the Patriot Hunters, a rather peculiar secret society, to liberate Canadians from their British rulers. Some Canadians were convinced that the unsuccessful rebellions had paved the way for an American take-over. They gloomily predicted success for the American invaders.

Is it accurate to say that the failure of Mackenzie's rebellion represented a rejection by Upper Canadians of "the American way"? Can it be claimed that the rebellion and the activities of the Patriot Hunters deepened the resolve of Canadians to remain independent of the U.S.? Why?

1. THE PROCLAMATION

Mackenzie issued the following proclamation in January, 1838.

For nearly fifty years has our country languished under the blighting influence of military despots, strangers from Europe, ruling us, not according to laws of our choice, but by the capricious dictates of their arbitrary power.

They have taxed us at their pleasure, robbed our exchequer, and carried off the proceeds to other lands—they have bribed and corrupted ministers of the Gospel, with the wealth raised by our industry—they have, in place of religious liberty, given rectories and clergy reserves to a foreign priesthood, with spiritual power dangerous to our peace as a people—they have bestowed millions of our lands on a company of Europeans for a nominal consideration, and left them to fleece and impoverish our country —they have spurned our petitions, involved us in their wars, excited feelings of national and sectional animosity in counties, townships and neighbourhoods, and ruled us, as Ireland has been ruled, to the advantage of persons in other lands, and to the prostration of our energies as a people.

We are wearied of these oppressions, and resolved to throw off the yoke. Rise, Canadians, rise as one man, and the glorious object of our wishes is accomplished.

Our intentions have been clearly stated to the world in the Declaration of Independence, adopted at Toronto on the 31st of July last, printed in the *Constitution, Correspondent and Advocate,* and the *Liberal,* which important paper was drawn by Dr. John Rolph and myself, signed by the Central Committee, received the sanction of a large majority of the people of the Province, west of Port Hope and Cobourg, and is well known to be in accordance with the feelings and sentiments of nine tenths of the people of this state.

We have planted the Standard of Liberty in Canada, for the attainment of the following objects:

Perpetual Peace, founded on a government of equal rights to all, secured by a written constitution, sanctioned by yourselves in a convention to be called as early as circumstances will permit.

Civil and Religious Liberty, in its fullest extent, that in all laws made, or to be made, every person be bound alike—neither shall any tenure, estate, charter, birth, or place, confer any exemption from the ordinary course of legal proceedings and responsibilities whereinto others are subjected.

The abolition of hereditary honours, of the laws of entail and primo-geniture, and of pensioners who devour our substance.

A Legislature composed of a Senate and Assembly chosen by the people.

An Executive to be composed of a Governor and other officers elected by the public voice.

A Judiciary to be chosen by the Governor and Senate, and composed of the most learned, honourable, and trustworthy of our citizens. The laws to be rendered cheap and expeditious.

A free trial by Jury—Sheriffs chosen by you, and not to hold office, as now, at the pleasure of our tyrants. The freedom of the Press. Alas for it, now! The free presses in the Canadas are trampled down by the hand of arbitrary power.

The vote by ballot—free and peaceful township elections.

The people to elect their court of request commissioners and justices of the peace—and also their militia officers, in all cases whatsoever.

Freedom of Trade—every man to be allowed to buy at the cheapest market, and sell at the dearest.

No man to be compelled to give military service, unless it be his choice.

Ample funds to be reserved from the vast natural resources of our country to secure the blessings of Education to every citizen.

A frugal and economical government, in order that the people may be prosperous and free from difficulty.

An end forever to the wearisome prayers, supplications and mockeries attendant upon our connexion with the Lordlings of the Colonial Office, Downing St. London.

What do you think?

1. Examine Mackenzie's proposals carefully. To what extent, in your opinion, do they stem from the American example? Support your answer with evidence.
2. Mackenzie claimed that his "Declaration of Independence" was supported in sentiment by nine tenths of all Upper Canadians. Do you think he was correct? Why?
3. Do you think Mackenzie's liking for American institutions and ideals contributed to the failure of the rebellion he led? Do you think it was an important factor in the rebellion's defeat? Why or why not?

2.   THE PATRIOT OATH

A British spy, William Jones Kent, described in October 1838, his Patriot experience.

I joined this lodge at the second meeting. I was taken into the lodge blindfolded. An oath was tendered to me. . . . "You swear in the presence of Almighty God that you will not reveal the secret signs of the Snow Shoe to any, not even to members of the society. . . . The bandage was then taken from my eyes after my being asked to see the light. A naked sword was then pointed at my breast, and two pistols flashed across my face. . . . The object of the society is stated after you have taken the fourth degree—also some of the plans and operations, but they do not communicate the whole unless to the grand master, commanders-in-chief, and others in whom implicit confidence is placed. The general object of the society is stated to be: "to emancipate the British colonies from British thraldom."

3.   SIR GEORGE ARTHUR REPLIES

On November 6, 1838, Sir George Arthur, lieutenant-governor of Upper Canada, reesponded to the Patriot threat in the Upper Canada Gazette.

Loyal Inhabitants of Upper Canada
Upon my arrival among you, early in the present year . . . I found you just recovering from the excitement that had naturally been produced by the then recent attempts of some infatuated and desperate individuals, both within and without the Province, to involve your Country in the horrors of a Civil War: and to subvert those long-cherished Institutions,

which your conduct has proved that you prize at the first of blessings—and are ever ready to maintain, at the hazard of your lives. . . .

The comparative state of tranquility . . . did in fact encourage me to hope that peace, with general harmony and good feeling, would soon be restored to the Province. To my deep disappointment, however, I have learnt from various sources . . . that, regardless of the friendly relations subsisting between Her Majesty's Government and that of the United States, and stimulated by the worst passions and motives, a number of American citizens, along our frontier, have formed a secret combination for another invasion of these Provinces, and that preparations on an extensive scale, for carrying this unprincipled enterprise into execution are, at this moment, in active progress.

It is further stated, that the members of this unholy union communicate by certain mystic signs—that they are possessed of considerable resources—that they have amongst them some individuals of influence; and are one and all bound by an *unlawful* oath to plunder you of your property —to destroy your Institutions—and to sever your connexion with the Mother Country. . . .

Relying on the amity and good faith of the American Government, I have made to wit . . . such representatives as will I trust, ensure it immediate and decisive interference, in suppressing those outrageous proceedings of its border citizens. . . .

It is but reasonable also, when the base design of unprovoked aggression shall become more generally known throughout the union, that I should look with full confidence to the great body of its respectable citizens, to rescue their country from the lasting discredit that will be entailed on it by the actual commission of the hostile acts contemplated by a licentious portion of its population, and the proceedings incident to which tend so fatally to interrupt that good understanding between the inhabitants of the two Countries, which their mutual interests, cemented by the endearing bond of a *common origin,* should lead them strictly to maintain.

But after all, it is less to the interposition of *OTHERS* than to *OURSELVES*—supported as we are by a just cause, and protected, as we may still confidently hope to be, by a righteous Providence—then we must look for safety.

With this in view I have directed . . . that several regiments of your gallant Militia shall be again embodied. . . .

Apparent as it must be to every one, that our security will chiefly depend on the preservation of perfect harmony and concord among ourselves. . . . I do therefore, most earnestly and most affectionately advise and recommend you . . . to drown all differences in a common regard for the public safety. Let the only contest between us henceforth be, who shall show himself the best man, and the most loyal subject.

INHABITANTS OF UPPER CANADA.

It is not to rouse your patriotism and loyalty—since they, I know, require no stimulant—but rather to allay any undue apprehension, or excessive excitement, which rumor may have produced, . . . and in requiring you to be prepared to repel, with steady heart and ready hand, the first aggression on the part of the lawless Brigoods, who threaten your security.

What do you think?

1. (a) What did Sir George Arthur think was the basic threat posed by the Patriot Hunters?
   (b) Which "institutions" was Arthur referring to? Why did the rebels wish to "subvert" them?
2. How did Arthur try to deal with the Patriot problem? How effective do you think his appeal was?
3. (a) What was the significance of the Rebellions of 1837-8 in forming Canadian attitudes towards the U.S.?
   (b) Why are the rebels now regarded as Canadian folk heroes?

4. DURHAM REPORTS CANADA'S VULNERABILITY

In 1837 Lord Durham was sent to Canada to deal with some of the problems which had helped to bring about the Mackenzie and Papineau Rebellions. Durham was certain that unless certain basic reforms were introduced the Canadas would be absorbed by the United States. Among other things Durham proposed a union of Upper and Lower Canada.

. . . a great and powerful people, which under the protection of the British Empire might, in some measure, counterbalance the preponderant and increasing influence of the United States on the American continent. I do not anticipate that a Colonial legislature thus strong and thus self-governing would desire to abandon the connexion with Great Britain . . . it can only be done by raising up for the North American colonist some nationality of his own; by elevating these small and unimportant communities into a society having some objects of national importance; and by thus giving their inhabitants a country which they will be unwilling to see absorbed even into one more powerful.

For it must be recollected that the natural ties of sympathy between the English population of the Canadas and the inhabitants of the frontier States of the Union are peculiarly strong. Not only do they speak the same language, live under laws having the same origin, and preserve the same customs and habits, but there is a positive alternation, if I may so express it, of the populations of the two countries. While large tracts of the British territory are peopled by American citizens, who still keep up a constant connexion with their kindred and friends, the neighbouring States are filled with emigrants from Great Britain, some of whom have quitted Canada after unavailing efforts to find there a profitable return for their capital and labour; and many of whom have settled in the United States, while other members of their families, and the companions of their youth, have taken up their abode on the other side of the frontier. I had no means of ascertaining the exact degree of truth in some statements which I have heard respecting the number of Irish settled in the State of New York; but it is commony asserted that there are no less than 40,000 Irish in the militia of that State. The intercourse between these two divisions of what is, in fact, an identical population, is constant and universal. The border townships of Lower Canada are separated from the United States by an imaginary line; a great part of the frontier of Upper Canada by rivers, which are crossed in ten minutes; and the rest by lakes, which interpose hardly a six hours' passage between the inhabitants of each side. Every man's daily occupations bring him in contact with his neighbours on the other side of the line; the daily wants of one country are supplied by the produce of the other; and the population of each is in some degree dependent on the state of trade and the demands of the other. Such common wants beget an interest in the politics of each country among the citizens of the other. The newspapers circulate in some places almost equally on the different sides of the line; and men discover that their welfare is frequently as much involved in the political condition of their neighbours as of their own countrymen.

What do you think?

1. According to Durham why were the Canada's being Americanized?
2. What arguments would you use to support Durham's view that "some nationality" was needed to deal with the American threat?
3. To what extent have Canadians succeeded in developing a "nationality" of their own?

5.   LESSON LEARNED

Nils von Schoultz, one of the leaders of the Patriot Hunters, was captured near Kingston, Ontario, and eventually hanged. Shortly before his execution in December, 1838 von Schoultz wrote to an American friend. His letter appeared in the Kingston Gazette *December 8, 1838.*

I wish my body delivered to you and buried on your farm. . . .

My last wish to the Americans is that they will not think of avenging my death. Let no further blood be shed. And believe me, from what I have seen, all the stories which were told of the sufferings of the Canadian people were untrue.

What do you think?

1. *How and why did the American invasions of 1775-6, 1812-1814 and 1838 differ?*

5

The Future?

As the U.S. capacity to supply its own energy needs diminishes, Canada will likely be regarded as a major supplier of necessary energy fuels. There has been a great deal of publicity in Canada recently about this likelihood, and the "energy crisis" experienced by the U.S. in the winter of 1972-73 brought home to Canadians the crucial importance of finding answers soon to the questions raised by the resource issue.

Will Canada and the U.S. become "continental partners," with Canada acting as a resource base for a continentalized economic structure? Or will the two countries act as "wary neighbours," with Canada zealously guarding its supply of natural resources for its own use or using them as bargaining counters in Canada-U.S. negotiations?

The authors have selected the "energy crisis" for this section in order to provide you with the opportunity of projecting into the future the contemporary and historical debate that you have examined so far in this book.

Why will the decision over the use of Canada's natural resources be of paramount importance to this country's future and its future relations with the U.S.? What economic, political and cultural issues that you have encountered up to this point are raised by the resource question?

Judging by past experience, what sort of decision will Canada be likely to make and why? What sort of decision *should* Canada make and why?

1. UNCLE SAM NEEDS US

Professor Fred Knelman, who teaches at Sir George Williams University in Montreal, documented U.S. energy needs in an article published in Weekend Magazine, *June 27, 1970. At the end of his*

article, Knelman posed some of the "vital questions" facing Cana-
dians over the use of Canada's natural resources. What do you think
they are?

With only six and a half percent of the world's population, the
United States consumes about 50 percent of all the world's energy and resources. This means that each person—man, woman and child—in the
United States on the average consumes eight times as much energy and
resources as each person in the entire rest of the world.

But even more than its present voracious consumption of fuel,
power, minerals, metals, chemicals, plastics, etc., the United States is
dedicated to an incredible growth in its use of all critical materials. The
average doubling period for the consumption of energy and key resources
in the United States is less than one generation.

There is another vital resource the U.S. is using far more than its
share of—the air we breathe. American industries are consuming an enormous amount of the world's oxygen.

Thus, early in 1980 it is estimated that the United States will
consume over 80 percent of the world's energy and major resources. Pro-
jections for the year 2000 are even more fantastic. The Gross National
Product will soar from just under $1 trillion in 1970 to over $3 trillion.
Steel production will triple or quadruple and electric power is expected to
go up by a factor of five.

In the past the United States has used enough raw materials to
account for half of the total world's steel output, more than half the world's
oil and 90 percent of its natural gas. But the growth rates now anticipated
will increase these proportions in the future. Should the rest of the world
achieve American levels of consumption, over a hundred-fold increase of
the world's energy and resources would be required.

Yet, from a resource viewpoint, the United States is a have-not
nation. Some 33 separate minerals and other basic materials are on a
"critical" list. Among those the United States must now import and continue to do so on an accelerating scale are crude oil (30 percent imported),
iron ore (40 percent), bauxite (95 percent), copper (75 percent), lead
(50 percent), zinc (55 percent), potash (over 50 percent), uranium (over
50 percent), pulpwood, timber, chromite (95 percent), manganese (95
percent), rubber (95 percent) and gold (95 percent).

What do all these figures mean? Actually, the arithmetic of resources is simple to understand. The United States cannot grow at its
present or intended rate without vastly increased dependence upon foreign
resources and energy. When we take into account that the entire developed
world and, in particular, the USSR and China, are equally dedicated to this
kind of growth, then the conclusion is simple. There is no way to share
the world resource pie. The pie itself is not large enough.

History has witnessed the rise and decline of supreme world powers from ancient Greece to Britain of the nineteenth century. Each in its time was a major consumer and producer. But nothing in the past compares to the world's localized affluence in the United States today.

What was once obtained by war and piracy, a technique not entirely abandoned, is now obtained by blackmail, barter or investment. There is truly an imperialist principle in resource exploitation, a resource drain to the United States, a resource glutton which consumes and is planning to consume the great proportion of the world's energy and nonrenewable resources. It is inevitable that Canada, resource-rich but population-poor, by virtue of its proximity to the resource-hungry but rich United States, will be the target of enormous pressures. United States corporations already control, among others, our petroleum, natural gas, paper, potash, nickel and copper.

It is well to understand the nature and point of attack of these pressures, as well as the principles and human values involved. Will we simply sell these "quick assets" irresponsibly or secure by hard bargaining the highest price short of extortion? Will we thus be reduced to a limited level of industrial development by this impoverishment of resources or restriction on manufacturing? If we resist will it be for venal patriotism, national resentment or clear principles?

What do you think?

1. (a) Why does the average U.S. citizen use "eight times as much energy resources as each person in the entire rest of the world"?
   (b) If the U.S. cuts back its energy consumption how would its economy be affected? How would the Canadian economy be affected?

2. Describe what you think Professor Knelman means by "enormous pressures." Do you think the U.S. will exert "enormous pressures"? Why or why not? How should Canada act now to avoid these pressures? Why?

3. How much of Canada's natural resources are controlled by U.S. investors? (See page 16) Given this situation, how can Canada effectively control the export of its natural resources, if at all?

4. What "human values" do you think are involved in the resource issue?

5. "If we resist, will it be for venal patriotism, national resentment or clear principles?" What "clear principles" do you think Professor Knelman refers to?

2.   THIRSTY OR HUNGRY?

This cartoon is by Duncan Macpherson of the Toronto Star.

What do you think?

1. How accurate an assessment of the energy situation do you consider this cartoon to be? Why?

3.   THE ENERGY NATIONALISTS

Thomas Hockin summarized in his book, The Canadian Condiminium *(Toronto: McClelland and Stewart, 1972) some of the arguments against Canadian energy "deals" with the U.S. How effective is the nationalist case?*

The growing realization by some Americans of the potential shortages of oil, natural gas, hydro-electric power and, potentially, even of water, in the United States has focussed attention on Canada's ability to alleviate these shortages. This realization extends far beyond government bureaucracies. Resource policy has become a pre-eminently political, not technical, issue. It is widely advertised in Canada as Canada's opportunity to deal with the Americans from a position of strength, or even as an opportunity to right the long-time imbalance of Canadian-American economic relations.

In order to join Canadian capacity to U.S. needs, American authorities have suggested a "continental energy policy." Any so-called continental energy policy would probably include natural gas, oil, electrical power, coal and nuclear energy, and later, water resources. American industry would have permanent access to these resources and a guarantee of no interference with future supply regardless of whatever needs Canada may develop in the future. It should be made clear, however, as intimated earlier, that quite apart from the lack of flexibility involved for Canada in becoming a committed supplier of U.S. energy, the new mood of Canada at present renders impossible any selling arrangement that would give the United States the appearance of such unilateral control over Canadian natural resources. In line with this emphasis, the present Canadian government has made it clear that it favours some sales to the United States, subject to conditions that meet ecological imperatives, and after the establishment of amounts surplus to Canadian needs.

The mood of opposition to any sort of "continentalism" now includes those who question the wisdom of any sale of energy whatsoever to the United States. Anti-Americanism motivates some nationalists in their disapproval of energy deals with the United States. They have no wish to see Canadian energy powering the military-industrial machine that fights the Vietnam war and exploits the rest of the world. James Laxer, a spokesman for the nationalist and most socialist wing of the New Democratic Party (the Waffle Group), has even suggested that Canada should leave untapped her supplies of natural gas until tanker export abroad becomes feasible. Since the Waffle Group has fairly ambitious social objectives, including widespread public ownership and restructuring of the economy, they take all the more seriously any implied inhibitions on Canada's future freedom of action resulting from a resource deal with the U.S.

Yet Canadian concern permeates a much wider spectrum of political opinion. It ranges from those who hesitate to commit all Canada's surplus resource eggs to the American basket because other nations might need these resources, to those who want more Canadian processing, to those who demand tougher conservation safeguards and finally, to those who worry about the erratic pattern of U.S. markets. (The story of the Canadian uranium mining industry vividly substantiates the latter fear, as it was largely built on American purchases. When the U.S. government's needs declined in 1959, it started to reduce purchases of Canadian uranium in order to maintain orders with American mines. This resulted in the virtual destruction of one Ontario mining town, Elliot Lake, and caused much bitterness in Canada.)

In short, energy nationalists, although a minority, are nonetheless an unusually potent force precisely because the topic of energy is one field in which public opinion is most favourable to their line of argument. Indeed, the ambiguities involved in energy questions probably increase, not decrease, the attractiveness of the position of the energy nationalists. The sense of sailing headlong into an uncharted sea provokes caution, not precipitate action. There is uncertainty about the employment effects and effects on the Canadian dollar of unprocessed energy exports to the U.S. since resource industries are more capital than labour intensive. American corporations, let alone Japanese corporations, involved in the Canadian oil and natural gas industry have not found it in their interests to greatly expand refining and processing operations in Canada. If Canada does not insist on more processing, the long struggle to diversify manufacturing may be conclusively lost, and the country will, in effect, have moved the terms of trade against itself. There is, then, real uncertainty as to whether surrender of some Canadian control of resources actually would bring the greatest economic benefit. There is also uncertainty about the demands Canada itself will place on its energy resources in the future. The National Energy Board's calculations on natural gas reserves in 1971 point to a near equality in Canadian domestic needs and supply. In the case of other kinds of energy, not only are detailed inventories lacking in some cases, but the possibility of large petroleum and natural gas discoveries on the Atlantic Shelf or in the Arctic makes accurate assessment of "surplus for export" extremely difficult.

The impact of large-scale exploitation of Canadian resources on the ecological environment also acts as a restraint on action. For example, will the Canadian Government be able to enforce the regulations appropriate to oil exploration in the Arctic on a multinational firm that can easily switch its operation to a more hospitable jurisdiction? In 1971 this concern focussed on the proposed shipment of Alaskan oil from Valdes to the Pacific Coast of the United States, with fears of disastrous oil spills near the coast of British Columbia running very high. On the subject of Canada's water reserves, McGill University geographer, Trevor Lloyd, has suggested that because of low precipitation in the North, much of Canada's fresh water cannot be considered as a renewable resource to be bartered away.

All these concerns combine in the demand that Canada maintain tight control over her energy resources through explicit national policies and priorities. Fortifying these demands is the undoubted fact that maintenance of Canada's heritage has become something of a shibboleth, the ultimate symbol of sovereignty in an age when concern about the ecology has become so widespread in North America.

What do you think?

1. *According to Professor Hockin what economic questions are involved in the resource issue? What cultural questions? What politi-*

cal questions? What is the position of energy nationalists on these questions?

2. (a) Does Professor Hockin suggest that energy nationalists are in better favour with the public than economic nationalists? If so, why are they?
    (b) Would a "nationalist" decision over resources be better received than a "nationalist" decision on foreign investment? Why or why not?
3. According to Hockin what is the present government policy regarding energy sales to the U.S.? Do you feel this policy is adequate? Why or why not?
4. What is Hockin referring to when he speaks of Canada's "heritage"? Does this "heritage" have significant cultural value for Canadians? Explain.

4.   ECONOMICS DEFEATS POLITICAL DREAMS

William H. Pugsley in his article "The Fallacy of Economic Nationalism," published in Canadian Business, *April 1972, argues that it is in Canada's best interest to become a source of raw materials for the U.S. Do you think Mr. Pugsley's case effectively answers the "energy nationalists"?*

If one condemns economic nationalism, one should put forward something in its place, Perhaps because, in the long run, economics has a way of defeating political dreams, we have become and are basically a source of raw materials for the United States, and a market for its manufactured goods (although this has been intruded upon by Canadian manufacture where the product and the market have made this practical). It seems likely that this will continue, and that to interfere with it for the sake of emotional political slogans will simply retard the advance of our living standards.

It has been argued that we should hold our irreplaceable raw materials, not sell them to the United States or anyone else. In the first place, if we do not use what we have found, no one will look for any more. In the second place, the materials we use will change in the course of time. We long ago used up the big timber in this country, but we have not really missed it, because when large timber is now needed, it can be made up by putting together smaller timber with modern synthetic resins that are stronger than the wood they join. Similarly, water power may soon give way to nuclear power as the main new source of electricity.

It is also argued that we should discourage development of resource industries because they are capital-intensive, and what we need is more labour-intensive industry. Resource industry is indeed capital-intensive, but at the same time, it produces a heavy proportion of our exports, it stimulates substantial employment in related industries, and it is more productive (i.e. can pay higher wages) than labour-intensive industry. . . .

The plain fact is that capital, in whatever form, is the greatest help to man ever found. What we need is more of it, very much more, so that industry can expand in capital-intensive ways that will make it possible to pay the best wages.

The basic trouble with economic nationalism is that it urges isolation. It offers emotion as a substitute for reason. It resents success instead of trying to emulate it. It would make us an economic ghetto with our backs to the Arctic. We are often told that Canadians are willing to accept a lower standard if this is necessary to remain Canadian, but one may suspect that the person who answers this way really expects someone else to do the paying.

Economic nationalism is a retreat, a denial of the principles that have brought the last century's huge increase in the excess of personal incomes over mere subsistence needs. Few would like to go back to the living of Upper Canada Village. If we wish to go forward with other nations, rather than cower in the background racked with envy, immaturity and self-pity, we must accept the challenge of our times, look on the whole world as our opportunity, and shrug aside the self-defeating negatives of economic nationalism.

What do you think?

1. ". . . and interfere with it for the sake of emotional political slogans will simply retard the advance of our living standards."
   (a) Compare Mr. Pugsley's views with those of the Gray Report (page 20) and Mr. Bonner (page 30).
   (b) Explain why you agree or disagree with Mr. Pugsley.
2. What arguments does Mr. Pugsley use to support the sale of Canadian natural resources to the U.S.? Compare his arguments with those of the "energy nationalists" in Mr. Hockins' article (page 230) and Mr. Gonick (page 25). Whose case do you support and why?
3. (a) In your opinion what would be the best course of action for Canada to take to meet the impending energy crisis? Can your solution be integrated into a scheme dealing with the whole issue of U.S. investment in Canada? If so, how?
   (b) Would you describe your solution as favouring
       (1) the status quo?
       (2) closer integration with the U.S.?
       (3) a more independent Canadian line of action?
4. Describe how you think your solution would affect the political and cultural aspects of Canada-U.S. relations, if at all. Would a decision on the energy issue have the same impact on political and cultural areas of Canada-U.S. relations as would a decision on the U.S. investment issue? Why or why not?

Suggested Readings

Contemporary

ATTWOOD, MARGARET: *Surfacing.* Toronto: McClelland and Stewart, 1972.

ATTWOOD, MARGARET: *Survival: A Thematic Guide to Canadian Literature.* Toronto: Anansi, 1972.

BALDWIN, DAVID and FRANK SMALLWOOD: *Canadian-American Relations: The Politics and Economics of Interdependence.* Hanover, N.H.: Public Affairs Center, Dartmouth College.

BARBER, JOSEPH: *Good Fences Make Good Neighbours.* Indianapolis: Bobbs-Merrill Co., 1958.

BREWIN, ANDREW: *Stand on Guard: The Search for a Canadian Defence Policy.* Toronto: McClelland and Stewart, 1965.

BURTON, THOMAS L.: *Natural Resource Policy in Canada: Issues and Perspectives.* Toronto: McClelland and Stewart, 1972.

CARR, JACK: *Cents and Nonsense: The Economics of Canadian Policy Issues.* Toronto: Holt, Rinehart and Winston, 1972.

CLARK, GERALD: *Canada: The Uneasy Neighbour.* New York: D. McKay, 1965.

CLARKSON, STEPHEN, ed.: *An Independent Foreign Policy for Canada?* Toronto: McClelland and Stewart, 1968.

COWIN, JOHN: *See No Evil: A Study of the Chaos in Canadian Defence Policy.* Toronto: Annex, 1963.

DOBELL, PETER C.: *Canada's Search for New Roles: Foreign Policy in the Trudeau Era.* London: Oxford University Press, 1972.

EAYRS, JAMES: *Northern Approaches: Canada and the Search for Peace.* Toronto: Macmillan, 1961.

EAYRS, JAMES: *In Defence of Canada.* Toronto: University of Toronto Press, 1965.

FULFORD, ROBERT, comp.: *Read Canadian.* Toronto: James, Lewis and Samuel, 1972.

GODFREY, DAVE: *Gordon to Watkins to You.* Toronto: New Press, 1970.

GORDON, WALTER: *A Choice for Canada.* Toronto; McClelland and Stewart, 1966.

GRANATSTEIN, JACK, ed.: *Canadian Foreign Policy Since 1945: Middle Power or Satellite?* Toronto: Copp Clark, 1970.

GRANT, GEORGE: *Lament for a Nation.* Toronto: McClelland and Stewart, 1965.

GRANT, GEORGE: *Technology and Empire.* Toronto: Anansi, 1969.

GRAY, COLIN: *Canadian Defence Priority: A Question of Relevance.* Toronto: Clarke, Irwin, 1972.

HERTZMAN, LEWIS, THOMAS HOCKIN and JOHN WARNOCK: *Alliances and Illusions.* Edmonton: M. J. Hurtig, 1969.

HOCKIN, THOMAS: *The Canadian Condominium.* Toronto. McClelland and Stewart, 1972.

HOLMES, JOHN W.: *The Better Part of Valour.* Toronto: McClelland and Stewart, 1970.

INNES, HUGH, ed.: *Americanization.* Toronto: McGraw-Hill, 1972.

JOHNSON, HARRY: *The Canadian Quandary: Economic Problems and Policies.* New York: McGraw-Hill, 1963.

KEIRANS, ERIC: *Challenge of Confidence.* Toronto: McClelland and Stewart, 1967.

LAXER, JAMES: *The Energy Poker Game.* Toronto: New Press, 1970.

LEVITT, KARL: *Silent Surrender.* Toronto: Macmillan, 1970.

LUMSDEN, IAN, ed.: *Close the 49th Parallel: The Americanization of Canada.* Toronto: University of Toronto Press, 1970.

LYON, PEYTON: *The Policy Question.* Toronto: McClelland and Stewart, 1963.

MASSEY, VINCENT: *Confederation on the March.* Toronto: Macmillan, 1965.

MERCHANT, LIVINGSTON G.: *Neighbours Taken for Granted.* New York: F. A. Praeger, 1966.

MINIFIE, JAMES: *Peacemaker or Powdermonkey?* Toronto: McClelland and Stewart, 1960.

MORTON, W.L.: *The Canadian Identity.* Toronto: University of Toronto Press, 1972.

NICHOLSON, NORMAN L.: *Canada in the American Community.* New York: Van Nostrand, 1965.

PEARSON, LESTER B.: *The Four Faces of Peace and the International Outlook.* Toronto: McClelland and Stewart, 1964.

PERRY, ROBERT L.: *Galt, U.S.A.* Toronto: Maclean-Hunter, 1971.

PURDY, AL, comp: *The New Romans: Candid Canadian Opinions of the U.S.* Edmonton: M. J. Hurtig, 1968.

REDFORD, ROBERT W.: *Canada and Three Crises.* Toronto: International Institute of International Affairs, 1968.

REDEKOP, J.H., ed.: *The Star-Spangled Beaver.* Toronto: P. Martin Associates, 1971.

REID, TIMOTHY: *Foreign Ownership: Villain or Scapegoat?* Toronto: Holt, Rinehart and Winston, 1972.

ROTSTEIN, ABRAHAM: *Independence: The Canadian Challenge.* Toronto: Committee for an Independent Canada, 1972.

SHEA, ALBERT: *Canada 1980: A Digest of the Gordon Report.* Toronto: McClelland and Stewart, 1960.

THOMPSON, DALE and ROGER F. SWANSON: *Canadian Foreign Policy: Options and Perspectives.* Toronto: McGraw-Hill Ryerson, 1971.

TUPPER, STANLEY and DOUGLAS BAILEY: *One Continent: Two Voices: The Future of Canada-U.S. Relations.* Toronto: Clarke Irwin, 1967.

WARNOCK, JOHN: Partner to Behemoth: *The Military Policy of Satellite Canada.* Toronto: New Press, 1970.

WILSON, EDMUND: *O Canada: An American's Note on Canada's Culture.* New York: Farrar, Strauss and Giroux, 1965.

WONNACOTT, RONALD J. and WONNACOTT, PAUL: *Trade Between the United States and Canada: The Potential Economic Effects.* Cambridge: Harvard University Press, 1967.

Historical

BELLASIS, MARGARET: *"Rise Canadians!"* Montreal: Palm Publishers, 1955.

BERGER, CARL: *Imperialism and Nationalism 1888-1914: A Conflict in Canadian Thought.* Toronto: Copp Clark, 1969.

BIRD, HARRISON: *Attack on Quebec: The American Invasion of Canada, 1775.* New York: Oxford University Press, 1968.

BREBNER, J.B.: *The North Atlantic Triangle.* New Haven: Yale University Press, 1945.

BROWN, ROBERT CRAIG: *Canada National Policy, 1883-1900: A Study in Canadian-American Relations.* New Jersey: Princeton University Press, 1964.

BRUNET, MICHEL: *French Canada and the Early Decades of British Rule.* Ottawa: Canadian Historical Association, 1963.

CLASSER, HANS GEORGE: *Thrust and Counter Thrust: The Genesis of the Canada-United States Boundary.* Don Mills: Longmans, 1965.

CREIGHTON, DONALD: *Canada's First Century.* Toronto: Macmillan, 1970.

DALES, JOHN: *The Protective Tariff in Canada's Development.* Toronto: University of Toronto Press, 1966.

D'ARCY, WILLIAM: *The Fenian Movement in the United States, 1858-1886.* New York: Russell and Russell, 1947.

DUNLOP, WILLIAM: *Tiger Dunlop's Upper Canada: Comprising Recollections of the American War, 1812-1814.* Toronto: McClelland and Stewart, 1967.

DURHAM, JOHN GEORGE LAMBTON, IST EARL OF: *Lord Durham's Report.* Toronto: McClelland and Stewart, 1963.

ELLIS, LEWIS: *Reciprocity, 1911.* New York: Greenwood Press, 1968, 1939.

FRAZER, BLAIR: *The Search for Identity: Canada 1945-1967.* Garden City, N.Y.: Doubleday, 1967.

GLUECK, ALVIN: *Minnesota and the Manifest Destiny of the Canadian Northwest.* Toronto: University of Toronto Press, 1965.

GUILLET, EDWIN: *The Lives and Times of the Patriots: An Account of the Rebellion in Upper Canada*. Toronto: Nelson, 1938.

HUTCHISON, BRUCE: *The Struggle for the Border*. Toronto: Longmans Green, 1955.

KEENLEYSIDE, HUGH: *Canada and the U.S. Some Aspects of their Historical Relation*. New York: Knopf, 1952.

KILBOURN, WILLIAM: *The Firebrand: William Lyon Mackenzie and the Rebellion in Upper Canada*. Toronto: Clarke Irwin, 1956.

JAMES, ROBERT: *Wartime Economic Co-operation*. Toronto: Ryerson, 1949.

LANCTOT, GUSTAVE: *Canada and the American Revolution*. Toronto: Clarke Irwin, 1967.

MASTERS, DONALD: *The Reciprocity Treaty of 1854*. Toronto: McClelland and Stewart, 1963.

NEATBY, H. BLAIR: *The Politics of Chaos: Canada in the 30s*. Toronto: Macmillan, 1972.

NEATBY, HILDA: *Quebec: The Revolutionary Age, 1760-1791*. Toronto: McClelland and Stewart, 1966.

PENLINGTON, NORMAN: *Canada and Imperialism 1896-1899*. Toronto: University of Toronto Press, 1965.

RAWLYK, GEORGE: *Revolution Rejected*. Scarborough: Prentice-Hall of Canada, 1968.

SMITH, GOLDWIN: *The Treaty of Washington: A Study in Imperial History*. Ithaca: Cornell University Press, 1941.

SMITH, GOLDWIN: *Canada and the Canadian Question*. Toronto: University of Toronto Press, 1971.

STACEY, C.P.: *The Undefended Border: The Myth and the Reality*. Ottawa: Canadian Historical Association, 1953.

WAITE, P.B.: *The Life and Times of Confederation*. Toronto: University of Toronto Press, 1962.

WAITE, P.B.: *Confederation, 1854-1867*. Toronto: Holt, Rinehart and Winston, 1972.

WAITE, P.B.: *Canada, 1874-1896: Arduous Destiny*. Toronto: McClelland and Stewart, 1970.

WILBUR, JOHN: *The Bennett New Deal: Fraud or Portent?* Toronto: Copp Clark, 1968.

WISE, SYDNEY: *Canada Views the United States: Nineteenth-Century Political Attitudes*. Toronto: Macmillan, 1967.

WRONG, GEORGE: *Canada and the American Revolution*. New York: Cooper Square Publishers, 1968.

ZASLOW, MORRIS: *The Defended Border: Canada and the War of 1812*. Toronto: Macmillan, 1964.

Films

New England and New France (1490-1763).   57 minutes 55 seconds   b&w   NFB 16mm: 106B 0167 106.

From the first uneasy contacts to the culminating conflict—the whole struggle of New England and New France, and the economic contest between the St. Lawrence trade system and the Atlantic-Hudson system, explored for the first time on film.

Canada and the American Revolution (1763-1783).   57 minutes 15 seconds   b&w NFB   16mm: 106B 0167 107.

The dramatic and fateful pattern of divergence between the ambitions of the American revolutionaries and the interests of the Canadian groups on the St. Lawrence. The flames of hostile rebellion spread northward but Canada resists encroachment.

The War of 1812 (1783-1818). 58 minutes 11 seconds b&w NFB 16mm: 106B 0167 108.
The Canadian-British-American struggle for the Ohio Valley, the War of 1812 and its contribution to American and Canadian nationalism, and some sardonic looks at the myths of that war.

Dangerous Decades (1818-1846) 58 minutes 20 seconds b&w NFB 16mm.
The contest for the continental interior. American advantages and internal Canadian troubles, the great dispute over the Oregon and Maine boundaries, American anti-monarchism, and a portent of a "transcontinental nation to come".

The New Equation: Annexation and Reciprocity (1840-1860). 58 minutes 10 seconds b&w NFB 16mm: 106B 0168 081.
The "one continent, one nation, one flag" concept had its strong supporters on both sides of the border, but in conflict were strong economic forces. All the ultimate alternatives for Canada—annexation, continentalism, free trade, economic nationalism—are illuminated in dramatic interplay.

The Friendly Fifties and the Sinister Sixties (1850-1863). 58 minutes 25 seconds b&w NFB 16mm: 106B 0168 082.
Here are interwoven several historical continuities in unique and unprecedented fashion—the whole complex course of relations between Great Britain, Canada, the North and South, before, during and after the American Civil War.

The Triumphant Union and the Canadian Confederation (1863-1867). 58 minutes 28 seconds b&w NFB 16mm: 106B 0169 012.
A fascinating study of the great and enduring principles and practices of international relations and the subtle, many-dimensioned geometry of war and peace: Canada and the American Civil War; Canada, Britain, the North and the South, and a dangerous diplomatic game.

The Border Confirmed: The Treaty of Washington (1867-1871). 58 minutes 30 seconds b&w NFB 16mm: 106B 0169 013.
The uneasy years after the Canadian Confederation when American attitudes to Canada were qualified and ambiguous. A critical period in Canadian-American relations is examined and the complex diplomacy of the Treaty of Washington is brought to life in striking fashion.

A Second Transcontinental Nation (1872). 58 minutes 36 seconds b&w NFB 16mm: 106B 0169 014.
For Canada the struggle to preserve the border continued. Emerging from the long historical background, and confirmed by it, the underlying factors, the great alternatives, the basic equations on which Canada's survival as a nation independent of the United States depend, now stand clear.